PENGUIN BOOKS

JUNG AND THE STORY OF OUR TIME

Laurens van der Post, C.B.E., was born in Africa in 1906. Most of his adult life has been spent with one foot there and one in England. His professions of writer and farmer were interrupted by ten years of soldiering—behind enemy lines in Abyssinia, and also in the Western Desert and the Far East, where he was taken prisoner by the Japanese while commanding a small guerrilla unit. He went straight from prison back to active service in Java, served on Lord Mountbatten's staff, and, when the British forces withdrew from Java, remained behind as Military Attaché to the British Minister. Since 1949 he has undertaken several official missions exploring little-known parts of Africa. His independent expedition to the Kalahari Desert in search of the Bushmen was the subject of his famous documentary film. (Other television films include *The Story of Carl Gustav Jung*, *A Region of Shadow* and *All Africa Within Us* [1975].) His other books include *Flamingo Feather*, *The Heart of the Hunter*, *The Hunter and the Whale*, *Journey into Russia*, *The Seed and the Sower*, *Venture to the Interior*, *The Lost World of the Kalahari*, *A Portrait of Japan*, *The Night of the New Moon* and *A Story like the Wind*. Many of these have been published in Penguins. His latest books are *A Mantis Carol* (1975) and *A Far-Off Place* (1975).

Colonel van der Post married Ingaret Giffard in 1949.

Is there a video of his progr. on Bushmen?
also

Laurens van der Post

JUNG

AND THE STORY
OF OUR TIME

*We live not only our own lives but, whether
we know it or not, also the life of our time*

THE DARK EYE IN AFRICA

Penguin Books

Penguin Books Ltd, Harmondsworth, Middlesex, England
Viking Penguin Inc., 40 West 23rd Street, New York, New York 10010, U.S.A.
Penguin Books Australia Ltd, Ringwood, Victoria, Australia
Penguin Books Canada Ltd, 2801 John Street, Markham, Ontario, Canada L3R 1B4
Penguin Books (N.Z.) Ltd, 182–190 Wairau Road, Auckland 10, New Zealand

—

First published by The Hogarth Press 1976
Published in Penguin Books 1978, 1985

—

—

Printed and bound in Great Britain by
Cox & Wyman Ltd, Reading
Set in Monotype Bembo

For My Wife
INGARET GIFFARD
who introduced me to Jung
and
'T–C' ROBERTSON
for many reasons inevitably evoked in the
course of fifty years of friendship, but here
mainly out of gratitude for what he has
done to make the earth of our native Africa
whole again as the example, which is the
subject of this book, exhorts us also to be
whole within.

CONTENTS

PROLOGUE

I have known, perhaps, an unusual number of those the world considered great, but Carl Gustav Jung is almost the only one of whose greatness I am certain. Time is relative in more dimensions than those of the continuum wherein Einstein's formidable equation places it. It has a knack of putting the truly great, as it were, well ahead of us, rather than in the past darkening so fast behind. As a result, most of those regarded as great in their own lifetime diminish once dead, and only the truly great increase in stature.

And this increase in stature precisely is what has happened to Jung, although he died only fourteen years ago. Today he looms larger on the scene of the human spirit than he did in his own lifetime. The books in which he recorded his quintessential self and work are more and more to be found in the pockets of the intellectual young. Words that he introduced in new senses into the modern English idiom have lost their elitism and are part today of our ordinary educated vocabulary. Terms like complex, extravert, introvert, persona, archetype, anima, animus and shadow, that we owe him, testify how wide and deep his impact has been.

But what this greatness consists of is almost impossible to define. I myself cannot attempt to do so as a specialist of any kind. Even if I could, I do not believe I would. I am not a psychologist. I was never a patient either of Jung, or of any of his distinguished collaborators, or for that matter of any other psychiatrist. I cannot even claim to be a Jungian in the only sense in which I believe he would have approved the term: that is, in regard to someone who has practised or taught the analytical psychology he pioneered. Used in any larger way and in particular as a label of discipleship, I know he rejected it, and voiced his objections to its use to me on several occasions in those plainest of terms of which he was a master. He did not like the idea of having disciples or blind followers, or even a school, and in his old age agreed most reluctantly to the establishment of the C. G. Jung Institute in Zürich for studies relevant to his own approach to psychology. Indeed, I remember him telling me that the Institute would be lucky if it did not outlive its creative uses within a generation.

Above all, he had a profound horror of "isms", and the adjective "Jungian", which could so easily be a doorstep to "Jungianism", was

ruled out in his own discipline of psychology. "I do not want anybody
to be a Jungian", he told me. "I want people above all to be themselves,
As for 'isms', they are the viruses of our day, and responsible for
greater disasters than any medieval plague or pest has ever been. Should
I be found one day only to have created another 'ism' then I will have
failed in all I tried to do."

Ours was, to use the term in its technical sense, a non-psychological
relationship. I was in it purely for the love of it. In so far as I could
make some small return for the immense amount his friendship gave me,
I believe it came out of this, so that no matter how much my lack of
specialist qualifications may limit my interpretation of the man, it is
just possible that my view may have a value which is not adequately
represented in the mass of material that has been written about him.

At the moment the world knows him almost exclusively as a psychologist and psychiatrist. Yet great and original as his contribution in
these fields has been, and unsurpassed as was his gift of healing the
abnormal and psychologically sick, his importance to so-called normal
man and his societies, I believe, is much greater. It is astonishing to me
how this larger aspect of the man has been overlooked by most of the
interpreters, who still come from far and wide, like multitudes of
dinghies with outboard motors chugging in the wake of a dread-
nought, home at last from a sea on which few of us have ventured.

Part of the explanation is that almost all the authors of this formidable
intermediary activity have been psychiatrists themselves, or started
out as patients either of Jung or of one of his collaborators. Such an
approach, of course, is perfectly valid, of great importance, and should
not be underestimated. It would be wrong not to recognise Jung for
the inspired psychologist and born healer he was. After all, he started
out in his career as a pioneer of psychiatry. Psychology and this applied
field of it were his medium and led him first to the discovery, and subsequently to the exploration, of a new world within the human spirit
greater and in my view far more significant for life on earth than the
world Columbus discovered in the world without.

Yet psychology and psychiatry are only a way and not an end in
themselves, and had the middle men between Jung and the public not
been so preoccupied with psychiatry, this salient aspect of Jung and his
work would not have been neglected for so long.

One has only to glance at Jung's *Memories, Dreams, Reflections* to
see how the man himself was full and overflowing with a greater concern. There one finds only one chapter, the fourth, entitled "Psychiatric
Activities". It is followed by one called "Sigmund Freud". Then

there comes "Confrontation with the Unconscious", where, much condensed, Jung gives his own account of a confrontation as portentous for the increase of human awareness as the dark night of exile in the Old Testament wherein Jacob, the father of Joseph the Dreamer, wrestled alone and long with an angel. Only then does one reach the chapter headed "The Work".

Understandable as the psychiatric concentration on Jung has been up to this point, it becomes less so subsequently in so far as it persists in presenting this "work" of Jung also as a mere extension of psychology and psychiatry, leaving the popular concept of Jung confined to what remains, despite the resultant enlargement, still a clinical cell.

Having never been in such a situation myself, I see it differently and, I believe, in the direction Jung himself viewed it, and I may therefore perhaps help in a small way towards another perspective of him. Even so, I cannot do this in terms of pure knowledge or as a product of any great research, nor as part of a particular discipline. I can only present it in the way it had meaning for me, and that was as a living experience in the context of a personal relationship. Moreover, since I came to the experience reluctantly, I believe that the difficulties from which it stemmed in themselves are a microcosm of the macrocosm of the problem Jung had in making himself and his work understood, and accordingly the problem his own time had in understanding him.

I am compelled, therefore, to begin with myself, not for any egotistical purpose but as the only way open to me if I am to render account of the man and his work as experience, and an act of knowledge rather than another of those abstracts of knowledge already so amply available. Also, I believe that by relating my own long-sustained imperviousness to Jung, I might help to expose in others the same process of negation which, although diminishing, is still astoundingly active in our time.

Finally, the European context of my life in the interior of southern Africa and its extreme Calvinistic mould, owing to its remoteness from the swiftly changing Europe of its origin, when communications were far slower and more difficult than today, tended to be so far behind the accelerating time abroad that, although born much later than Jung, I experienced a version of life with a religious emphasis and tensions of mind and spirit that might almost have been drafted from a blueprint of the Protestant Switzerland into which he was born.

A certain detailed reconstruction of the parallels of that world which, in our permissive and technological retrospect, appears even stranger than fiction, may help therefore to illuminate how formidable in Jung's day were difficulties whose resolution now is taken for granted. Out of the nature of their constriction they provide a measure of the originality, courage and pioneering quality of the man, showing a spirit great enough not only to surmount the almost impossible odds mobilised against it, but to overcome them and make his life and work a new universal point of departure for our dangerously arrested time.

THE TIME AND THE SPACE

And Joseph dreamed a dream, and he told it his brethren:
and they hated him yet the more.

Genesis 37:5

For me it all started as a child in the interior of Africa. In the clear light of a certain *esprit d'escalier* that comes to one on the way down from one's own little attic in time, I seem to have had an inborn predisposition towards the area of meaning in which Jung's abundant spirit, unknown to us, was already embattled. I had always had what seemed to my own family and friends an inordinate interest in dreams. I was always dreaming, and dreams, from the beginning, meant something to me that they did not to the grown-up pale-faces of my world. The pink, marshmallow material they were in the minds of governesses trained in the Victorian order of these things became suspect to me at an early age. Even worse was their dismissal as some sort of poor rich trash of the imagination by the hearty male teachers of our extravert society who followed on where wistful spinster ladies left off. They would pass sentence on one's dreaming processes with a phrase that filled me with dismay, "But my dear boy, it was only a dream."

That "but only" of theirs became increasingly discredited when I saw how it was automatically part of their judgement of almost everything that mattered to me as a child. Growing up in the European way began to appear to be not so much a process of growth as a dangerous reduction to a provisional "but only" state. I feared it accordingly, and so acutely that the fear is still with me, for it is continuously encouraged by the loss of power of increase that I see in men and their societies, because how can there be either growth or renewal in such reductive soil of the human spirit?

My one defence against the condemnation of adults was the effect on me of the dreams themselves. Almost nightly I was reminded, by yet another dream, of their vitality to persist undiminished against the constant opposition of the adult world. Also they would continue to have marked effects on the mood and atmosphere of my days. There was more to dreaming, I suspected, than my elders knew or supposed.

I had, of course, good dreams as well as bad. The number of good may well have exceeded the bad, but I had nightmares enough to prevent me from thinking of dreaming as an altogether comfortable process. The good and the bad seemed part of one indivisible reality which.

for all my inability to define or explain it, I could neither ignore nor depend on as a source of comfort.

I soon took this to be axiomatic because, for a period of about a year, I tried hard to fashion dreaming to my own prescription. I would go to bed determined to inflame my sleep with dreams of wonder or fulfilment. But not once was I able to have the slightest influence on the dreams of my sleep. I knew a brief period when I even tried to enlist the help of our Calvinist Almighty in the matter.

Like all children of my world, I was compelled to say my prayers every night before going to sleep, although our evening meal always ended with a long reading from the Bible, an even longer improvised prayer, with all of us kneeling on the hard, polished wooden floor of the dining-room by our rather medieval chairs and their carved frames and high backs, and a final singing of a psalm. Later, an African nurse or senior member of the family was always there to supervise this last ablution of our minds from the stains of the sinful day. They would see to it that one knelt down by one's bed and ran silently through the prescribed formula for invoking divine protection for parents, brothers, sisters, friends, not forgetting a perfunctory plea for one's own redemption from a state of sin—which one did not feel but had been talked into accepting as an inborn element of one's being.

I never minded the occasion and invariably took to my bed afterwards mysteriously relieved and rather startled by how often the long white, home-made candle by the side of my bed would look transformed into a lighthouse poised on the rim of the great sea of African night, lapping at the lip of the shuttered window, and sanctifying my room with a sort of pentecostal glow. I would stare for a moment at the brass rails of my bed rendered gold before glancing up to see candle and flame stand transparent on the glass within the frame which enclosed on the wall above my bed the text, stitched in blue gothic letters on yellow silk, "The Lord is my shepherd, I shall not want." After that, I could have no doubt of finding safe harbour in sleep, and in sleep the dream I had secretly placed on my prayer list. But no such dream ever came.

There followed some months of agonising questioning and self-examination when I woke up so often, to prod myself on to greater dream exertion, that I got up in the mornings looking exhausted and had my parents thoroughly worried. But somehow, I made my peace with the fact that I myself could not fabricate dreams. Far from lowering the process in my estimation it increased my respect for the dream, since I concluded that with a will and a way all its own it was greater than both I and prayer combined.

By this time my obsession had become common knowledge. In so affectionate a family, even so large a one as ours, it was astonishing how one's most secret thoughts and aspirations were enticed from one. In particular, one's sisters seemed to have a special nose for divining secrets and then spreading them around. If they were found to be at a tangent to the family norm, one instantly became the subject of endless teasing. I would try hard to fall back on a previously prepared position (as military strategists would say), and take refuge in a secrecy I should never have abandoned. I no longer confessed my dreams or fantasies inspired by dreams to anyone. But the damage had been done and inevitably I was nicknamed, "Joseph the Dreamer".

If I had to choose one moment rather than another in which I first became aware of a deep feeling of isolation in an essential part of myself from the community in which I was born, it was when fond family officialdom labelled me thus.

Had it remained merely a matter of the affectionate teasing from my family, I believe I could have kept up my own end by retreat into a secret self. But unhappily, this dreaming process had a knack of following through into my waking imagination in a way judged highly reprehensible by a pioneering society, still engaged in a battle for survival which demanded focussing of the attention of the faculties of all its members on the physical world. Again and again I would be forced to recognise that the recollection of a dream of the night before and a train of imaginings sparked off by it had taken my mind away from the immediate business of the day. Unwittingly I had put myself in a position of being reproved for lack of appropriate attention.

The reproof in the beginning was mild and little more than some tart exhortation to the assembled family or classroom, like "Look at him! He's been at it, dreaming again", or, more sarcastically, "Would you be good enough, sir, to step out of your trance?" But as I grew older, this deficiency was seen more and more as an enemy of virtuous concentration and the seducer of will so essential for facing the facts of life which, of course, meant the facts of the physical world and the practicalities of the urgent pioneering day. That dreams in themselves were facts and whether we liked it or not were of considerable practical importance was a notion either dismissed or instantly aborted in a ridicule of reasoning.

In time, reproof led to punishment for my transgressions in this regard. Somewhere I still had some protection in a suspicion that it could be not I, but the world, that was at fault? But I could not possibly have known how to put forward the proposition in my own defence and claim that what I was suffering from was not a lack of the power of concentration but that all my symptoms of inattention were evidence of a natural capacity for concentration of another kind: concentration on significant aspects of reality of which my elders and betters seemed insufficiently aware. I seemed to have been born profoundly pre-occupied another way and could ultimately do nothing much about it.

Divided in this way by my own private and personal pull towards an inward direction, and the tug of the world to keep me focussed on the life outside me, I was overwhelmed by guilt and a belief that I was born incompetent in all that mattered most in life. I do not know how this newly withdrawn and secret dreaming self, so vulnerable, in-experienced, and gradually compelled in this and other ways to fall out of love with itself, would have survived if help had not come to it from unexpected quarters.

It first came from my wise, stern and upright old grandfather. He was already very old when I was very young. Indeed, the difference in our ages was so great and the span of years between us so long that I can remember him telling me in great detail of a battle in which he had fought against the English in Africa in 1848. It seemed to me that there was almost nothing that could happen to human beings this side of the grave that had not happened to him, things both bad and good which his faith and courage somehow had not failed to contain if not alto-gether to resolve.

Help came from him on a night when I was staying with him alone in the home which he built for himself on his broad farm called Boesmansfontein—Bushman's Spring. The moment possesses a start-ling, timeless, Vermeer-like clarity. The great table in the dining-room had been cleared after the evening meal. All the household servants had been summoned to join us and taken up their positions squatting against the walls. They seemed to represent all the races and variations of colours of the men who made up the population of the interior of southern Africa. They had a look in their eyes that seemed to go back to the beginning of life on earth, particularly so in the light which illuminated the room at that moment. The light came from a single and immense oil lamp suspended from the centre of the ceiling by three silver chains joined to a bronze hook. The glass of the lamp was always cleaned and polished by the senior servant of the house every morning, since my grandmother was no longer alive and all his daughters gone. The elaborately wrought-iron frame which held the bronze lamp and contained the oil had a kind of Byzantine look and, somehow, whenever I heard the parable of the lamps in the New Testament, a miniature of this sort of flame always glowed in my mind.

For me there was no artificial light so beautiful as the light from that lamp. Wherever its light fell it charged even the most insignificant physical objects with wonder, and the smallest space became vast with the cosmic quality of the shadow cast. I had only to see it lit to experience a confirmation of a promise of life unfailing. It seemed right, therefore, that it should lie like a reflection in water within the sheen of the heavy, olive-green velvet of the after-dinner table cloth held down along the edges by heavy golden tassels and spread evenly across the surface of the table. Elongated, the flame of the lamp would shimmer there in front of the huge family Bible like a reflection of one of our poplars shaking the yellow evening sun, flake by flake, from its trembling leaves. On either side of the Bible two of the tallest household candles would be set, I suspect, not so much to aid my grandfather's eyes as to complete the symmetry of the unique image his instinctive sense of the occasion demanded.

It was significant that my grandfather never referred to it as the Bible but always as the Book. He had such a feeling for the Book (which had been almost his only reading because he had never been to any school) that he had a special ritual before reading. He would reverently lift the large, heavy leather covers of the book with their metal clasps that shone like silver and open it slowly on the first ivory pages, smooth them out with his long, brown hand and then let them lie there exposed on the table a brief moment. I think perhaps he did this so that he could survey the large, green family tree with its spreading branches painted across both pages, and seek out, among the leaves, the names of his forefathers recorded there from the time they had landed in Africa as refugees from persecution in Europe some two hundred and fifty years previously. I suppose this silent roll-call of family history was necessary to quicken in him his feeling of continuity which, as he became older, appeared increasingly threatened by the discord gathering in the spirit of his people. I believe his instinct told him that it was only through a feeling of continuity within oneself that one could be linked to a beginning where awareness of origin in the human imagination, no matter how keen, is exhausted on the marches of consciousness. The living thread has to be rediscovered in the kind of experience communicated through stories such as those recorded in the Book open in front of him. Only when he had done with this silent dedication of his mind to the spirit of continuity would he turn over the heavy pages until he came to the part he had decided to read.

On this particular occasion it was the story of the young Joseph and his blood-stained coat of many colours, which remains for me as one of the greatest stories ever told. To my joy it was being read from beginning to end. Suddenly there came the indication that the story had been chosen for my special benefit. My grandfather looked up from his reading (I believe he knew that part of the Bible by heart) and, with his eyes directly on me, declaimed, "And Joseph dreamed a dream and he told it his brethren: and they hated him yet the more." Whenever he came to a dream thereafter, his eyes left the book to seek me out, while he spoke the piece from memory.

Finally, when the text had been read and the last prayers said, my grandfather's favourite commando hymn (which was also my father's) had been sung, and the servants dismissed, my grandfather withdrew to his favourite leather armchair by the fire. Those who stayed were speaking in lowered voices, for the atmosphere left behind on these occasions was always solemn. But once seated and at ease, my grandfather did not call but beckoned me to him and took me on his knee. He addressed me by my full name, as he always did when he had something of particular importance to say to me: "Laurens Jan, always remember what the Book says about Joseph and his dreams. Remember that though his brothers hated him for it, had it not been for his dreaming, they would never have found corn in Egypt and would have perished as you have heard in the great famine that was still to come."

I wish I could remember the precise words of the elaboration that followed on the theme of Joseph and his dream. But I have not words so much as the feelings left in me and know little more than that over the years to come they started a process of widening comprehension.

Of the words themselves I remember that almost every one of his paragraphs began with a *Ja-nee* (literally "yes-no"). My grandfather used this expression only when he talked about things of ultimate importance to him. The expression taken literally, of course, consists of words that cancel each other out and leave one, logically, with a non-statement. And yet, taken with the tone in which it was uttered, it was a pointer to a homespun philosophy full of meaning because it was based on utter acceptance of the fact that at heart, life and the nature of truth which gives life its direction, are inexorably paradoxical. All, he knew, was both a "yes" and a "no". To contain this paradoxical challenge of reality was for him the most honourable pursuit and source of dignity available to man.

But incapable of the least appreciation of paradox myself and longing passionately for no noes at all and only an endless chain of affirmations for a tentative self, that evening left me with an intuition of real
significance. Its recollection flares up in a living emotion still burning
and bright enabling me to see today that my grandfather had been
aware of my dilemma in a manner that I was not. He saw dangers in it
that I could not possibly foresee at that moment, and he wanted to
convey to me both a warning and an encouragement. The obvious
encouragement was that however much the dream might be suspect
for others, it was as valid for him as it was for the greatest authority he
recognised, the Book of Books.

I was much older before I realised how subtly and wisely my grandfather had implanted in my highly impressionable imagination both a
sense of the role of paradox in the meaning of things, and also a warning against taking the dreams of Joseph too literally. He had done much
to prevent me from over-identifying myself with the Biblical example.
Indeed, the immediate effect of his concern for me seemed to have ensconced me more firmly in the state of secrecy regarding my dreaming
life which I have mentioned. And this meant that in one vital aspect I
was more and more isolated from family and friends.

I was protected too from hubris by the fact that the dreams of Joseph,
themselves, did not impress me as much as perhaps they ought to have
done. I was never over-fond of the dream spectacle of the sheaves of
corn, as proxies of Joseph's brethren, bowing their yellow heads
obsequiously before the one that represented his dreaming self, and
could well understand why it was regarded as an egotistical presumption that had to be resisted. But, all in all, my reaction to Joseph's
dreams, of course, was purely instinctive and I could not possibly tell,
as perhaps I can today, that what really limited their appeal was that
they appeared over-confined to a kind of fortune-telling role, largely
contrived to help Biblical man in his struggle for physical survival.
That, of course, was not to be despised. Nothing could be more natural
than that the dreaming process should have a vested interest in the survival of the vulnerable flesh and blood which have to live the dreams
that so mysteriously impel them. But once a particular battle was won
there appeared some uneasy truce in an endless campaign as, for instance, after the flood and famine, fire and brimstone which destroyed
the cities of the plain, after which man is brought back starkly over and
over again to the real business of living, namely the task of living a
life of increasing meaning as the only answer to the problem which
provoked the very act of creation in the beginning.

When and how such a feeling was made known to one, I could not say. It would seem perhaps as if always in one's deepest potential there is axiomatic conviction that life was created as a means of answering a universal question, and that when the question is ultimately answered, life will be put, as it were, out of business and something else will come to take its place.

But how and from where did man find the power and the courage to do so? And what or whom guided him to the true end? And what even then, did it all mean? I did not know. Some instinctive sense perhaps made me turn to the first dream recorded in the Bible, the dream of Jacob and the ladder. This was to me, the greatest of all dreams, the progenitor of all the visionary material and mythological and allegorical activities that were to follow until the traffic and travail of the human spirit hesitate, fearful, on the lip of an immense apocalyptic vista where Alpha and Omega, first and last, speak as one in the Book of Revelations. This dream seemed to be, in a sense, an "absolute", existing outside space and time, for it had lost none of its freshness and excitement. Even now I have only to close my senses to see in the darkness within a ladder pitched on the stony ground of a great wasteland and reaching to a star-packed heaven, with the urgent traffic of angels phosphorescent upon it.

I was not in the least surprised that this dream should have obsessed the imagination of artists and poets as no other dreams have ever done. I cannot pretend to understand all that the dream is meant to convey. The dreaming process and the symbols through which it seeks to communicate with life still seem to me always more than I for one can say about them. How much more so were they, therefore, to a boy?

Only the dreaming process itself can know fully what it is, and what its purpose with us can be. So this dream, with a fateful grasp of what is appropriate, begins by defining, in unmistakable imagery, what the dreaming process within itself is. Moreover it does so without any of the oracular ambivalence of so many of its successors, declaring simply that it is the way between life and its ultimate meaning. For that, I believe, is what the image of the ladder and its positioning between Heaven and earth is intended to convey. It asserts that through it men and the source of all their meaning will, forever, be in communication. That is what I suspect the traffic of angels on the ladder represents since angels (as the Greek derivation of the word so clearly denotes) are messengers and visualisations of the means by which the dreamer and cause of dream can speak to each other. No matter how abandoned and without help either in themselves or the world about them, the dream, using Jacob's state and the great and perilous wasteland through which he is fleeing in fear of his life as imagery of man at the end of his resources, affirms that man is never alone. Acknowledged or unacknowledged, that which dreams through him is always there to support him from within. And Jacob had not even had to ask for help. The necessities of his being had spoken so eloquently for him that the dream brought him instant promise of help from the source of creation itself. All this made the coming of the dream appear to me to be as fateful for life within as had the coming of fire for life on earth without. For great as the service it has already performed is, the dream is not complete with only this preamble of intent because of its immense practical implications.

Up to this moment, ever since the expulsion from the Garden, the life of Biblical man had been a singularly one-sided affair. It was a progression ordered entirely by command and the direct voice of God or His visionary plenipotentiaries as, for instance, those who came to warn Abraham and his kinsman, Lot, of the imminent destruction of the cities of the plain. Man himself had no direct say in the matter. He had not to reason why. He had but to fear and obey or face the most catastrophic consequences. With Jacob's dream, however, all this suddenly changed and the whole relationship between creator and created became reappraised.

The traffic of the spirit which had been so uncompromisingly from above to below, now was suddenly transformed into a two-way affair also possible from below to above. This would seem to be the meaning of the fact that in Jacob's dream the angels are both descending *and* ascending the ladder. The created is told, in the most authoritative manner, that he has an inbuilt system of communication for transmitting his needs to the creator and so receiving help in proportion to the will and purpose of creation inflicted on him. As the phrase would have it, for the first time a dialogue becomes possible between God and Man. Further, the dream seems to imply that the creator has delegated some of his own infinite power to the created. There is more than a hint in the symbolism evoked that the source of creation has, in a small but significant degree, diminished its own role in order to increase that of the created. It is as if creator and created, through this dream, are being joined in an increasing act of partnership. Indeed, it almost seems as if the dream has taken charge both of God and man, and made them, however disparate the degree of their relationship, servants of a common purpose. Obedience is still as imperative as ever, but it is obedience henceforth to an authority no longer one-sided and impervious.

Of course it may have always been so. The God that appears in this dream of Jacob's might only be an aspect of God, and God in the ultimate entirety remains the originator of the dream. It would be only too easy to evade the overwhelming import of this particular dream by a shift into the semantics of the matter. But since the dream and its symbols are always more than we can say about them, it is best left for us all to draw such meaning from it as we can for ourselves.

Speaking only for myself, all that has come out of the impact of the dream in my early imagination shows that my feelings about it, and its importance, have not changed. They still come straight out of feelings belonging to that remote African day when I first heard the dream. So much so that I understood, even as a boy, and without surprise, how the tortured soul of Francis Thompson could write:

> "Cry; and upon thy so sore loss
>   Shall shine the traffic of Jacob's ladder
>   Pitched betwixt Heaven and Charing Cross."

Such examples seemed to suggest this, although Jacob first dreamt the dream, the process of dreaming itself was already there to bring order out of chaos, light out of darkness, and draw both God and man together.

The ancient Chinese have defined meaning as "that which has always existed through itself". This dream for me was an intimation that the dreaming process must always have existed through itself, and that when the last secret of nature has been unveiled and the final problem of creation resolved, however opaque the heart of all matter, and swiftly changing as may be the many-faceted and elusive spirit, we shall still find, like stars in the night, images of the dream that always existed through itself. Many years later, I was greatly moved when one of the first men of Africa, a Stone-Age hunter in a wasteland greater I believe than even the wasteland in which Jacob dreamt his dream, informed me, "You know, there is a dream dreaming us." To this day I do not know anything to equal this feeling for what the dreaming process is to life or the implication that it is enough for creation to appear to us as the dreaming of a great dream and the unravelling and living of its meaning.

In the years that followed, I could easily have been talked, badgered and teased out of my belief in the importance of dreams, if it had not been for this dream in particular, and in general the significant role allotted to them in the stories of the Old Testament that we all knew by heart, and treasured long before we could be fed on other nourishment as in the collected works of the Brothers Grimm, Andrew Lang, Hans Andersen and the stories of Africa. As one moved out of the world of fairy-tales and was exposed to the onslaught of so-called realism, one became more vulnerable. Even so I was helped by the frequent appearance of dreams which had come at crucial moments in the history and literature of the past and which already in Homer's *Iliad* and *Odyssey* were clearly an instrument of the gods themselves.

I remember, for example, that when at a very early age I read in an anthology called *The Tales of Troy* that Zeus decided to inflict a dream on the great foredoomed Agamemnon as the indispensable overture to the sombre orchestration of Homeric men in conflict, this added to, and confirmed, the role of the dreams in the Bible that I already knew so well. From then on I assumed that was how everywhere, and at all times, and for all men, the dream was a kind of Admiralty chart especially designed for their searching selves by which their lives were navigated. Evidence to confirm this assumption was emphasised by the Arab proverb, "Tell me what a man dreams and I will tell you what he is." Significantly for me (who always wanted to be a story-teller) it made me believe that in some inscrutable way the art of writing, indeed all art, was a continuation by one's daylight self of a process begun in some dream conceived in the darkness of sleep.

I could not see how otherwise events so remote as those that occurred in the world of Joseph, or the great plain of Troy, could matter so much to a boy in the interior of twentieth-century Africa. What was it, I wondered, that made the whole Homeric world so real to us that some of us immediately were passionately on the side of the Greeks, others as zealously on that of the Trojans, and prepared with ardour to play at going to war with one another? Perhaps then I realised that all men were born either Trojans or Greeks? And all this somehow suggested that, no matter how rational and egotistical our attitudes, there existed a reality not only without geographical and cultural bounds but also outside space and time. That was both one of the most significant and the most mysterious elements for me about the world of religion and art. I have never been able to separate the two. I knew, of course, that even in a conventional reading of time Homer was nearer to us than men realised, only some seventy generations away. But in actuality I had only to read the *Iliad* and the *Odyssey* as I have many times in many languages, and instantly I felt as if I were shaking Homer by the hand.

So out of this, in time, there was to grow in me an awareness of the great company one kept in this overall dimension of life which enabled one not to be surprised even by the negative consequences it produced in my fellow-men. I was not amazed, for instance, that Shakespeare was so real to a person that George Bernard Shaw regarded him as a dangerous rival and because of an absurd streak of vanity was incapable of accepting his pre-eminence. It was perhaps a measure of Shaw's own quality that he could pick on the greatest as cause for envy and subject of malice. But the point is that his jealousies illustrated this timeless area which I had in mind and without which my own isolated self would have succumbed.

Nor must I fail to mention how lucky I was as a child by being sustained in my instinctive self by the primitive world into which I was born. Dreams to my black and coloured countrymen were real, vital and decisive facts, rivalling the reality of any in the objective physical world around them. As a child already they made manifest to me that for them, as Lévy-Bruhl was to proclaim later, the dream was the real god of primitive people. My own special Bushman nurse even had a father whose spirit was vivid with manly pride in the name of Dream bestowed on him at birth.

Yet once the need for more schooling drove me from my home, sustaining this particular note in my imagination became increasingly lonely and difficult work. It was not until my last year at school, when a master who had just come from Oxford and to whom I owe much, lent me Freud's *Introductory Lectures on Psycho-Analysis*, that this dishonoured state in myself became re-invested with honour.

The excitement caused by those volumes was intense. We all had to work part of the time during our holidays on the farm which was called "Wolwekop" ("The Mountain of the Wolves"). I found I could not leave my books at home when I had to go to work but had to take them with me. On one long, cold winter vacation, my particular task was herding a precious flock of ewes and their lambs in the hills not far from home. I do not think so valuable a flock has ever been better protected by Providence, for I was too preoccupied with my reading of Freud to watch it properly. Just the memory of those days brings up the sound of ewes bleating, demented by the disappearance of their offspring and the far-off, high-pitched quavering replies of lambs who had fallen asleep behind a boulder and so had been left far behind, exposed to the jackal or hyenas that might have been on the prowl—a situation that, ostensibly, I was there to prevent.

The recollection of that oddly Biblical sound remains charged with an agony of nostalgia not just for a golden moment in the blue of southern Africa, suspended as it were from on high in a witch-bowl of unclouded time and space, but also for another moment, infinitely more remote, which accompanied the movement of the human spirit in another wasteland farther and farther away from the garden that nourished it at the beginning. Africa has always been Old Testament country for me, and this was a singularly Old.Testament atmosphere in which to be introduced to such an Old Testament prophet as Freud. I may not have been able to articulate it at the time but I believe I had already an inkling that Freud's was an Old Testament temperament, trying with the inspiration of genius to give an Old Testament sense of the overwhelming importance of the hidden world to which the dream was an unique gate, its relevant, scientific and contemporary idiom. It was my first intimation of Freud as the Old Testament prophet of modern psychology. Jung, I was to find much later, was the exponent of the New.

Even so profound a nostalgia, however, cannot hold back a resurgence of the excitement which accompanied my reading of those dark blue volumes and which was my salute to them as a great breakthrough in the human spirit. For me they remain the best of Freud.

Yet thereafter I turned to everything Freud wrote with growing disappointment. He had less and less to say to me, personally. Even the language which was so simple, lucid and adequate in the beginning, seemed to become more and more obscure. An urge to invent hideous, lifeless words of his own and abandon the inexhaustible idiom of the European spirit takes over, and his own attitude becomes more dogmatic, letting a kind of metaphysics of sex usurp the place of the unclouded observation and deduction that had excited me in the beginning. The self-defeat implicit in this which already many years before, unbeknown to me, had worried Jung in his relationship with Freud, was, as far as I was concerned, final.

Nothing should have made this aspect of Freud more plausible and its appeal greater than the puritanical Calvinist world into which I was born. There in a one-sided, man-dominated world sex was, at best, a necessary evil. The community's attitude was invested with an abomination of it and woman as great as that expressed by Calvin's fanatical disciple John Knox, whose church really fathered the Dutch Reformed Church of my world and not that of the Holland of which it was ostensibly a branch.

Indeed the vast complex of the consequence of a compulsive suppression of sex in the mind and customs of man was so great that one could easily see why, as Freud implied, it could appear as the villain in almost every piece of human folly and individual and cultural derangement. Even the Victorian dancing, just becoming fashionable in our late-Edwardian colonial day, was regarded as sinful. A young girl I knew, for instance, was badly beaten with a length of rope by her eldest brother because she had taken part in an impromptu dance in a house where she happened to be staying. Woman's place was so much confined to the home, kitchen and nurseries, that one of my own sisters had sermons preached against her in our local church because she had had the presumption to become one of the first of her sex to go to a university and take a degree.

Obviously, in such a world, this aspect of Freud's approach had to have a certain compelling validity. Yet for me it failed because, ultimately, sex remained a part and not all, nor, indeed, even the greatest of the sources of life's energies.

Again, I found Freud's excursions into the field of religion and art inadequate. I could never remember a moment when the Christian church as I had encountered it in the interior of Africa had not only bored me unspeakably but seemed to me to have become an aberration from the main movement of the spirit recorded in my Grandfather's Book of Books. It was the Book to which I constantly turned, although even that was not wholly satisfactory. I knew that the movement of the spirit it represented was for me the most significant of all aspects of reality. But neither Freud nor any single church that I knew of, least of all that of my own people, seemed to throw any new light on, or to be remotely worthy of the two Testaments of the experience of faith that presided over my own beginnings.

On the contrary, the later Freud and the church both got in the way of what, in my imagination, seemed the direct experience of a meaning beyond my own immediate state of being. In that at least, I was not alone. In my own family the widening schism between science and religion had a devastating impact on my brothers and sisters who studied the sciences rather than humanities at their universities both in South Africa and abroad. One of my brothers to the end of his days devoted most of his energies in an effort to reconcile the claims of Darwin and Calvin on his spirit. For my own part, neither the attitude to religion which made a friend describe a church spire as "the hypodermic steeple, ever ready to inject the opium of the people", nor that of the master at school who had introduced me to Freud, which made him maintain that Salisbury Cathedral, spiking the blue as no other church does in the Constable canvas on which a reproduction hung over his desk, was nothing but "a glorified phallic symbol", made any sense to me. Religion and art and the search for living truth which my instinctive self held to be among the highest of values, were, I was oddly certain, greater than either. For me the passion of spirit that we call "religion", and the love of truth that impels the scientist, came from one indivisible primordial source, and their separation in the life of my time was a singularly artificial and catastrophic amputation.

By that time, Freud's name was no longer alone in the world. It was one of the awesome psychological trinity of Freud, Adler and Jung. Since they were bracketed together by everybody, I had no desire to look any deeper into the credentials of the other two, but assumed that Adler and Jung had to be likewise partial. With the typical capacity of a child of my time for pre-judgement and prejudice, I refused to read them, and so denied them the right, which no-one even lesser than they should be denied, of speaking for themselves. Accounts of how the three had disagreed among themselves convinced me how right I was to be no longer interested. Jung in particular, or so claimed the intellectual establishment of my world, had not only betrayed Freud but was just a woolly and unscientific mystic. Somehow I was induced into holding on to this odd belief.

By this time, what had started out as a feeling of isolation in the midst of my large family whom I loved, had assumed formidable and, for me, dangerous proportions. It had spread to a total dissociation from my own people in their attitudes to my black and coloured countrymen and the whole complex of that subtle and mysterious entanglement of spirit called colour prejudice.

At the age of seventeen already I found myself in active rebellion against the prevailing racial and colour prejudices. Whereas the rest of my family had all gone to universities either in the Cape or abroad in Holland and America, I had refused to follow their example. Despite my love of literature and history formal education had suddenly become bankrupt for me. As a first step towards writing I went to work on a newspaper in Durban on the East Coast of Africa and began to earn my own living. There in due course also I joined the poet Roy Campbell and William Plomer in the running of a literary magazine called *Voorslag* (Lash of a whip), one of whose main targets was racial discrimination.

Growing up as I had, in intimate relations with our black African countrymen, this prejudice had just been left out of my make-up. More, I was convinced it was not natural and instinctive in any of us.

I was certain we all started with a great love of our black and coloured people and I was convinced that we had been educated into the prejudices that divided us from one another. The violence and un-reason of these prejudices seemed to me proof of how self-doubt was at their source of origin. Others, of course, had felt the same, and had taken them to be peculiarly local phenomena condemning them, as Olive Schreiner had done so bravely and eloquently, on purely ethical grounds.

But to me there appeared to be something fundamental to all man-kind involved in the problem. Might not what we called colour prejudice in Africa be merely one manifestation of an inaccurate con-dition of spirit that afflicted human-beings all over the world in other forms? For that reason I suspected it was symptomatic of one of the most fateful issues of our time. Indeed, so fateful did I feel it to be that the hero of a book that I was trying to write experiences the hidden conflict of spirit to be a dangerous sickness of his body. This book, in many ways, was to prove prophetic. But it was also an intuitive antici-pation of what I was later to find empirically explained and confirmed by Jung. Today the whole range of psycho-somatic phenomena is taken for granted because of Jung and more often than not without much acknowledgement of the debt owed to him in that regard. But in this, my first book, *In a Province*, the decision of the hero to detach himself from all the collective prescriptions for the problems of life, and his determination to live them out alone in an individual and natural context of his own choosing, was important. In this sense too the book was somewhat prophetic and the hero became, perhaps, the first "drop-out" on literary record. Anyway he reflected my own growing isolation and antagonism to the mind, mood and trend of the pre-war world.

So far did it go that I abandoned the literary scene in London and went to live on a farm in the West Country of England, to practise what my book had preached. Art even then seemed to me a vocation that had not only to be expressed but lived as well. Ever since a chance journey to Japan in 1926 had not only confirmed my hatred of racial and colour prejudice but inflamed an inborn longing to see and know the world of my own time, to such an extent that I had once even worked my way as a stoker from Cape Town to Southampton, I had experienced life in an unusual variety of ways and settings. I had worked as a freelance writer and journalist through the great world recession in London, at times running out of money and going short of food. Speaking fluent Dutch, German, French, Flemish and of course English, my number of friends was as varied as it was large and unusual, and even on the farm it seemed to grow and diversify because I continued to commute from there also in my capacity as a diplomatic correspondent in London; but this inner isolation and emptiness did not diminish. Even the fact that my book made an immense impact on critics like Herbert Read and poets and writers of my own generation did not give me the meaning or purpose that I had hoped it would. Whenever, between farming and writing, I looked into myself, a feeling of inexplicable and unfathomable evasion grew. I was appalled by the cataclysmic split in a spirit once so profoundly committed to a dream reality.

I had been born with as great a passion for history as for stories—not surprisingly as both are part of the same indivisible process. History presents the story as lived. The story presents the options and possibilities of life that might have been and still can be lived. There are moments of national and individual crisis where the past is not an inevitability but presents life with the opportunity of a creative course of new action. I read history continually but this interest had already rendered me dissatisfied by the factual way in which history was written, and the seeming lack of interest of historians in the nature and meaning of the historical process itself. It was as if the recording of events was all that mattered. With one or two honourable exceptions like the great Burckhardt, they appeared to judge the book of life by its cover. I had a hunch that throughout the decades profound elements and energies, which had never been assessed or acknowledged, were at work; and that myth and legend and even dreams were as much historical material as anything preserved in the orthodox archives. It was not surprising, therefore, that the first wedge driven into my own inhibitions and resistances against the new psychology was provided by my sense of history.

I had been watching the rise of Hitler in Germany with terrible foreboding, increasingly dismayed by the inability of the English and French to see the phenomenon for what it was. All the reasons Hitler advanced to excuse, justify and explain himself and his movement made no sense. In the course of the slow, impervious and sullen pre-war years of ranting he seemed always to be speaking out of a tranced, mediumistic state. Hitler said only one thing that struck me as real, and that was, "I go the way fate has pointed me like a man walking in his sleep." That, and his own account of the dream which purported to have saved his life in the first World War, had an alliance of unholy meaning for me.

According to Hitler, in World War I he was asleep in an advanced salient of the German trenches when he dreamed "that he was about to be engulfed in an upheaval of earth and mud". He broke out of this nightmare with the utmost difficulty. Feeling suffocated and fighting for breath, he stumbled out of the dug-out for air. He had hardly got clear when an enemy shell hit the post and killed all his companions. He himself looked upon this dream as an act of Providence intervening to save him for a greater destiny. But the conviction that he was under the special protection of fate accelerated the process of inflation to which he was already prone.

One could not doubt, of course, that on the literal level in its special context of war the dream had indeed saved his life for the moment. But there was for me another dimension to the dream, even more important. I thought that it addressed also the most urgent of warnings of another kind of peril to the dreamer himself. It seemed to be trying to tell him that he was in imminent danger of being overwhelmed, not so much by the physical earth as by what the earth stood for in the imagination.

Always it has been one of the greatest images of titanic forces and urges of life that have their source below the daylight of reason in some dark underground of the human spirit, as great trees have their roots deep down in the blacked-out recesses of the earth. This dream, I felt, could not be warning the dreamer more clearly that he was in peril of being overwhelmed and suffocated in an upsurge of some dark, instinctive, unrecognised collective aspect of himself. Unless he woke up, in the sense that was an image of a process of being self-aware, and removed himself from the mass, the crowd, the collective pressures of whom his fellow soldiers were the image and their sleeping state the sign of their unawareness of their condition, he and they would all surely perish. The dream seemed to stress that his salvation was possible only in finding himself as an individual. But content in the purely literal surface manifestation of the dream, he neglected the cataclysmic warning latent in it. Reversing the deeper trend of his dream, he embarked on a course of rejoining the mass, the great mindless German collective compulsions to rally his countrymen round him in greater and more solidly congealed numbers than even the Kaiser had done. The whole of Germany swarmed to him like bees around their sovereign. It was transformed at once from a dream metaphor into a proposition of a direct and profound scientific exactitude. I was convinced that Germany and, by hypnotic induction, the whole of western Europe was at that moment walking towards unimagined disaster in a nightmare of sleep.

History, the legends and myths in which it has its roots and of which the dreaming process seemed so dynamic an element, appeared to be written in a way that offered no explanations and threw no light on its latent meaning. It seemed to ignore some unrecognised new meaning that was trying to draw attention to itself through war, social upheaval, racial conflict, individual tragedy and disaster that had been inflicted upon the human race since its expulsion from the Garden at the beginning. There seemed to be an underworld of history filled with forces far more powerful than the superficial ones that history professed to serve. Until this world was brought out into the light of day and recognised and understood, I believed that an amply discredited pattern of self-inflicted death and disaster would continue to reiterate itself and dominate the human scene. I had even coined a name for it and called it the "mythological dominant of history".

I came also to suspect that this area in myself from which my childhood interest in dreams had come was connected with it in a way not yet understood, because it was itself the subject of one of the most dangerous errors in our thinking. We assumed that "without" and "objective" were one and the same thing, as were "subjective" and "within". I believed that they were by no means synonymous and that there was something as objective *within* the human being as great as the objective *without*. If that were so, then men were subject to two great objective worlds: the physical world without; and a world within, invisible except to the sensibilities of the imagination. This objective world within had its own irrefutable geography and laws that one ignored or defied at one's mortal peril. One broke one's neck if one defied the laws of gravity in the world without. Equally, some disaster overwhelmed one and one's community if one ignored the facts of life and transgressed the laws of the world within.

That dream of Hitler, for instance, seemed as objective a fact as a cloud foretelling a storm to come. The lesson I had learned in childhood that no-one could subject dreams to his own will or fancy had gone deeply enough to make that clear. Dreams had a will of steel, and a way of their own in their role as direct manifestations of this inner objectivity. They were incapable of falsehood. Only our reading of them was liable to error, and I had an inkling that they, and the prompting of this other objectivity within, were the true sources of mythology, religion, legend and art, seeking and re-seeking recognition and expression through our several histories. If denied those by fair means, they sought them by foul. Refused admission at the front door of the spirit, they came in by force or stealth from the rear.

Gerard Manley Hopkins had already said it definitively when he wrote that there were not only "landscapes" for us but "inscapes" as well, or as he put it in one of his greatest poems,

"O, the mind, the mind has mountains,
cliffs of fall,
Frightful, sheer, no man fathomed."

It always seemed to me that this was a statement not just of great poetry but also of some scientific axiom. I already believed that poetry and art possessed their own transcendental importance for the spirit of man because, without them, no full statement of the truth is possible.

Truth is always greater than so-called fact. Until all things have been expressed not only in their scientific and religious aspects but also with full relevance to art and its graces, and all these aspects then translated precisely into living behaviour, they have not been expressed in their totality. Surely that is Blake's ultimate justification for predicting that when the arts decline, nations decay? Art, for me, became increasingly a manifestation of pentecostal spirit, seeking to make men aware of a greater reality. It introduced the seed of a greater becoming in the midst of our being: and out of this element of becoming we derived our senses of meaning and belonging. I saw art as a kind of magic mirror making visible what is invisible in us and the life of our time. An instrument also for making what is oldest in the human spirit contemporary and new. It was an unfailing source of increasing human awareness, and by such increase enabled life to renew itself in greater and more authoritative expressions of itself. Without art truth was not whole.

Examples in art of great scientific pronouncements on the matter appeared abundant enough, from Lucretius' poetic anticipation of the atomic theory millennia before Eddington, up to Shakespeare's "prophetic soul of the wide world dreaming on things to come", or most impressive of all, in his last play, where he begs that image of his future self, Ferdinand, full and complete in his betrothal at last to Miranda, Prospero's soul and daughter that was mother of his spirit, not to be dismayed because "we are such stuff as dreams are made on".

Germany in the 'thirties seemed to be of such stuff as nightmares were made on. Everyone in it was goose-stepping towards an abyss in a terrible dream of sleep. I thought to see the new German hordes in the grip of a long unacknowledged mythological dominant, grown terrible and angry through neglect and about to revenge itself not only upon Germany but an entire culture that had been indifferent to the legitimate claims of the forces of this "inscape" within themselves.

I could not accept that the explanation lay in the so-called injustices of the Treaty of Versailles concluded at the end of the 1914–18 war. That might well be the plausible excuse in which established history specialised and which made it so superficial an exercise for me. Surely the real motivation came from that underworld of life's past which is beyond articulation and where our several histories, unrecorded, defying articulation, are lodged deep as our own psychology? I believed that unless Hitler was stopped and stopped quickly, the greatest of all world wars would be upon us. We had only to study German mythology to see how the German spirit was fully mobilised for a mythological charade of the most shattering proportions that the world had ever seen.

I failed to convince even my closest friends, and in the end began a book to show how a mythological design obsessed the Hitler phenomenon. That was by far the most frightening part of it. German mythology was the only mythology that I knew in which the gods themselves were overthrown by the forces of darkness. In Hitler's Germany, surely we were watching precisely a massing of the forces of darkness for the overthrow of such forces of light as were still in the European spirit? We were witnessing, in fact, another horror instalment in the long serial of history similar to the 1914–18 war, on the eve of which a British Foreign Secretary pronounced the words, prophetic in more dimensions that he knew or consciously intended, "One by one the lights are going out all over Europe."

Although I had a mass of urgent practical duties to attend to, the running of my farm and days in London as a diplomatic correspondent, I yet worked away at the writing of my new book. Then, suddenly, I was sent to Germany to report on the terrifying Nuremberg Rally, and returned to England more dejected than ever before. At that moment Jung reappeared in my retarded reckoning.

I met a remarkable American journalist called Knickerbocker. He had just come from Zürich where he had interviewed Jung for his newspaper. He could talk about nothing else. He kept on saying that Jung was the only man who really knew what was happening in Europe, that none of the statesmen and politicians had any idea of what all this ascending volcanic rumbling on the European scene portended. Only Jung knew.

I listened, oddly rebuked yet fascinated. Of the many examples he gave me of Jung's present-day understanding, the one that stands out most clearly in my memory happens to be the one most relevant to Jung's wider significance. It emerged from a distinction that Jung drew for Knickerbocker between Mussolini and Hitler. Mussolini, according to Jung, could at a pinch be said to rule Italy. In no way whatsoever could one say that Hitler ruled Germany. That would be a cardinal and culpable error, Knickerbocker reported. "Jung told me never to forget for a moment that Hitler has the power he has, not because he rules Germany but because he *is* Germany. He is more of a myth than a man. He is the loudspeaker that makes audible all the inaudible murmurings of the German soul." And these murmurings, Jung had made it clear to Knickerbocker, had long since ceased to be a mythological reactivation of the German spirit: but instead had become black portents of a catastrophe of universal proportions.

There were, it is true, observations by Jung in this reported conversation with which I could not agree. His excursion into the political aspects of the problem of dealing with Nazism, such as his suggestion that Germany should somehow be induced to spend this archaic upsurge of itself in a war on Bolshevik Russia, seemed to me an evasion of his own profound insight into the nature and mythological origin of the problem. Later, he himself, when he came to reconsider, corrected it in depth. And I remember many post-war occasions when he spoke with increasing urgency of the necessity for us all to understand that the Russian problem in the external world could never be resolved without more disaster unless we first dealt with the "Russia" in ourselves. But at the time, my reservations were insignificant compared with the illumination and dawning confirmation of my own tentative quest conveyed by Knickerbocker's account of his meeting with Jung. These feelings finally overcame my resistances. I knew somehow then that I had been not just prejudiced but exceedingly silly, rejecting the one spirit that could have helped me in an area of unknowing wherein I myself had been groping in a singularly ill-informed fashion. But by then the war was almost immediately upon us. I managed to sell my farm and on the first of September volunteered for active service. Starting as a private soldier in the British Army, I was after some months recommended for a commission as an officer, and on completion of my training applied for commission in a famous British regiment. The Colonel who interviewed the five of us who had applied for commission saw me last because all the others had family connections with the regiment and I none.

"What made you pick on us?" he asked, genuinely bemused.

"Well it is quite simple, sir," I told him. "In 1848 we fought a battle against the British in South Africa and a platoon of the Regiment captured my grandfather, who was fighting against them . . . Then in the Anglo-Boer War in 1902, a company of the same battalion captured my father . . . So I thought it must be a pretty good regiment."

At that he beamed, saying: "Come on in. Come on in!"

Yet I went to war strangely comforted. Whatever the odds against us, I never doubted that Germany would be defeated, because Hitler was going against the titanic import of his own dream. Motivated by the logic of a mythology which demanded so dark and tragic a fulfilment as did the Teutonic one, I was convinced that he would be compelled to conduct the war in a manner that would make defeat inevitable. Then, in the twilight hour before the fall of the final night, like the lame god in the turgid myth of the overthrow of Valhalla, the crippled European spirit might snatch some light from the burnt-out ashes of an inadequate pattern and so rekindle a greater fire for itself than had been possible before.

During this period of war, whenever I had a moment to give to the world within myself, I realised that my former inner preoccupations were growing even greater than before. All sorts of things had happened during those long years of unreason which convinced me that this other dimension, below the manifest pattern of our private and personal, social and international lives, was one wherein the main character of the future was determined. Moreover, my own war which took me from North Africa, Ethiopia and Asia Minor on to Malaya and South-East Asia, had given me some inkling of the universality of the phenomenon. In particular, war against the Japanese in Java, where I was sent in 1942, and three and a half years in their prisoner-of-war camps, seemed to reveal how, despite pronounced differences in race, culture and history, and vast differences of space and time between the two countries, the forces which impelled the Japanese into war were akin to those that had overwhelmed the Germany of Hitler. The many plausible differences paled into insignificance before the similarities of the equinoxial pull which had drawn the Japanese like sleep-walkers stepping out in that oddly Germanic goose-step of theirs called "Hochi-tori" into the nightmare choreography of a similar mythological dominant. The parallels were not only close but often refined in detail. For instance, the sun, which is the image of the light of reason in man and walks as a god tall in most highly differentiated mythologies, was for the Japanese the same feminine phenomenon that it was for the Germans. Yet the infinitely renewing and renewable moon that swings the sea of change and symbolises all that is eternally feminine in the spirit of man, by some ominous perversity of the aboriginal urgings of both Germans and Japanese, was rendered into a fixed and immutable masculinity.

Nor was it an accident that both were fundamentally "father" countries. I had always thought it important in the psychology of countries as to whether they thought of themselves as "father" or "mother" countries. One had only to hear the crowd at Nuremberg singing of the *Vaterland*, some hundreds of thousands of individuals joining in one mindless voice, to realise how much an unyielding "father" was in charge of the German spirit. The bonds between this "father" dominant and some submerged Wotan element of ancient Germany had somehow bypassed Holy Roman transformation and remained intact.

As for the Japanese, despite the presence of a goddess in their sun, theirs was a similar father-dominated spirit which sent them swarming like bees not around a queen-bee but a king-bee in the person of their emperor. It was no accident that of the three great proverbial terrors of Japanese life, "Father, fire, and earthquake", "father" was the greatest.

But perhaps the main lesson for me was that war did not come to us by some form of spontaneous generation in the human spirit. Nor was it a design imposed on us by greedy, ambitious men, armament manufacturers, international financiers, freemasons, Jews or any of the conventional scapegoats upon whom societies choose to inflict their own inadequacies. It was monstrously born of the way we all lived what we called "the peace". I felt, in a way that I could not define, that we too had contributed to the reaction of Germans and Japanese to the reality of our time. We too, therefore, had to share some of the responsibility in the matter. Through our deeds of omission, we too were the accomplices before (but I hoped not after) the fact of the war which we were fighting. Only by understanding how we were all a part of the same contemporary pattern could we defeat those dark forces with a true understanding of their nature and origin. This was vital if we were to be free to embark on a way of peace which would not lead to a repetition of the vengeful past.

But even more, I began to have a firmer intimation of how much greater the role of symbolism was than either I, or my generation, suspected. I had already accepted that it had a dynamic, initiating function in the imagination of man. Symbols seemed to be the imposed first material out of which we fashioned new ways of thought and spirit in order to achieve greater quality of being. I had been unable, although I had tried, to look on symbolism as the Freudian-inclined intellectual elders and betters of my generation were increasingly doing. Even then it had seemed as absurd to me as it does today, to hear them talk of Freudian, Jungian or Adlerian but, of course, mostly Freudian symbols. None of these adjectives or, for that matter, any others borrowed from intellectuals and artists marching under the fly-blown banners of nineteenth-century pioneers of symbology to their latest existentialist inheritors. seemed to me appropriate. They were a complex phenomenon issuing from the great objective within and were the property of no single mind, however original or exalted. Any proprietorial rights in the matter belonged to life and not to any particular man. I could not accept that symbols were devices of the human spirit for hiding an abhorrent self. If symbols did this, it was only because we failed to accept their pre-eminence on the scene of our spirit.

On the contrary, I saw them as part of a natural function striving night and day to inform us of our deeper, more meaningful and authentic selves. I could not go with an intellectual fashion which claimed on scientific grounds that every man invented his own symbols. I was not even sure, except within the limits of a painfully prescribed comprehension, that man did all his thinking for himself. I had a feeling that even our own capacity for thinking shrank into painfully humble proportions compared with another kind of reality which was, as it were, thinking through us.

Yet even these reservations about human thought-capacity were trivial set against my conviction that we were utterly incapable of inventing the content of symbols. They seemed to issue straight out of our deepest nature as starlight out of the night. Whether we liked it or not these symbols were inflicted on us as a spur to a widening vision. I had never seen so clearly as during the war how symbolism infected the human spirit and imagination, and compelled human-beings to act them out in blind, ritualistic behaviour. For me that was final proof of our incapacity for inventing them. Already I held it as axiomatic that human-beings on their own were incapable of inventing anything that was greater than themselves. Whatever we created, however truly it reflected our creation, was always invested with something more powerful than the selves which had produced it. The power and glory was at our service, but never of our invention. The trouble was, as exemplified by the war, that despite the light of all our knowledge, reason and perception, we had failed to live out our symbol meaningfully. By taking it literally we had pursued its many-dimensional reality in a one-dimensional way.

For instance, it would seem that the Germans behaved as they did to the Jews because they were symbolic to them of their own inner darkness. So, in persecuting them as human beings the Germans themselves lost their own common humanity. We are all mirrors which reflect back to us, from without, that which we despise and reject within ourselves. But by destroying the enemy without, because of what he reflects, we do not rid ourselves of the enemy within.

I remember one particular day in prison when the nature of all this seemed clear to me. It was a day when one of those strange outbursts of hatred against us exploded among our "hosts" (as we called the Japanese). They had us absolutely in their power. We had no resources of defence except what we possessed in natural spirit. And these explosions were usually unpredictable. They would occur when we ourselves had done nothing, however trivial, to provoke them. Then some of us suspected that these outbursts were impelled by some connection with the waxing and waning of the moon. We had noticed that as the moon filled out the more it seemed to swing a sea of unreason in the minds of the Japanese. It drew it like a great neap tide high up into the foreshore of their imagination. Then as the moon began to decline, a dark insecurity often seemed to overcome our captors. It was then that they would be compelled to inflict the worst and most indiscriminate of their beatings, and the most horrific of their cruelties upon us.

I became increasingly aware of this compulsive mechanism in their spirit and perpetually sought for a way in which we could mitigate the process. But protest, verbal response, or silent acceptance only aggravated it. Our only protection was to follow the example of Job on his ash-heap, accepting all his dangerously unjust afflictions with similar patience, dignity and some intuition, perhaps, that it was all part of some universal purpose.

This particular enlightenment to which I have referred was on just such an occasion. We had all been beaten up for no apparent reason. As always when this happened, I had noticed a strange, unseeing look in the eyes of the Japanese. It was focussed not at us but at something beyond us. Were they afraid that, should their eyes focus on us, they would recognise our common humanity, and so the cruelties they were inflicting would not only be challenged but extinguished?

Yet there was again something extraordinarily familiar to me about this look. Where had I seen it before? In the eyes of my men and fellow-officers there was an expression of utter bewilderment. Yet that, too, seemed just as familiar to me as the look on the Japanese faces. Then suddenly I had it! I had seen that look of bewilderment so often in the law courts of my native South Africa when some black native countryman was being tried in a language he could not understand, and for a breach of laws that often he did not even know existed. And even when he did know of their existence he certainly had no understanding of the assumptions that served as their justification. The judges too, in passing sentence, rarely looked at the uncomprehending accused. Their eyes too were generally focussed on some abstract of vision beyond the ragged and tattered creature in the dock, as if afraid that one glance would deprive them of their capacity for passing judgement.

The implication followed the recognition. We too treated the black man in Africa as we did because we had abstracted him from his human reality and allowed him to become a symbol of our own unawareness. We were projecting upon him an unknown part of ourselves; punishing him and at the same time punishing a dark, rejected aspect of ourselves. It was another intimation of the symbolism of colour in producing specially acute forms of racial differences in my native country.

Gradually I became more and more appalled by the collective failures in this regard not only of a single nation but of the cultures of our time, indeed of the whole civilisation that had nourished them. The same mechanism, too, trapped smaller groups, from parents and children, husbands and wives, lovers and enemies, down to individuals like myself in our relationships with one another. I was appalled by a roll-call of human errors I myself had committed out of the same unseen projections in my own life.

It seemed important to maintain the proportions in the delicate balance of both collective and individual values which were involved in a symbolic dimension of reality. Human beings could be too "good" in both the collective and individual senses, and so call down upon themselves an horrific revenge for having neglected other valid collective and individual values. I reflected in this regard on two strange social phenomena that I had encountered both in Malaya and Java.

In Malay it was heralded under the cry of *Amok* which is one of the most frightening I have heard. In Java it went under the name of *Mata Kelap*, or the Dark Eye. In both instances some man was involved—I have only encountered it in men—usually at the age of forty, which is, significantly, at the beginning of the second half of life. The man was invariably someone who had done his duty by wife, children and society with the utmost circumspection down to the minutest detail of the elaborate conventions governing behaviour in these matters in that part of the world. Then, without warning, he would snatch his kriss* from its sheath. Kriss in hand he would rush out to kill as many men, women and children as were near him, though up to that moment he may have loved them, and none of them had done him any personal injury.

What made this outburst of individual violence even more significant to me was that both Javanese and Malays individually and collectively set such store by gentleness, grace, delicate and considerate manners. Some of this is implicit in the name Malay, applied to the peoples of Malaya and of the coastal belts of those South-East Asian archipelagos, shining like strings of emeralds in the blue seas, and made more profound by tall, monsoon clouds reflected below the brilliant surface of the blinding ocean. The word Malay, derived as it is from *malu*, gentle, denotes that they think of themselves as an essentially gentle people.

Were they over-gentle and hence the relapse into violence? Was there a connection between the two? Was goodness not subject also to the laws of proportion and had to beware of its own excess? From where did these laws issue? What made them reach out with so long, strong and murderous an arm into the dark around us? Of course, I could not tell. But the question remained with me.

None the less, the Javanese term *Mata Kelap* and its intimation that the eye of the man who ran *Amok* thus had suddenly darkened, seemed to be full of potential meaning. It lived with me, as a seed, out of which grew, in time, a feeling of a certain understanding not only of colour prejudice and intolerance in South Africa, but of prejudice, intolerance and other forms of fanaticism in every nation and human soul. Many years later I was compelled to orchestrate such conclusions as I could draw in a book I inevitably called *The Dark Eye in Africa*. Today I could widen its conclusions and call it "The Dark Eye of the World".

When eventually I came out of prison to begin another and even stranger round of soldiering in South-East Asia, I was to find that the indigenous people there too had congealed into a mass collectively. So darkened and charged were they with the strange electricity of injured spirit that they ran *Amok* among the Dutch who had been

* The Malay and also Javanese dagger.

their masters for more than three hundred years. I was intimately involved, therefore, for nearly three years with a contemporary example of what happens when a natural, collective value had its validity denied, as it had been by the Dutch for the Indonesians. The British in India and the French in Indo-China had followed the same pattern. All had used their power to bestow many material benefits but in the process had prevented those peoples from living out their own ancient cultures.

In the beginning, in Java, I had to deal with riots and murders in the streets. But on a more tender occasion I saw Sukarno on a pilgrimage to his mother in Eastern Java whom he had not seen for many years. As he knelt at her feet to receive her blessing, I found myself profoundly stirred. More, I, who did not really respect him, despite his immense charm, was nearly choked by the collective emotion of the crowd of seventy thousand who had followed him and were sobbing with relief because the suppressed and accumulated longing of centuries to see someone of their own kind leading them again now had found a living symbol at last. But again, where did such volcanic forces in the human being come from? What gave them such overwhelming power over men? How and what did one and societies do to contain them?

The question stayed with me through all those long inarticulate and random years of war, imprisonment, and then subsequent war. I suspected that we would never know how to set about dealing with these dark forces until we knew more of their origin, nature and areas of growth. I was encouraged in this because of the extent to which I had achieved some understanding of these great non-rational imponderables in the Japanese during our years of imprisonment. And understanding helped me to invest our experience with some of the humanity that it so sorely lacked. What is more important, perhaps, it helped the two of us in the prison camp who were chiefly responsible for bringing some six thousand men through the experience, to do so not only without any feelings of bitterness for the Japanese, but with that extraordinary liberating conviction that our enemies had been forgiven because they truly "knew not what they did". One and all, we ended up, in the main, with nothing but compassion for the Japanese that they should have been so unselved as to commit such atrocities upon us.

That encouraged me. Compassion leaves an indelible blueprint of the recognition that life so sorely needs between one individual and another; one nation and another; one culture and another. It is also valid for the road which our spirit should be building now for crossing the historical abyss that still separates us from a truly contemporary vision of life, and the increase of life and meaning that awaits us in the future. Somehow we have to understand the intimations which come at us out of our natures like lightning in the dark, and which are portents of great possibilities of new being, preparing to fall upon our arrested and arid lives like rain on desert earth. Accordingly it seemed more and more to me that we needed to serve and express them with all that we have of light, reason, endurance and fortitude.

In particular I began to re-examine what I recollected of history in order to see what connection there might be between history and the denial of symbolism in our life. Perhaps history, properly observed, was not the rationalistic pattern presented by historians. Was its deepest meaning an expression of unrecognised or misunderstood mythological pressures within the human spirit? Were symbols the first utterances of a submerged thrust of new being in man himself?

By what we call chance I managed to find a remarkable authoritative and detailed Dutch translation of a lengthy German study of the myths and legends of Greece and Rome abandoned, of all places, in the corner of a Japanese prison store. I re-read the Classics, particularly Homer and Virgil, and Dante, all in various languages, as well as the incomparable Shakespeare. I then read the Bible from beginning to end in its authorised English version as well as in Dutch, French and German translations. I was amazed how this vast world, apparently lost below the horizon of Time, could still hound my imagination with undiminished vitality.

Above all I was particularly struck by the extraordinary phenomenon of the Renaissance. It seemed to me that it was so precisely a re-awakening and rebirth of all that was best in the vast complex of the history of the Western world that had preceded it, because the extremes of the human spirit which had been at war with one another were joined in it for a while in harmony with a third; the Roman and the Greek with the Hebraic.

On one hand was the highly organised Roman aspect of a spirit dedicated to law and order and life's need for spiritual authority. It was also a protracted exercise of an alert, observant and wide-ranging intellect. On the other hand there was the world of ancient Greece which, as a result of the fall of Constantinople and the flight to safety in the West of the scholars with their books and archives, brought the Christian-Roman attitude into contact (after centuries of crippling separation) with an approach to life based more on feeling and a recognition of the non-rational factors. That search of the many-sided Greek spirit for balance, proportion and a condition of a sanity of mind and body was one of the most impressive excursions in whole-ness to which European man had had access. Suddenly its openness to the claims of both external and internal realities was held up as a clear mirror wherein Europe, already straining to escape from its long medieval preoccupations, could see how slanted and partial it had become.

However impressive the totalitarianism of spirit of the Christian church of Rome and the centuries of profound intellectual rationalisa-tion of the original inspiration and experience of Christianity which supported it, this ancient Greek world seemed a more naturally religious world than the Christian world in which the Reformation was about to explode. Even at the greatest period of Greek history and at its point of loftiest achievement in arts, science, philosophy, politics, and affairs of religion, the gods themselves did not hesitate to come down from Olympus and participate, in some shape, in the heat and dust of the battle to live out the meaning that invested life on earth. Indeed the fact that the gods themselves were housed on their native Olympus seemed to be significant proof of the close and inti-mate connection of Greece with its religious experience. It was also significant that Greece's decline started with a relegation of its gods to the planets and outer spaces. It seemed a self-evident truth that some-how the sheer geographical distance between a man and his "religious" images reflected the extent of his own inner nearness or separation from his sense of his own greatest meaning. If so this made the con-ventional Christian location of a God in a remote blue Heaven just as alarming as, conversely, the descent of his Son to earth was reassuring.

More, what made this period of history so peculiarly significant was that although it was without any religious dogma, although it had temples, it had no organised Church or priesthood in the Christian-Roman sense. It has been dismissed as pagan and praised by the rationalists of today for having been one of the most impressive efforts ever to live life without religion. My interpretation was that it was a truly religious age. Every man and woman in it walked by day, slept and dreamed at night, in the company of their gods. It was surely a religion based on a continuous religious experience rather than on dogma or metaphysical speculation. The meaning it gave to the imagination of man accordingly prevented it from becoming static and pinned down to one immovable interpretation as in the world derived from Rome.

Most moving, too, was the role allotted to Fate in the Greek world. It was not "fatalistic" as in the Arab sense. It only intervened in the lives of men when, through hubris or unawareness, they exceeded their proportions. In so far as it was aware of and obedient to proportion, the human spirit could have been freer in Athens at its best than in any other age. Obedience, too, was easier because the gods themselves set men the example. Even the greatest of them, Zeus, was subject to Fate and could not interfere with its processes. Fate was the overall law of creation in its totality, and whatever had created it was subject to his own creation.

To put it in our own religious terms, it demonstrated that God, the Creator, had surrendered some of His authority in the very act of creation, and had set himself not above, but freely subject to His own laws. This subjection, as also in the Greek example of Fate, was for me one of the most meaningful and moving manifestations of the ultimate in religion. But where and how had it obtained its power over our imagery of God and man?

I realise of course how much of a simplification this is of history. But it gives some idea of the exhilaration conveyed to me in my Japanese prison contemplating the vista of the vast inheritance we had received from the Roman lawfulness in the human spirit, and at the same time observing its cross-pollination with the Greek sense of fatefulness in our midst. But what did Europe not owe to the Hebraic contribution? The unfailing struggle of the Jewish people to serve, even at the cost of forsaking all others, those great, invisible values of the One that was also the infinite many, seemed to have inflamed the Renaissance spirit with an unparalleled passion for fullness.

The role the Bible itself played in all this, of course, was immense. The rediscovery of Greece coincided with the world's rediscovery of the original Biblical material which dogmatic authority had so long kept to itself in its privileged capsule of the Latin tongue for a Catholic elite. Suddenly, as a result of the invention of the printing press, the Bible was translated into English and German and widely disseminated among ordinary men and women. Suddenly western man became a living trinity, creative and renewing. A new excitement impelled his spirit, and a boundless curiosity his senses. He began to explore the world without and within in a way hitherto unknown. For the greatest characteristic of Renaissance man, whether artist, philosopher, humanist, explorer, king or councillor of state, seems to be that they all lived and worked with the whole of their personalities. Leonardo da Vinci, the artist, scientist, and engineer, and the companion of

kings, was a classic example. In the great humanists like Erasmus and
Thomas More, past, present and future were not fragmented but
were a part of, and the whole spiritual inheritance of, European man
from its remote pagan origin to its tumultuous present, not only made
whole but transformed into examples of living behaviour.

Even in the Britain I had learned to love, no period of history seemed
to me to have produced the equal of Elizabethan man, the true Renaissance phenomenon. For him, the idea and the capacity to act on it
was a unified whole. Never has the world produced so complete an
awareness of this as, I believe, in Shakespeare, matched with such an
unparalleled gift for expression.

As a result, when I thought of how slanted and partial we had all
become, I felt great despair over the vista of decline and fall evoked.
For alas, this Renaissance unity of extremes did not last. The power of
the negation of the long centuries of arrested introspection which had
gone before, induced it to evolve into another opposite. More and
more committed to extraverted expressions of itself, it broke from
the wholeness which this kind of trinity of spirit had briefly accomplished. As a French proverb says, men have to become that which
they oppose. As the Reformation orchestrated, spread and became
more commanding, men set out on another one-sided road of advance
that was almost exclusively directed to the external world. It concentrated more on a tangible, ponderable reality which had had its claims
ignored for so long.

Profound acts of separation from our totality of spirit, such as this,
may well have been necessary for the evolution of human awareness:
provisional stages needed on the way to totality. Yet there would
have been more comfort in this qualification if history had not made
plain how difficult it was for human beings to relinquish, of their
own free will, an evolutionary approach that had not only outlived
its uses but become a danger to the men and societies who persisted in
still promoting it. History teaches that men as a rule do not break
with specialised processes which apparently have served them well,
without the help of disaster. The firmer and more intellectually
plausible the grip, and the longer the habit of a specialised development, then the greater the disaster and catastrophe needed to free the
human spirit from the drowning embrace of exclusive conditionings.

I had only to think of the war that was raging all round me to have
overwhelming proof of this fact. Already I saw how Clausewitz's
definition of "war as a continuation of policy when all other means
had failed it" could be re-phrased in depth. It could be seen as a con-

tinuation of a profundity of spirit trying to be lived but hampered by sharply-sided men who not only failed it but tried to pin it down to the one aspect of itself which they found desirable. This explained to me the strange relief I had observed in many beings at the outbreak of the war. It was not just relief that what had appeared for long to be a menace was about to be fought and overcome. It was also a relief that a way of life which had been apparently devoid of purpose had now, with the declaration of war, suddenly again acquired meaning.

Men could once more serve a cause greater than any egotistical pursuit of themselves. War, I concluded, was perhaps a terrible surgeon of life called in to cut away some atrophied limb of the human spirit. And this war in which I was engaged had been made inevitable, I suspected, by another one-sided extraverted process of evolution after the Renaissance. This process too had now served its purpose. Outworn, it had to make way for something greater. But since we had lacked both the vision and the vitality to clear the way of our own volition, one more war had come as the terrible healer to this tragic bedside of our spirit.

What was remarkable was that we had not seen it coming. Yet, ever since the Reformation the signs and portents had been warning that, unless we renewed ourselves, disaster after disaster would crowd in on us and our societies. There had been a terrible succession of religious and other wars inflicted on Europe as a consequence of the strange barbarian that European man had become in the name of civilisation. Yet surely the most precious value implicit in the coming of Christ and the New Testament was that of an individual capable of taking upon himself the great universals and making them specific in his own imagination and being? But the concept of the individual had been almost smothered by the Roman emphasis on collective and communal values. It was alarming how soon after the Renaissance this view of the individual had lost its wholeness and declined into an increasingly arid intellectualism.

Had this egotistical upsurge confined itself to individuals, the consequences might perhaps not have been so catastrophic. Unfortunately the majority of individuals who rejected the Catholic collective seemed darkly compelled to gang up in their new egotistical yearnings and to form sharply-sided collectives of their own. This applied not only to Reformers but to states, nations and races, leading to a proliferation of nationalisms ultimately to be called (as a passport to intellectual respectability) "self-determination". But this splintered Europe as if it were an exploding grenade. This nationalism increasingly resembled the collective equivalent of egotism uncontained in any value greater than itself. European values of the spirit seemed increasingly subservient to purely rational concepts of reality. A consequent tendency to assume that what was visible, concrete, and externally demonstrable was the only meaningful reality, divorced European man more and more from his natural, instinctive and intuitive self. Naturally this produced a great decline in the feeling values; a great fall in man's instinctive reverence for life; and encouraged such an arrogant assertion of the rational side of man that it usurped the power of the whole and introduced, in reverse, as great a spiritual tyranny as the one which had preceded it. Soon European man had raised the "idea" to such a height that humans would kill one another for it. This was the hubris, I felt certain, which had provoked the cataclysmic disaster which I was experiencing in part; and which was a disaster of surprisingly long and steady growth.

Perhaps the example of this proliferation in European man which is most relevant occurred in France at the end of the eighteenth century. This century which was, and still is, labelled as the century of Reason. But despite its resplendent by-products of art and philosophy, it was one of the most alarming periods in modern history. Rare achievements in art, philosophy, science and religion cannot be measured in terms of their pretensions and must be assessed in the context of their age and their consequences in the lives of living men. Judged by those standards, the results in France of this age of pure reason were appalling, ending, as it did, in the monstrous phenomenon called the French Revolution.

Again because conventional history takes so limited a view of its own processes, we tend to regard it in unconnected segments of comparatively limited duration, instead of seeing the long, slow growth of which they are an integral part. We think of the French Revolution as something gone with the wind, and Napoleon. Whereas the process (of which it was only a symptom) goes on to this day, and not only in France, and is widening at a terrifying speed the post-Renaissance salient in the classical defences of the spirit of Europe.

The Russian Revolution, so much a product of a kind of sterile, excessively political and economic Calvinism, so much the child of ideas, is another example that made its French antecedent look like an amateur amongst these disasters increasingly rooted in ideological abstracts of humanity. Like the French Revolution, it too is far from over and goes on in the spirit of modern man. Both were states of mind long before they became political and sociological phenomena. So again the world is threatened far more by the partiality of spirit that is Communism than it is by any particular social or political manifestation of the Marx–Engels–Lenin complex. As always, long before the riots and barricading of the streets begin, the spirit of man starts barricading itself and then proceeds to throw stones through the windows of the mind. Both the power and devastation of these and similar explosions in the European spirit appear to have increased with geometric progression in relation to man's technological advance. As his capacity to exploit nature and its resources accelerates, rational, extraverted assumptions dominate his way of life.

Most relevant too in this aspect of reappraisal was the Seven Years' War of Frederick the Great. Here was a prince so in love with eighteenth-century France that he spoke German with a French accent. Here was a man so devoted to Voltaire, the prophet of reason, that he made him live for years at the Prussian Court. It was, in fact, the beginning of an unmistakable Brandenburg prelude to the orchestration of the larger Wagnerian theme demanding the Götterdämmerung of Germany to produce also the last world war. Yet terrible as Frederick's war was in the context of its age, it was infantile in comparison to the succession of wars and the devastation of classical Europe, initiated by Napoleon. But even these Napoleonic wars were mere gladiatorial exercises compared to such horrific manifestations as the American Civil War, which too is still persisting in another dimension in the spirit of the Americans, the first World War and finally this last war. All seemed continuations of the same chain of continuations, of the same chain of volcanic eruptions of some submerged spirit of man. And these major demonstrations on the debit side of the negations deployed since the Renaissance of course leave out of the reckoning all the minor colonial wars, rebellions, social upheavals and outbursts of violence sloganised as "rights of self-determination", and "validities of nationalism" which scorched the international scene in-between. When added up these constitute a formidable and horrific sum of disaster.

One of the most interesting things about the unreason produced by the assertion of pure reason as the dominant in our values was the fact that, in the midst of all this, it was as if human beings instinctively had an inkling of the cause of these horrific exercises in destruction. For instance, the guillotine was invented to behead the victims of the Revolution as speedily and impersonally as possible. It was as if the populace of France knew that the offending member, the culprit in this Grand-guignol aspect of history, was the head, the seat of logic and reason. So they had tried to dispose of all it represented in this senseless, ritualistic and literal symbolic manner. After all, one cannot overlook the symbolic importance of the fact that, when the French Revolution was perpetrating its greatest inhumanities against helpless men and women, it officially deposed God and in His place actually crowned a goddess of Reason in Notre-Dame in Paris.

Then, as this wave of unreason curved high to break over France, there came the strange appearance of Jean-Jacques Rousseau. Whatever the approximations of his approach to reality, he had an unerring intuition to which he held, although the whole trend of his time worked to contradict it. Somehow he knew and proclaimed eloquently that the inadequacies of nis day were due to a profound neglect of natural man, the first begetter of our spirit. He then proceeded to demand a new social contract from life based on more natural and greater feeling values than those then in command of the human scene. All this was summed up in his concept of the "noble savage".

If taken literally, it does not take us far. However, taken symbolically as a personification of a vast area of neglect in the modern spirit, out of which new and greater human values might be extracted, this concept seems to me to have been extremely accurate, and of the highest importance to our present future. It certainly made me look at the scene of my own native South Africa afresh and to realise in a new way how the indigenous people of Africa, although no longer primitive in the sense that the Stone-Age aboriginal Bushmen of the Kalahari were, they were, for all their relative sophistication, far closer to their natural selves than we were. As a result they had become more and more something of a mirror reflecting a forgotten and fast-receding part of ourselves. Perhaps for this reason they inevitably provoked a desperate reaction from the Protestant-Calvinist, rationalistic Europeans that we were in Africa. What, elsewhere, were just racial tensions, in South Africa acquired another dimension and a greater intensity.

I did not overlook in all this the importance of the decline of religion in the Greek and non-institutional sense. That seemed to me the master dimension of all. Only religion gives life the over-riding value to which all others are subservient, and on which a life of meaning depended. I was painfully aware how the loss of religious power had increased as this gap in the spirit of man widened. It seemed to me no accident that what had started as wars of religion in Europe, became converted into upheavals like the French and Russian revolutions. One of the main targets of the instigators of violent change was always religion. One knew how unrelenting the perpetrators of the Russian Revolution had been from the beginning in their attack on religion. No-one could be a member of the Communist Party unless he was a professed and dedicated atheist.

In so far as these objections to religion were directed against the churches and organised religious institutions of our time, I could see a certain validity which the excesses of the argument did not impugn. There was, for instance, this progressive rift between religion and the scientific spirit. At their best, both seemed to be bound on the same quest. But I was as dismayed at their mutual failure to understand each other.

Moreover, as I saw it, the churches had abdicated their religious task for a more worldly involvement in the political and social issues of the modern age. The example of Christ implied such a profound revolution in society and the practical life of man precisely because He was concerned with the fate of man before and beyond any particular social issue of His day. When He exhorted the Pharisees to "render unto Caesar what was Caesar's and to God what was God's" He was stating a resolution of two valid extremes always in conflict within any given community.

I had only to look into my own life to realise how, ever since my childhood, the church into which I was born and all the other churches I had encountered, far from promoting the natural interest I believe I have always had in religion, seemed to come down like an iron curtain between me and my own religious feelings. This reaction was something that came about despite itself. I tried hard to like the church. I fought my natural reaction away from it for years because of the history and cultural conditioning of my family, the example of parents I loved, and the precepts of friends and masters I respected. Also I acknowledged the need for churches and religious institutions in the collective life of man. I was born profoundly biased their way. Wherever I went in the world I took great comfort in looking not only at Christian churches but also entering the temples of countries as far away as Ceylon, India and Japan. Indeed, any ground consecrated by pagan, Hindu, Buddhist or Christian in the name of their gods had similar numinous effects.

For instance, I was deeply moved at the sight of the modest piles of stones raised at random by the almost vanished Hottentots to their god-hero Heitse-Eibib in some wasteland of southern Africa. Heitse-Eibib was a divine intangible for them, revealing himself in the red of dawn as a spirit coming home bleeding after battle fought on behalf of light against darkness and who, though often killed in his role as their god-hero, was unfailingly resurrected, and always reminding them of his re-ascension in the rising wind. Often I have sat with one of these vanishing copper-coloured men in the heat of summer under some great camel thorn tree, and heard my companion say with profound satisfaction that it was the spirit of Heitse-Eibib that had come to extract so silky a rustle from the green above us, as a sign that no matter where they went he would always be and go with his people. As a child no church brought my native sense of religion alive more acutely than that.

So wherever I went in the world I never failed to go into churches and temples, and visit the places held to be sacred by the peoples of the many lands I had visited before the war, not only because of my own need but also out of a feeling that otherwise I would not know the peoples themselves as I should know them.

The trouble for me only began when I joined congregations in such places and was compelled to listen to the priests and their utterances. Instantly I was dismayed, and whatever there had been of God in the church or temple fled. Fortunately, I never fell into the error of looking upon organised religion and the aboriginal hunger in the spirit of men that we call religion as completely the same thing. However organised creed came between me and religion: between me and the New Testament and the utterances of St Paul, particularly in his thirteenth chapter of his second Letter to the Corinthians, which I still find one of the greatest utterances of the spirit ever penned. I knew that the churches tried to serve what was most important and vital for the continuation of the human spirit. But did that make them more adequate for the unacknowledged and desperate religious necessities of my time? Could it perhaps be another form of religion? For it was another of those prison perceptions that became axiomatic to me; only religion could take the place of religion. Religion, I was convinced, could not be pinned down to one final dogmatic interpretation, nor even to one final revelation. The Book of Revelations already was final proof for me that the Bible ended with the drawbridge of the Christian citadel let down and the road open once more for the spirit of man to travel to the end of time with a renewing and infinitely renewable capacity for fresh religious experience and revelation.

I had a conviction that I cherished dearly, namely that repetitions of amply discredited patterns of history were neither inevitable nor necessary; indeed that history itself sought nothing more ardently than to be delivered forever from the dark negations hitherto implicit in its processes. But it was a lonely, ill-armed sort of belief. So isolated was I in this area of myself that I came back from war more lonely than I had ever felt in life before.

The war ended officially in 1945 but my war went on longer. I was compelled to go straight back from a Japanese prison into active service in Java in order to deal with the revolts of the islanders against their former Dutch masters. I had a brief two weeks of urgent duty in Europe reporting to Mr Attlee, the Prime Minister, and various members of the British War Cabinet who sent me on to Holland to try and persuade the Dutch Government to adopt a truly contemporary policy towards their former Empire. I returned to Java as Lord Mountbatten's military and political adviser and was involved in more years of war, half-war and uneasy periods of brittle peace. I stayed on even after Mountbatten's departure as Viceroy to India and the ultimate withdrawal of British forces from South-East Asia as military representative of the United Kingdom. I returned to Britain therefore nearly three years after the end of the war. Despite tempting offers of promotion I resigned a permanent commission in the army. The day I left the army, however, was one of the saddest I had ever experienced because I was leaving the truest community of men I had ever known.

So long and unbroken had my war service been that I still had some fourteen months of accumulated leave. But I soon found myself appalled by the extent to which the war, already, after only three years, had been forgotten. The cause for which I believed we had fought it seemed to be obliterated from the consideration of men. I was appalled by the selfishness, deviousness and the extraordinary greed of ordinary men and women. The army behind me seemed to be a compassionate order of mercy compared to the bitter, competitive civilian world that I now entered. Politicians, artists and intellectuals seemed to have taken up the very partialities of mind and slants of spirit which (I thought) had produced the war. The loss of a sense of history was almost more frightening than their seeming oblivion of the more immediate war. I had done all that I could in prison to try to correct what seemed to me inadequate and inaccurate in my own way of life. Now I set out once more, as I had done first as a boy of seventeen, to try and do something to prevent the same cataclysmic tragedy which had overwhelmed the Dutch in South-East Asia from overwhelming life in my native continent of Africa. But even in the midst of trying, I was aware of the fact that somehow there was lacking the language necessary to unite the Babel of tongues raised in high-pitched argument along the peripheries of the central issue involved. I was aware that some new language of the spirit, some new truly contemporary way of looking at the reality of our desperate day was essential, if the screaming arguments were to be resolved.

I remember a despairing White Father in the Belgian Congo saying to me, "There is another great age of darkness closing in on the life of man and all that we can do is to create little fortresses wherein the authentic light of the spirit can be kept burning. Then, one day, when men wish to reach out for light they will have places in which to find it. But for the rest, we must just accept the inevitability of disaster."

"Perhaps you're right, and disaster may have to come," I had replied. "But as a matter of honour I believe we must go on working to prevent disaster, if only to make certain that if it ultimately has to come, it is the right kind of disaster life needs."

But I felt increasingly isolated. Equally I thought I had never known a world so full of isolated and lonely people. This gave me comfort of a sort. Perhaps this loneliness had its origin in the same area of the spirit as mine? I began to meet people in remote parts of the world and to receive letters from people I had never even met that made me see these lonely spirits as being members of a new community which, as yet, had no institutions to express it. I re-read the moving correspondence between Erasmus and Sir Thomas More. The latter was perhaps one of the most saintly of men because he never sought a saintly role but had it thrust upon him. In an age of disintegration just as fateful as ours, such companionship was enough for the two of them because they knew that in the dark night of the soul only the lonely speaking to the lonely can be companion to the other. It was in such an age that Nietzsche (just before the doors of his mental prison closed about him) observed that there was room in the world only for hermits; or at the most, hermits in pairs.

Yet for all these remote contacts I was not relieved of the feeling of isolation. The numbers of people I met who suffered similarly added to my alarm. Was not this "aloneness" a sickness of our time? But I was empty of answers. And that set the seal on my isolation. There is no loneliness so great as the unanswerable, not in terms of the mind but of the feelings. And where had these feelings gone? It seemed that as I travelled a well-worn beat up and down Africa, the Far East, India, England and Europe that I had not really moved far from the moment when my grandfather read out of the leather-bound family Bible how Joseph had dreamt a dream, told his brethren and been hated yet the more for it . . . So what had happened to that great dreaming process? What of the ladder, phosphorescent between a star-packed heaven and stony wasteland earth, charged with angelic messengers ascending and descending it? When I looked around me it was not only as if the dream had vanished in the debris of war and disaster behind me, and the ladder between men and their greatest value removed, but that they had lost their capacity to dream. If I went by what men in command of the social, intellectual, scientific and artistic scene said, that wide, prophetic soul of the world of which Shakespeare had spoken in one of his greatest sonnets seemed utterly deprived of its dreaming on things to come and civilisation no longer in possession of any great dream to serve. And yet deep within myself the process went on and I knew that I was doing the little I did on account of a kind of dreaming that clothed the memory of my beginnings, as with a Joseph's coat of many colours, and went on providing the flicker of such little light as I walked by tentatively in the dark hour around me. I knew that somehow the world had to be set dreaming again, but what a laugh that raised for being the whimsy and Barryesque sentimentality it was generally taken to be, if I ever dared mention the fact to even the most perceptive of my contemporaries.

THE MAN AND THE PLACE

And the slumber of the body seems to be but the waking of the soul.

SIR THOMAS BROWNE

It was when this feeling was at its height that I came back from the last of a series of ventures into the interior of Africa to join my wife Ingaret Giffard in Zürich. She it was who as a young woman before the war had urged me again and again to read Jung. Yet so profound were the resistances ostensibly produced in me by disillusionment with Freud that I rejected even her urging, although she had exceptional claims to be heard. Her mother was an intimate friend of Dr Godwin ("Peter") Baynes who had been for many years a colleague and close friend of Jung's in Zürich, and had come to live nearby in England. So through personal association and extensive reading, my wife already had an unusual knowledge of the work of Jung and insight into its meaning. Moreover, between making bombs in a factory in London and serving as an air-raid warden by night during the war, she had started psychiatric studies and training with Dr Alan McGlashan who was to write that remarkable manifesto of the spirit of our time, *The Savage and Beautiful Country*. From there, soon after our marriage in 1949 she had logically gone on to complete her training at the newly formed C. G. Jung Institute in Zürich, working in particular with Toni Wolff, without whom the great confrontation of Jung with his own unconscious could perhaps not have been carried to so great and creative a conclusion, and Dr C. A. Meier, who had become Jung's principal male collaborator and to this day holds Jung's former professorship at the Federal University in Zürich. Technically I was still in the British Army, raw with experiences of life and death, unshared and perhaps unsharable with men who had not known them. I could not have been, in one sense, less prepared for the Zürich of Jung and his fellow workers than I was then, despite the fact that I had never forgotten how just before the outbreak of war just one remark of his had injected light into a dark, enigmatic moment of time.

However, much as I felt a fish out of water, I could not refuse to accompany my wife to a celebration over which Jung was presiding. Aniela Jaffé, who had been a patient of Jung's and was later to become his secretary and biographer and a beloved friend of mine, had had a conviction that the two of us should meet and somehow contrived the seating so that I sat on Jung's left at the head of the principal table.

It was an already late afternoon. The party was in one of those old Guild houses founded by knights in Zürich in the fifteenth century. Through the windows with their stained heraldic designs, I could see the troubled waters of the historic Limmat with white Lohengrin swans blown sideways by a keen, precise wind of early autumn bringing up snow from the Gothard Oberland beyond. Grey-green church spires, their bells tolling with medieval peals, and the stone attics of tall buildings, lined the ancient quay, erect as any brigade of guards. Just across the disturbed water and white ruffled swans, I could see the walls, grey with history, of the house in which Paracelsus once lived. He was one of the first frontiersmen of this no-man's land between "landscape and inscape". Looking out, a sense of the great European past came easily into my reckoning.

The timbered hall had far too many people in it. They talked too loudly for my liking. But it seemed the right sort of place for a meeting with someone who had so much to do with my burdened imagination as Jung. When I was shown to my place at his side, he was already deep in conversation with a distinguished professor.

I remember distinctly that they were talking about primitive ways of making fire. I thought how strange that one should begin such a meeting at such point: the natural leap forward into new human awareness. Fire, after all, was the great cross-road in the human journey behind us. It was the event that set men apart not only from the animals and the natural world to which, without self-doubt or feeling of guilt, he belonged. It also removed him one degree further from blind obedience to the gods who previously had had him in their absolute power. It had always been, for me, the great image of the spirit made conscious of itself. So I sat back eager to hear what they had to say about it.

Jung was not speaking at the moment but listening with great attention. That was one of his most moving characteristics. He himself was full and overflowing with ideas. He had only to begin speaking for one to realise that his was a mind perpetually in flood. Yet he managed to be one of the best and most understanding of listeners. Listening, I had time to observe him because both he and the professor were too engrossed to do more than acknowledge my presence with punctilious politeness.

He was a big man, bigger than his photographs had led me to expect. Physically he seemed to match the scale of his spirit. He gave out, too, an air of great well-being. From that moment on until his death I thought of him physically as the best possible advertisement for his own attitude to life. His eyes were larger than they appeared in photographs, and alert, utterly without solemnity and full of somewhat puckish humour and fun. A fanlike pattern of the finest creases at the corners of his eyes clearly came not from exposure to the sun but to the strong light of a continuous and continuing love of laughter.

He looked neither like a doctor nor a professor, nor did he strike me as particularly Swiss. His dress was far too casual. Indeed, there was something oddly English about his appearance. He was wearing a brown Harris tweed sports coat, lightly chequered sports shirt, woollen Paisley tie, cardigan, grey flannel bags and brown shoes. He had a pipe in his hand which he had long since forgotten to puff.

When finally he did speak, he spoke in English and with obvious relish. This love of the Englishness of the English went very deep in him. It was difficult to think of him as the redoubtable Swiss phenomenon that he was. But this, too, constitutes an important nuance in the character of Jung. It demonstrated the universality of his being as well as his work. Nor was I alone in this reaction to the man. I was to discover how Hugh Walpole, the novelist, shared my impression and had tried to define it in the terms both natural and most evocative to persons of his generation. "He looked like some genial English cricketer", he said, describing Jung at their first meeting.

I only regret that Jung himself may never have known Walpole's comment. Although he and I discussed the novelist and his work in detail he never referred to it. Had he known it I am certain he would have been highly amused if not gratified. For Jung regarded games as of the utmost importance to the sanity and well-being of men and their societies.

"Civilisations at their most complete moments", he once told me, "always brought out in man his instinct to play and made it more inventive." He would point out how in the Greece that he loved, games had a religious origin. In fact he was to give me a long exegesis on the origin and meaning of tennis and how the modern game, derived from Real Tennis, began in the quadrangles of medieval monasteries as religious exercises. Even today, if one looked closely at Real Tennis, one would see within it the impact of its original monastic design.

"One of the most striking testimonies to the quality of the English spirit", he told me once, "is the English love of sport and games in a classical sense and their genius for inventing games. One of the most difficult tasks men can perform, however much others may despise it, is the invention of good games and it cannot be done by men out of touch with their instinctive selves. The English do it. And, by Heaven, they even taught us Swiss how to climb our own mountains and make a sport of it! That made us love them all the more. And their Wimbledon, did they but know it, is a modern version of an ancient ritual!"

The instinct to play was still active in him and he could relax into an almost schoolboy playfulness at times. My first impressions of him were, fittingly, very varied. I was ultimately to settle for the image of "the squire", and in this I was anticipating proof of an important fact, for I was to find that he had an immense respect for the way in which chivalry (in the Round Table sense) continued to play a living role in the life of Britain, in that high service was still rewarded with knighthood.

So there was, I believe, a special part of him that was also naturally a kind of England. He had, I was to discover, long ago got friends to teach him to sail in the English Channel and he had become a dedicated wind and canvas man. Even his way of speaking English, apart from a slight Swiss accent, had an unusually casual, almost schoolboy flavour to it.

"It is hellishly difficult", he was saying now at our first meeting, speaking in a deep, animated voice to the professor, a smile forming on his face, "to know what you are trying to get at in all this unless you can tell me what fire means not to primitive people, but to you yourself. It is its meaning for you, not to others, that matters."

The professor seemed taken aback. Then he said, rather perfunctorily, as if assuming that fire could only mean one thing to all men, "Why, it means energy, of course."

For a moment I regretted I had come, so blank and aridly over-intellectual did the answer sound. I thought, dismayed, "Dear God, how unnatural and unreal these Europeans have become. It's worse than before the war. You wouldn't think to hear him that fire was a divine gift stolen from the gods, that Prometheus suffered the cruellest of punishments, and that what he and fire stand for in all of us still suffers because of that precious gift. Besides, it is light in darkness, safety against the beasts and animals that prowled and threatened life in some long-forgotten prehistoric night; it is warmth against cold; it is what brought us from an age of ice, to this privileged moment in time, cooking the food we are to eat, warming this room against the winter which that cold wind outside is bringing up so fast. It is all these and many more things before it becomes an abstract of energy in the mind of a professor, however eminent."

All this flashed through me not as words but as one searing feeling, and I heard the voice of Jung with great good humour teasing the professor in similar though far better and more gracious terms than I had used to myself. Indeed, the professor looked so abashed that instinctively I tried to change the subject by saying that I had listened with immense interest to their discussion of the various primitive ways of making fire, but that there was one way which I had encountered which they had not yet mentioned, and I wondered whether they knew of it.

For the first time Jung turned to give me more than a polite look. I was amazed to notice how his face possessed what I think is permitted to the faces only of those who are naturally and permanently filled with reverence for all the multitudinous detail of life, however drab, for whom there is no frontier between what is ordinary and extraordinary, great and small, but where all are equally charged with their ration of universal wonder. His face just then, and he was in his early seventies, looked truly young and innocent.

Then I told them quickly how during the war, in a jungle of South-East Asia, I had encountered a small yellow aboriginal people who lived for ever in a world of green leaves, sodden moss, dripping tree-ferns and perpetual rain, and where making fire by friction, in the classical primitive manner, could not possibly work. They had accordingly developed a method of making fire that I had seen nowhere else. Each of these little men carried suspended from a leather thong tied round his naked waist, a longish square block of wood. This block was divided into two sections. It had a solid hard-wood lid out of the centre of which protruded a long, tapering rod of wood with a deep niche carved into its end. This rod fitted tightly into a narrow tapering cylinder bored into the main block of wood. When one of these little men wanted to make a fire, all he did was to undo his leather thong, extract the rod from its cylinder, take some very fine dry moss from a leather satchel he carried over his shoulder, insert the moss into the niche at the bottom of the rod, fit the rod into the opening of the cylinder and then, with his hand, slam the rod hard and fast, as deep as it could go into the cylinder. That done, he would quickly pull the rod out and one would see that the moss was on fire. And, I added, the first time I saw fire made in this way, a senior R.A.F. engineer officer on my staff was standing beside me. As he saw the glowing moss extracted from the cylinder, he turned to me, his face comic with amazement and exclaimed, "Good God, Colonel, the Diesel engine!"

I was about to add that this, of course, was precisely the principle on which the Diesel engine worked and that here, unbeknown, in one of the greatest jungles of the world, primitive human-beings who had never had any contact with our own civilisation, which we thought so superior, had for centuries been applying a principle of ignition which we had only recently discovered and whose application to the Diesel engine we regarded as one of the brightest of our inventions. But of course Jung had already grasped this point and for the first time I heard him laugh.

That laugh of his was one of the more memorable events of that afternoon, as far as I was concerned. It was both Olympian and intensely human at the same time. It came out of that big man sheer and immediate, with no inhibition at all between the impulse to laugh and the laughter itself. I had only heard such laughter before among the Bushmen, the first people of my native country, whose brightest possession it is and whose capacity for laughter had impressed and moved me so much in the past that I had felt I would not hesitate to sell everything I possessed for the gift of such laughter.

"How can you do it?" I was to say to him often. "You are the only person I've met who can laugh like a Bushman." And he would just laugh all the more.

Later, when I met Olga Fröbe-Kapteyn, the remarkable Dutch woman who organised the Eranos meetings where Jung delivered some of his most momentous lectures, she told me more. She said that in between lectures at her home at the Casa Gabriella on the shores of Lake Maggiore where Jung and other distinguished speakers came to talk, they would sit in the open at a great round table under the trees in the garden of her house. There, from time to time, this laughter would break out from Jung. On many occasions, she told me, tourists travelling on the main road from Italy to Switzerland which passed by her house, would pause and perhaps wander in with a look of amazement begging, "Signora, please forgive my intrusion, but who was it who laughed just now in so wonderful a way?"

Later, when I had to speak about Jung at the Memorial Service held in New York after his death, I begged everyone there not to forget the laughter, because it was a laughter possible only to those blessed with some of the insight of the gods themselves.

If I had still any doubts about the quality and calibre of Jung, that first laugh of his settled them. There are many ways of laughing but the greatest is that which comes from the sheer joy of seeing disproportion restored to proportion. And Jung's laughter came out of a profound love of the ancient proportions implicit in the original blueprint of life. His laughter was delight in the triumph of the significance in the small over the unreality of excess and disproportion in the established and great. I never knew him to laugh at but rather with life. It was inevitable that from then on he made me laugh, not only by the infection of his own example, but because of his wit and sense of fun and spirit.

The detail of the conversation that followed does not matter. Jung clearly had little interest in promoting any argument with the professor and, when he decently could, decided to leave the party. He bent down, picked up a knobbly walking stick of rough wood which had been lying beside his chair, which added yet more to the country squire in his appearance. For a moment he stood impressive and tall against the slanted light streaming in through the windows where the heraldry of the knights of Zürich had now been blazoned with a pattern of the sinking sun.

A feeling of disappointment assailed me. I was full of things I would have liked to ask Jung. And full of resentment too at having avoided him for years. Then, unexpectedly, he asked me to go home with him, and not long afterwards we were sitting in his library, where we talked for five hours. We talked, to my surprise, a great deal about Africa.

There is a kind of conversation I have hardly ever experienced except in Africa, when one is alone in the bush or desert with little to diminish the impact on one of that great swollen sea of land, its skies, winds and clouds and abundance of vivid and infinitely diversified natural life. Subjects come up fast in one's senses and the voices of one's African companions, as a rule pitched singularly low out of the instinctive reverence induced by that natural surround, so one can, simultaneously, overhear the intimate conversations of nature. The voice of the lion; the intense cough of a leopard; the sound, like a pistol shot, of an elephant tearing a strip of his favourite bark from a tree; the night-plover's sea-pipe call; the bush-buck barking to keep up its courage; a baboon whimpering in some unfathomable nightmare of the tangled bush; the croaking of frogs by some precious star-filled water; the sustained Gregorian chanting of the cricket priests of the night; and, overall, the smell of the incense of the devout earth evoked by the first fall of dew.

It is a kind of conversation that certainly one never hears in Europe. Yet, on this occasion, although I was sitting in comfort in a historic city, in a library full of books, and although it had gone black outside and a hungry European night was pressing against the window like the muzzle of a great bear on the prowl, I had an extraordinary feeling that Jung and I were only technically there. In reality we were back in Africa in the way I have just described.

It all reached such an intensity that again I had another enigmatic variation of the feeling at the party, that I was actually warming myself by one of the first fires with one of the first people to promote its discovery.

Part of all this, I am sure, came from his own attitude to fire. He never took it for granted; it always seemed to remain something of a miracle for him, and always sacred. He had a way all his own of laying and lighting fire, except in so far as his way had a touch of the primitive people I had seen making it with great precarious difficulty, preparing it with infinite solicitude as if it were a matter of life and death that, once made, it should not die.

He did it instinctively, as if performing a religious rite, and as the Hindu flame leapt up, the light on his face would show an expression devout as of that of an archaic priest.

The impact of the coincidence that we were there continuing a conversation begun at such an unexpected beginning was too striking to be ignored, particularly when it was reinforced by another. Until that moment I had not known of his love for Africa. I had not known that he had gone on a long, far safari through it and had even lived for months among the ancient Elgonyi of Mount Elgon in East Africa in the year 1925—the time I myself went to that part of the continent for the last time.

Coincidences, instinctively, have never been idle for me but as meaningful, I was to find, as they were to Jung. I had always had a hunch that coincidences were a manifestation of a law of life of which we are inadequately aware and which, in terms of our short life, are unfortunately incapable of total definition. Yet, however partial the meaning we can extract from them, we ignore them, I believe, at our peril. For as well as promoting some cosmic law, coincidences, I suspect, may be some sort of indication as to what extent the evolution of our lives is obedient or not to the symmetry of the universe. Coincidence was nothing if not an expression of a symmetry of meaning. That symmetry of meaning, I felt that night, had demanded not only that Jung and I should have been to the heart of Africa at a similar moment in time; but also that fire should have been my first introduction to the world of his mind and his nature.

Also, my experience of Africa and above all what it evokes in human imagination have been the source of almost all that has concerned my imagination. I have walked through vast areas, from the Cape of Good Hope to the baroque mountains and deeply wooded valleys of Ethiopia on my flat feet. And travelled in other ways through other areas. I thought that if I came near to knowing and understanding anything, it was Africa and its peoples. Yet I was finding, as we talked, that Jung understood its aboriginal patterns of life even better than I and, if anything, revered them more.

Although there were moments when I felt a little abashed that a Swiss, however eminent, should know my native continent quintessentially better than I did, any possibility of resentment was cancelled by the confirmation and support he gave to my own intuitions and feelings, and their wider significance for the life of our time. It warmed me to hear him too imply that the balance between the primitive and the civilised, the Jacob and Esau, of which I had spoken, had never been honourably struck. Many of the troubles of modern man came from the fact that he himself had a deep, warm, primitive self from which he had not only allowed himself to be divorced but which he had proceeded to despise and repress with deadly ruthlessness.

Africa, it became clear, meant much to Jung but not only because of itself. He called it always "truly God's country"—and in a tone that made it sound not like the cliché it is for most men, but a profound and original observation. He loved it among other things because it had finally settled whatever doubts he might have had as to the validity and universality of an area of the human spirit shared by all men, no matter how different their cultures, their creeds and their races and colours. Of this great hypothesis of his for which he coined the term "collective unconscious" I was as yet unaware. But it was almost as if the basic imagery of that untravelled region itself had been made visible for him by Africa.

So there was for Jung something specific and personally significant about Africa. Africa in a profound sense had been the most subjective of all his journeys in the physical world. All the others, in Europe, Britain, America, North Africa, the Middle East and India, had had an over-riding objective concern. He travelled them well protected in the purpose of his main work. I am struck how in comparison with his other journeys, India made no great impact on him and gave him perhaps less than any country. It seems, in retrospect, to have been an almost irrelevant and redundant exercise. But Africa penetrated to a deeper subjective level of man where only a complete submission to the experience for its own sake enables one to achieve a relative objectivity. The journey itself, Jung told me, was the most impulsive he ever undertook and he came out of it with a sense of having been challenged to a personal confrontation with the reality of primitive Africa.

So deep had been his anticipation at having to meet Africa face to face that he prepared himself with greater thoroughness than ever before. In the voyage out, for instance, he spent most of his time learning Swahili. So when he landed at Mombasa, he told me, he surprised the black porters and stewards by addressing them in this ancient esperanto of East Africa! His instincts about his own inner motivation for the journey were confirmed immediately because the next morning when he woke up in his train in the interior of Africa and through the dust of a scarlet dawn had his first glimpse of the land, a lone Masai warrior leaning on his spear, a great Euphorbia candelabra lit like a Byzantine cathedral by the fire of the new day . . . and a prodigious, volcanic surge of animal life soaring over the long yellow grass . . . Jung had the most extraordinary feeling of a remarkable certainty that he had seen it all before. So certain was he that he gave a cycle of time to it and called it "some six thousand years before".

The deeper he went into Africa the wider and the closer his identification with Africa became. Once ensconced in the mountain fortress of antique man that the immense Mount Elgon and its forest were in those days, the identification was as healing as revealing; and in the end almost overwhelming.

Jung always claimed with justice that outer events and their physical detail of matter and men were relatively unimportant to him. Hence the lack of physical and human detail in his *Reflections*. But in Africa the "without" and the "within" were so interdependent that he spoke of it with astonishing detail. Perhaps the most convincing single testimony of his identification with Africa came towards the end of his stay on the frontier of Uganda and the Sudan. There one night he became so excited by a dance of African warriors organised by a local young chief that he liked, that he could not resist jumping up and joining in the dance. It was, I gathered, some sort of a war dance and, swinging his rhinoceros whip over his head as being the nearest thing to a weapon he possessed, he leapt and stamped around with a horde of men whirling spears, swords and clubs, in the ascending rhythm of some archaic possession of their spirit. At this high point of the dance, an aspect of himself of which he had not been aware before emerged. Despite his involvement in the accelerating pattern of the frenzied dance, suddenly he felt the danger inherent in it: and saw himself in a position of special responsibility towards it. Immediately, despite the chief's protests, he called off the dance. He tried to disperse the roused warriors with gifts of tobacco and, when that failed, he leaped at them again swinging his whip at them with a laugh that concealed an urgent truth in the jest that it pretended to be. His eyes would brighten as he spoke of the tensions of the moment. Also it was the turning point in his relations with Africa. Soon after that he had a dream which is recorded in detail in his book and which warned him, in unmistakable imagery, how close he had come to "going native".

When, after this, I told him of a book I had just written about Africa which had as its text a quotation from the Elizabethan Sir Thomas Browne, "We carry with us the wonders we seek without us: there is all Africa and her prodigies in us", he was deeply moved. He wrote it down and exclaimed, "That was, and is, just it. But it needed the Africa without to drive home the point in my own self."

Although Africa had thus given him final confirmation of his recognition of the "collective unconscious in man" he spoke to me on that same evening of three other personal values extracted from Africa. He stressed that his and everyone's first duty was to his own culture, place and moment in time; and the material on which he had to work was always what was nearest and came most naturally to hand. The second point was that Africa confirmed his suspicions of the motive behind the growing habit of the European to travel the physical world as communications became easier and faster. There was, for him, in this a certain element of evasion. Without denying the validity of travel for specific ends, travel for travel's sake was another matter. He saw it more and more as a substitute for a far more difficult and urgent journey that modern man was called upon to undertake into the unknown universe of himself. Finally, as far as Africa itself was concerned, his own experience had shown him how the Dark Continent and its aboriginal peoples attracted Europeans, because through its own physical character and example it provoked what was forgotten in their primitive selves.

He generalised at length from his own experience in this regard. He impressed on me how the primitive inevitably provoked in the white man a great temptation to revert to an utterly uncontemporary version of himself. This was all the more powerful and difficult to resist because in most cases it was unconscious. As a result, the resistances of the white man in Africa to "go black", or "native" as he put it, produced so powerful an undertow in his spirit that it caused tensions which were almost unendurable. These either caused him to succumb, or to reject and hate the dark man who had served to evoke these tensions.

The farther man grew from his instinctive self the more intense was the rejection in the European that we call prejudice and hatred. It was precisely because Catholic man tended to be in closer touch with his own collective primitivity, through the symbolism of a maternal church, that colour prejudice in Catholic contexts tended to be less than in the Protestant. The Protestant rule was the product of a more exclusively rationalist development which cut man off more from his natural self. But either way, it was an evasion because the task of modern man was not to "go primitive" in the African way. Rather he had to discover, confront and live out his own primitive self in a truly twentieth-century way. Not the least of Africa's services to Jung, personally, was that it had confirmed and emphasised the reality of his own primitive nature which had already caused great conflict in him in his student days. He referred to the clash between his "country or natural mind" and the "town mind" in his encounters with professors and fellow students in the 'nineties at the University of Basle. This experience seemed to me to have blown into full flame the fire necessary for transcending two extremes that had long burned in him, not vicariously through Africa, but at home in his own context.

It happened to be a moment also when Schweitzer and his work in Africa were beginning to attract world-wide attention, and his name inevitably cropped up in our talk that night. I noticed Jung's concern never to denigrate any areas of thought or ways of life that gave meaning to the lives of others. He was not once reductive about the achievement of Schweitzer (whom he had known briefly). Though Jung had profound reservations of his own on the subject, he felt compelled out of respect for his own truth to allow himself the general comment that there was an element of some evasion in Schweitzer's choice to live out his life in Africa.

He had to say this also out of a clear conviction that Europe and European man had no longer moral energies to spare for others. They needed all they had of these for themselves. According to Europe's success in dealing with its own divided self, its resources of moral energy no doubt would increase out of the living example it set, enabling it to re-acquire a real capacity for service to others. But for the moment the precept that charity, in its original meaning of the objectivity of love, began at home, was never more relevant and urgent for the West. Only an example lived truly and fully out in the life of our time could help and save. Preaching and continuation of efforts to convert others in our own confused image would only imperil both ourselves and those we presumed to serve.

None the less, a living nostalgia for Africa was always there in Jung. Writing to me once about a book of mine which he said had brought back to him the sights, sounds and smells of unforgettable days and nights spent in the bush, he declared that he would never cease to thank whatever gods had woven the pattern of his fate that they had also included Africa and all its wonder within it.

He longed to go back to Africa and had his heart been less responsible might even have done so. But he felt he had little enough time for the work he wanted to do to go back over a page already turned.

Once, when I thought I had almost persuaded him to come back with me, he said, "I'm afraid after hobnobbing for months with witch-doctors and delving into their witchcraft in Africa I was amazed, on my return to Zürich, to find how many witch-doctors and how much witchcraft there was in it, and in the Swiss mountains and beyond! Until I have learned all I can about them I feel I have not the right to go back."

From that moment on I hardly ever went to Africa as I was doing just then, once or twice a year, without calling in on him at Zürich. By some curious process of "synchronicity" as he called it, these visits of mine invariably coincided with an aspect of the work he happened to be doing. So I was often referred to, laughingly, as a sort of messenger boy between him and Africa.

However, concerned as I am more for the feeling of the man than the knowledge that came out of our meetings, I leave aside the details of the rest of our conversations. We have knowledge enough of the man and his ideas. But, beyond the shrinking circle of those who knew him, little imaginative, rounded record of the dynamic, life-giving feeling that emanated from him.

What was of overwhelming consequence to me was that as we sat there talking, something was communicated to me of what Jung was in himself, rather than out of his ideas. In this process the feeling of isolation and loneliness in a vital area of myself which had haunted me all those years vanished. I was no longer alone. I had company of a noble order. For the first time in my life I had a neighbour in the inmost part of myself. I was also having an elementary lesson, in the fact that men, women, ideas and the causes which are singularly our own, are often those which we most brutally reject. Perhaps there is something in all of us that demands a "journey to Damascus" of our own before we can discover in a single, blinding, decisive flash that light which we are, in the innermost nature of ourselves, contracted to seek.

Jung certainly was a great and inspired neighbour. He had a genius for propinquity. He was companion to all sorts and conditions of men and women from the most despised and rejected to those overcome with vertigo from the intellectual heights they had achieved. He is a neighbour to millions that are yet to be born. His gift for propinquity brought him near to all manner of men and women. From deeply disturbed spirits shut away in some asylum to some humble negro barber in New Orleans; the "Mountain Lake" of an almost vanished American Indian entity; a Hindu guru; just a despised and persecuted primitive or Zürich lake-sided cellarman—they understood and felt near to him when some of the great minds of his own day dismissed him. I personally found that he gave me the feeling that there could be a valid meaning to this loneliness regarding Africa and also this other "dreaming" area of myself which I had carried about with me for forty years. He performed precisely the same service for countless others.

For example, he did it for the distinguished scholar, Richard Wilhelm, the translator of the *Golden Flower* and the *I-Ching*, or Book of Changes, which is perhaps the oldest book in existence today. Wilhelm carried about with him the loneliness of an experience of China and its ancient culture which he could not share with others. Nor could he integrate it with his European self. Wilhelm had a concern and understanding of the first experience of an immense proportion of the human race which not only made no sense to the Germany and the Europe of his begetting, but was rejected by it as incomprehensible Orientalism. As a result the loneliness vanished when he met Jung. He found that his experience could immediately be decoded and rendered into an idiom which made sense to Europe and became, as introduced by Jung, a source of enrichment of its own culture. Today, for instance, Wilhelm's *I-Ching* which some fifteen years ago was available only as an expensive hardback publication, is a paperback selling annually by the thousand.

At our first meeting when Jung heard that I had been to the Far East as a boy and what a great impact it had made on me, he asked me instantly if I knew of Wilhelm and his work. He then proceeded to give me the best possible introduction and preparation I could have had to a Wilhelm I had never met. I realised Wilhelm had been a kind of Columbus to Jung's own wide-ranging spirit and had opened up as a great new world to him. This world of course was the ancient civilisation of China a thousand years or more before Christ and on which the culture of the West for so long had turned its back, to its impoverishment and peril. It did not concern me that the excitement caused by this re-entry from the outer space of European abstractions into this organic world of China where dark and light were equal and indispensable elements of creation and harmoniously at one, led Jung to generalise somewhat naively about the East and West, as two definite and clearly defined opposites of spirit and culture. I knew that, at a pinch, one could regard Western cultural projections in the Americas, British Commonwealth and Europe as one and the same complex of spirit. It did form a loose union called the "West". But one certainly could not do that to the East.

There is no such thing as the "East" in similar form. It is extraordinary, for example, how little impact China has made on India over the centuries, particularly compared to the immense consequences both for China and Japan of the influence of Buddha and the Upanishads which they imported over the centuries from India. Indeed, Buddhism continued to flourish and grow abroad long after it had been reabsorbed and sunk almost without trace into the ocean of the Hinduism in its native India. More particularly, through its evolution in Zen in those lands, Buddhism assumed a much more dynamic and contemporary form than it ever did in the country of its origin. India, in a sense, was a "European" inset in the complicated and cultural diversified intaglio of the East. It was part of all that had issued out of the spirit of what I had long called to myself Sanskrit Man—a fact that makes us, too, who are heirs and successors of a common Sanskrit ancestor feel so close to India and induce us both into having so strange a political and cultural love–hate affair with one another. The East was a geographical, not a cultural or spiritual entity. And China was quite apart from India. But through the Upanishads, India had given Jung a great deal, far more than his visit to the sub-continent ever did. But it was a gift in a known and pre-experienced form.

China, however, was truly a new world, a unique and infinitely meaningful universe of its own, and when Jung spoke of the East as he often did, the East that he had mainly in his mind was that represented by China into which he was conducted by this rare German scholar who had continued the exacting work already started by his father and was to have carried on by his son. He felt himself so very much enriched by Wilhelm that he felt as if he had received more from him than from any other person he had ever known. Wilhelm had so endowed the meaning of our time, he felt, to provide an Archimedean support in the European spirit from which it could perhaps lever itself out of its own dead weight.

Little as I knew of all this that night, I was moved by a special note

that came into Jung's voice whenever he mentione ! Wilhelm's name.
It was a note of grateful, loving remembrance of someone who had
meant a great deal to him. I was not surprised to see later in his letters
to Wilhelm how this concern was expressed. He already feared that
Wilhelm was dying. For Jung's primitive, intuitive self knew as clearly
as any African witch-doctor in charge of the "soul" of his tribe, how
perilous was the absorption of a whole new culture to the men and
people called upon to promote it. He knew that a culture so fundamentally alien to all Wilhelm's own European values could be interpreted not just by translating the words in which this ancient China
had fashioned it. Also it would have to become an organic part of
Wilhelm's own imagination so that his whole flesh and blood would
have to be translated in the same idiom as well, and the basic image of
the man transformed into a reality for which he had no historical and
cultural immunities. The experience, Jung feared, would be a kind of fire
that could burn out all Wilhelm's energies. Hence his ever-increasing
anxiety over the physical well-being of Wilhelm and his constant
pleading that he should take greater care of his physical self. The immensity of Wilhelm's endeavour, its dangers and Jung's fear of their
consequences found verification, alas, in Wilhelm's untimely death.

Yet without this cross-pollination between Jung and Wilhelm both
Europe and China would have been the poorer. We are only at the
beginning of the effects of their partnership on the European spirit, as
the example of the impact of the book of the *I-Ching* shows.

Only this was implicit in the little said that night. But it was enough
to make me realise how Jung, solely out of his own profound loneliness,
despite the close support of a unique circle of friends, could so recognise and understand the nature of the loneliness in Wilhelm. As a
result he was able to provide the companionship needed for completion of the tremendous task heaped on so sensitive a spirit. I have yet
to meet in history, or life, the human-being who has been able to find
and evolve himself without some act of recognition of his mind from
another he respects.

When Jung's storm-battered book *Answer to Job* first appeared, he
had a most moving and tender correspondence with a white nun in
a convent in the Black Forest of Germany. She found that, for the
first time, someone had enabled her to see meaning in the concept of
the Trinity. Shut out for so long by her doubt of a vital concept of
the faith to which she subscribed, she had suffered a form of loneliness
of guilt that made her feel almost untouchable in her community. But
long before this correspondence was ended, she saw herself again as

part of a living human procession. She was, as the Kalahari Bushmen say, "walking again with the moon and stars".

Then there was the doctor with a practice in a remote mountain district of Switzerland who asked Jung to see a simple girl of the hills whom he thought was going insane. Jung saw her and realised at once that she had neither the intelligence nor need for a sophisticated and intellectually demanding analytical treatment. He talked to her quietly in his study and came to the conclusion that all she suffered from was the fact that her community, in a sudden enthusiasm for what was thought to be modern and progressive, had poured scorn on all the simple beliefs, ideas, customs and interests which were natural to her. Her own natural state, her primitive self, had lost such honour with herself and others that her heart wilted because of a lack of incentive in the kind of prospect life held out for her.

Accordingly he got her to talk to him at length about all the things she had enjoyed and loved as a child. As she talked, almost at once he saw a flicker of interest glow. He found himself so excited by this quickening of the spirit of a despised self, that he joined in the singing of her nursery songs and her renderings of simple mountain ballads. He even danced with her in his library, and at times took her on his knee and rocked her in his arms, undeterred by any thought of how ridiculous if not preposterous would be the picture of him in the eyes of orthodox medical and psychiatric practitioners.

At the end of a few days the girl was fully restored to a state of honour with herself and he sent her off in high spirits to her home. She never again regressed. Indeed the result appeared so miraculous that the learned doctor in the mountain wrote to Jung and asked him how it had been achieved. Jung wrote back to the effect, "I did nothing much, I listened to her fairy-tales, danced with her a little, sang with her a little, took her on my knee a little and the job was done."

But he never persuaded the doctor, he told me, that his leg was not being pulled, although the girl stayed what the world termed "cured".

I myself remember a beautiful, unusually sensitive girl not yet in her twenties whom Jung, at the age of over seventy, at a time when he was trying hard to put analytical treatment well behind him, had reluctantly taken on as a patient. I still recall vividly the wonder in her voice when she talked of how in all the years she worked with Jung, he never once took her outside the range of what she could understand; how always he respected her own limitations and capacity for experience. Through his own respect for what she was, she re-centred herself and thereon flowered out of her own desire and volition.

Finally, I knew a remarkable woman who was so terrified of herself and of Jung, so ignorant of analytical psychology, although she was a person of great culture, that she went to see him three times a week for six months without being able to speak. Yet on each occasion he just talked to her about all the things he thought could matter to her as much as they mattered to him. Suddenly at the end of six months she found her own voice within her and spoke out more and more confidently. Soon her isolation from a vital part of herself and therefore from others too, vanished. She became what she is today, a person with a unique creative voice and meaning of her own.

This sort of approach to his practice was not without its embarrassments. Almost all his life Jung was confronted with misunderstandings as much among scientists, theologians, as philosophers and psychologists who confused Jung's method in the practice of analytical psychology with its scientific aspects.

"I had to point over and over again to pompous asses", he told me once with a laugh, "that I obviously drew a firm line between psychology as a science and psychology as a technique. I shocked a great scientific excellency once by telling him that when cases seemed to warrant it I had no compunction in speaking to them of spirits instead of complexes and archetypes, with the reservation of course that what appeared to them as spirits could merely be personifications of something unconscious in them, and when truly made conscious, might vanish. I was compelled always in the beginning to respect my patients' own truth and idiom and never treated two patients alike."

He used the word patient with great reluctance because he felt that people in trouble with themselves gave him precious insights he could never have obtained any other way, and preferred to talk not of patients but persons working with him. It was the artist in him, and his dislike of inventing technical words that gave him no great liking for the American substitute, "analysand".

I could multiply these examples a hundredfold, each with a significant nuance of its own. I could elaborate on how his gift of propinquity and respect for what I called the essential "otherness" of all persons and things enabled him to enter into the spirit of life so remote from his own as is the aboriginal life of Africa. He could extract from its customs, its rites, its witchcraft, black magic and all that was universally dismissed as sheer superstition, meanings which he told me were more valuable than any learned from his exalted professors at Basle.

My interest, arrested through disillusionment by my first tentative reading of Freud many years before, began to flow and gather momentum again. The "inscape", "mythological dominants" and "underworlds of history", the impact of dreams on everyday life which had perturbed my imagination for so long could no more be dismissed as "fantasy". They were, on the contrary, increasingly broadened by Jung's empirical demonstration of their validity as facts of natural science. As I saw it, neither psychiatry, nor his enlargement of the field of psychology, were his major achievements. They were by-products of the discovery and evaluation of an as yet unmeasured potential that followed his breakthrough into this great new world within. It was as momentous as the breakthrough into the nature of the atom. Again the fact that both coincided in time suddenly seemed significant.

Indeed it is almost as if the synchronicity of the two developments imply that they are concerned with two aspects of the same reality. Perhaps even the atom, nuclear in its fission, could be regarded as a physical metaphor of the "inscape" of man nuclear in fission of a conscious and unconscious self. Relative to the position from which we view them, one can be seen utterly from within, the other only made visible from without.

The relationship between spirit and matter, world within and world without, is transcendental and incapable of total expression in non-transcendental terms. These two great objectives to which we are subject play on us like some great symphony of music which we cannot describe save through its effect on us. We are condemned to know them in part and only through their consequences in us, even though they circumscribe us in full. Yet this much seems certain. Less and less can we maintain that there is a cast-iron division between the inner and outer worlds. Today even the most rational of scientists incline to consider the possibilities of their being aspects of one and the same greater whole. I myself never doubted that the physical world is spirit seen from without; the spirit is the world viewed from within.

It does not surprise me that in the final analysis, at the point where our dreams vanish over the rim of sleep, we meet matter receding fast over the horizon and, in the process of the most powerful electronic microscope, behaving less like solid, predictable material but more as the swift changing texture of living thought. We pass from one to the other like Alice in Wonderland through a looking glass, to find that the objective mystery which faces us macrocosmically in the night skies above, confronts us microcosmically in reverse. In the depths of our own mind, beyond those "cliffs of fall, frightful, sheer, no-man-fathomed" of which Hopkins wrote, symbols, images, patterns of meaning with all the immense energies at their disposal, are constellated and in orbit and strangely akin to the minuscule solar systems, planets, Milky Ways, comets, nebulae and black holes of anti-matter, dynamic in the heart of the physical atom. How could two such discoveries coming at the same desperate moment in time, therefore, not be another of those strange affirmations of the symmetry of meaning?

But immediately one faces a common misconception—the belief that Jung's over-riding concern was the unconscious in man. Jung's breakthrough as a result of his descent into this Dantesque underworld was a result of his over-riding concern for consciousness in man. Metaphorically, he was concerned with making fire for greater light out of the darkness of the mind; and to determine among other things what it was in man that so often arose to extinguish such little light as he possessed.

Great as is the mystery of so vast an unconscious area in life there is a yet greater mystery involved. There is the mystery of consciousness and beyond that the ultimate wonder of how and for what purpose these two-in-one are directed. The mystery is not lessened because it is articulate. The light the fire throws does not diminish the aboriginal mystery because of its power to illuminate some of the night. On the contrary, the mystery grows with the growth of consciousness. Consciousness could not have the importance it possesses for life, nor could it have survived the onslaught which is symbolised in the Flood of the Old Testament, and made visible and active in all the wars, disasters, revolutions, social and individual tragedies inflicted on the human race if in some way consciousness had not had the support of the collective unconscious. All that is unconscious in life must aspire to consciousness. Consciousness is meaningful, I imagine, precisely because in some way it serves the greatest longing of the collective unconscious. It is, as it were, the deepest dream of greater spirit in this underworld of life. It is only when consciousness betrays the longing and the dream which gives it birth, that it is overwhelmed and temporarily destroyed. Temporarily, I suggest, because always, hitherto, the dream and the longing have never failed to return, and consciousness been refashioned. Yet there is a lesson here as portentous as it is difficult to declare.

The mystery and the unknown before and after, are not the synonyms we may take them to be. Mystery includes the known as well as the unknown; the ordinary as well as the extraordinary. Once the feeling of mystery abandons our travel-stained senses in contemplation of the same well-worn scene, we have ceased, in some vital sense, to know what we are observing. What that mystery is, is beyond verbal definition. We know only that its effect on us is either positive or negative. It is, perhaps, most creatively, the feeling that in the midst of our own partial knowing and experience of life there is the presence of a something far greater than man can comprehend. Reality, no matter how widened and heightened our perceptions, never ceases to be an infinite mystery. Again, Shakespeare expresses it better than anyone else when he makes the doomed Lear say to Cordelia, "We shall take upon us the mystery of things and be God's spies." In other words, awareness of the mystery of things acknowledged and revered, though inexpressible and utterly non-rational, is also a vital form of knowing which enables the human spirit to pass through the defence lines of what he knows, and enter the territory of an embattled unknown like a spy to prepare the way for the mobilised forms of consciousness to follow and so extend the area of his awareness. And it is in all these senses that this ever-recurrent process of the dream, the longing in its keeping and the consciousness which emerges from it, is one of the most moving and life-giving aspects of the mystery that motivates our brittle lives.

In this great abysmal underworld, to which Freud had opened the gate, and through which Jung had passed and continued to become the first to penetrate them in depth, the dream and its longing were never permanently discouraged. They rose phoenix-like out of the burnt-out ashes of a conscious expression which had failed its unconscious motivations and soared, again and again, to compel life anew for another effort at greater consciousness. It is perhaps not odd that Jung had a phoenix in his family coat of arms, and that he was so young, both in person and name, the youngest and most childlike wise old man that one could meet, as if to leave no doubt that he was uniquely charged to make what was oldest in life young and new again. In this manner he was the very first great explorer in the twentieth-century way. And to understand what he was and accomplished and the immense hidden distances he travelled, I myself go back not only to what others close to him told me over the years but most of all to the little he told me about his own beginnings and the feelings it evoked in me. Without these feelings and the impact of the man, such knowledge and statistics as the world already possesses could not have lived as they still live and shine for me like a fire of my own in the African night.

THE LAKE AND THE RIVER

Lakes resting on the other.
The images of the joyous.
Thus the superior man joins with his friends for discussion and
  practice.

I-CHING

Jung was born on July 26th, 1875, at Kesswil on Lake Constance. When he was barely six months old his father, who was a clergyman, poor even by the standards of a poorly paid vocation, moved to Laufen almost at the foot of the first great falls of the Rhine. Some four years later his family moved again to Klein-Hüningen, a small hamlet just outside Basle, but still on the Rhine. For the next twenty-one years Jung went on living there, so that for nearly a quarter of a century, the presence of this great river, the view of its swollen, thrusting, on-flowing water and its sound as of the wind and stream of time itself was in and around his senses. It was not until December 1900 that he left the banks of the Rhine to settle in Zürich on the shores of another great inland sea, where he remained until the end of his days.

I always begin my contemplation of the man and his work by reminding myself of these apparently sober geographical facts of his beginning and movement from childhood into early manhood. I stress them because they were of immense importance to him physically as well as being, I believe, a dynamic element in the evolution of his character and work. He himself was fond of saying that, as a child, he was already convinced that no-one could live without water. He did not mean of course the physical fact that without water people died of thirst. He meant the presence of water in lake, river, and lake again, and its unfolding significance within man's awareness. He would recall how as a small boy on a visit to the Lake Constance on whose shores he was born, its water to him was a vision regained of an incomparable splendour ringed with a bright circle of certainty that one day he would just have to live near a lake. He had this unshakeable conviction at so early an age, I believe, because water, in lake and river, already was a basic element in the opening movement of the orchestration of his own spirit.

He told me repeatedly, as well as recording the view in several of his books, essays and letters, that the nature of the earth itself had a profound influence on the character of the people born and raised on it. He could not define it. Nor was there any scientific means by which he could prove it. Yet he maintained that, for instance, the German national character could not have developed as it did had it not also been an expression of the nature of the dark soil of Germany. He believed that any other race who migrated to Germany, even without any definite cultural process to encourage them, would have acquired, in time, some of the fundamental aspects of the German character just because of their nourishment and participation in the nature of the earth of Germany. He stated, using the most improbable parallel accessible to him, that even a remote Siberian aborigine brought to settle in Switzerland would change out of all recognition and in time become a good, solid and respectable Swiss citizen! He would say this with a certain indulgence of the irony and humour native to him, knowing how such a thought would tease his more stolid countrymen, rooted in the assumption of their own unique and inalienable Swissness.

He declared himself thus without doubt, I believe, because nature in all its forms was not a cold, impersonal, objective reality but was rather an expression of symbolic form, evocative of all that was symbolic within the spirit of man. The symbol made manifest in what is called inanimate matter, regarded with the utmost relativity, is the symbol given its final and unalterable form. Or, to use the language of physics, it is the symbol made static and the energies at its disposal locked up within a closed circuit of its own constellation of logistics. After all, that so-called inanimate matter had energies of monstrous proportions has been proved with disastrous finality by nuclear fission.

The symbol within on the other hand is in a condition of thrust and movement, and the energies at its disposal are highly kinetic. That is why a contemporary artist like the sculptor, Henry Moore, for instance, makes so great an impact. He has a genius for joining the symbolic in nature without to the living image of its symbolic equivalent within. For these reasons I always found it necessary as a preliminary to understanding what I experienced of the man to look as precisely as I could into what lake and river have tended to represent at all times and places in the imagination of man.

The lake is one of the most telling images of a great universal made specific. The macrocosmic sea, microcosmically contained in the earth, is so made a comprehensible source of nourishment to the life and spirit of man. It reflects and draws down into its own deeps and so into the heart of the earth all that its opposite, the sky, represents and possesses of illumination and height, become a kind of mediating factor between two great poles, two opposites of reality: a dark, earthly principle and another of light and celestial sky and all the values they stand for. In other words, the yin and yang of Tao, the ancient Chinese concept of the one and only living way as set out in the *I-Ching* of Wilhelm that was to give Jung so much. It is for me the most comprehensive, precise, and authoritative study of living symbolism and its role in time, space and the evolution of creation and being which is its purpose.

This Book of Changes personifies the lake and makes it the image of the feminine value with the greatest future and possibilities of increase, calling it the youngest of all the daughters in a house of many mansions, describing it as a source of joy, as for instance in the extract quoted at the beginning of this chapter. But the river is another matter. It is an image of water already in movement, finding its own way through great ravines, carrying all over cataract and rapid and through conditions of external danger, to emerge intact and triumphant for union with the sea out of which it rose as vapour at the beginning. It succeeds in doing so only because it finds its own way without short cuts, straight lines, or disregard of any physical impediments but in full acknowledgment of the reality of all that surrounds it, implying that the longest way round is the shortest and only safe way to the sea.

As a result, the *I-Ching* emphasises that water represents the nourishment that comes from above for life on earth, where it is transformed into an element which leads the heart of men to the soul locked up within the body, reflecting there a light that is enclosed in the dark. Above all, the water which the river conducts so untiringly to the sea itself, this ancient book stresses, is a master image for what is abysmal in life.

Considering how Jung, almost from the moment of self-awareness at the age of three, was dedicated to the end of his days to the understanding of what is abysmal in life and man, these images of lake, river and again lake, seem so apt and complete that I cannot believe his early associations with them were accidental. The fact that the chosen river should have been the Rhine also seems the most portentous event if the child Jung were to succeed in becoming so truly himself.

The Rhine is one of the great mythological rivers of the world, not yielding place to the other immense mythological rivers representing the searching and inquiring spirits of men and their cultures, such as the Ganges, the Nile, the Yellow River of China and so on. But unlike those rivers which appear as rivers of light, resolution and are full of a natural, maternal solicitude for life, the Rhine is a dark, angry and outraged masculine stream. It is as dark and in as strange a rage and passion to reach the sea as is the Congo issuing straight out of the darkest centre of the heart of darkness of my native Africa.

I have travelled the Rhine as I have travelled both Blue and White Niles from source to sea. But I have never found the ease on it that I have felt on the Nile and its tributaries. It was as if the Rhine had its source in the heart of the darkness of European history. Even its course followed the direction of European history, for as the name Europe itself suggests (in its derivation from a Sanskrit root) it was in the beginning the land where the sun went down, the *Abendland* of the Germans. Though it streamed out of the morning as did the Barbarians who over-ran the Roman Empire, it found the sea unerringly at the point of fall of the night. I myself having once sailed down the Rhine to the sea understood as never before its role in Teutonic mythology together with the prophetic associations of Wagner's equinoxial music, which Jung himself, in so far as he allowed himself music, preferred.

Like Heine, I could not understand why it should make me feel sad when the tops of the hills above the Rhine sparkled in a long evening sunlight of summer. I wondered why the story of the Lorelei should trouble me? The very same Lorelei that, when I travelled the river, the Germans still celebrated by drinking endless mugs of black Pan-Festival beer and singing with the all too ready collective tears streaming down their cheeks. Perhaps it was because the imagery evoked by Heine of the feminine being of irresistible beauty and siren song, combing out her hair of gold with a comb of gold, represented all the feminine values which European man, particularly German man, had rejected. German culture, embedded as it was in a civilisation almost entirely man-made, was deliberately and wilfully masculine. Consequently Heine's poem of the Lorelei and the doomed boat (which in itself is an image of the means whereby men find their own conscious way over the rivers and seas of what is unknown and abysmal in life) was an intuitive intimation of disaster already at work in the European spirit and particularly in the German version. One can stress in this regard of course the Protestant rejection of all that was feminine in Christianity, and its increasing abhorrence of the symbolism that had illuminated it for so long. In the process this too had encouraged a general masculine authoritarianism in the cultures within which it had found shelter and taken root.

The most striking external example, of course, was the strange Seven Years' War of Frederick the Great who followed faithfully, but utterly without love, in the wake of his father, the terrible Elector of Brandenburg. This war gave much sinister impetus to this destructive progression. Ostensibly it was a war fought to uphold an ancient law and was justified by many a rationalisation of the rights of Germans to reunite (or to congeal) archaically again. But what was this law which served as pretext? It was a law that forbade woman, even as queen, to inherit as a man inherited. It was a law against a self-evident and natural feminine right and was fought even against a queen, Maria Theresa. Looked at, as it should long since have been done, in this deeper level of the symbolism involved, it was a most savage denial of the feminine in man conducted by a prince of will and reason who hated woman and loved men, a fact of which his monstrous father so disapproved that he had a boy-friend of the young Frederick brought out and shot in front of his son. And Jung, one should not forget, was born as part of the Germanic complex of culture and religion as expressed in its unique Swiss annexe. Above all Jung was raised on the banks of the unconverted and unrepentant Rhine. It is only when set against this uncomfortable inheritance that one can measure how remarkable was Jung's metamorphosis of a Swiss-Germanic self into a universal personality, one of the greatest since the Renaissance.

So I have elaborated on this role of the Rhine in European imagination because it had an uncanny pre-association with the Jung whose whole work, in one main and final appraisal, was the rediscovery of the great feminine objective within the objective psyche of man, as to make possible as never before a reconciliation of the masculine and feminine elements in life.

I conclude this consideration of Jung's physical beginnings, therefore, with a certainty all the greater because Jung himself stressed to me more than once how profoundly symbolic his native land was to him always, from the moment when at Laufen on the Rhine—so far back that he could not be certain who it was except that it was a woman, probably an aunt—firmly anchored in the sea of his memory his first glimpse of the distant Alps by exhorting him to look on the storm-tossed waves of mountains and observe how red they were.

"I never looked at the Swiss scene again", he told me, recalling that moment, "without feeling myself in the presence of a great mystery. I never could look at the mountain tops without also looking at the valleys and their rivers and lakes and thinking of them all as a great and mysterious whole."

There was to start with, therefore, this unusual combination of physical externals to make a lasting impact of nature on him. Always he was to stay close to the earth; that earth which in the imagination of man, whether of the Stone-Age Bushmen in the Kalahari, the Greek of Hesiod and Homer or the Roman of Virgil, was essentially feminine, a Great Mother producing and nourishing all forms of living things. So much so that in Jung's case in both plants and trees he felt himself closer to the act and deed of creation than in any other physical manifestation of life. They were never just trees, plants or flowers to him. He was to call them "thoughts of God", expressing not only the mind of the creator but also the magnetic beauty of the instant of creation. I remember one evening at Bollingen when a wind was raising a remote Merlinesque moan from the trees he had planted so thickly around his tower. The lake was lapping at the shore hard by. He could never, Jung said, go along with the concept that man alone was created in the image of God. That wind, those trees, the water that we heard, those contemplative plants and flowers outside, the valleys and the great mountain tops with their fall of snow, reflecting sun, moon and stars beneath, all seemed to him, as a boy, to be an expression of the permanent essence of God more true and wonderful than any in men and their societies. It was to them that he turned when the world, for the moment, defeated his questioning self. Animals, much as he loved them, were already one dimension further away because of their ability to move at will. They were, to put it symbolically, both in being and spirit already uprooted, and cut off from that which had made them. Although, he hastened to add, it was God's will that moved them and not their own. But even with such a will they represented already a step towards the exile that men today call consciousness.

One has to stress this to show how all important this was to him from the beginning and how at one with his destiny. When his own resources of foresight and reasoning failed him, this pre-association and continuing bond with the earth provided a non-rational wayside hospice which refreshed him and set him back on his way again. There was, for instance, their reappearance in the dream which came to him in a moment of great irresolution when, his school-days over and entry into a university before him, he did not know what courses to follow. He was at his wit's end, with argument and counter-argument continually raging within, when out of himself there came a dream which put him back in a dark wood on the banks of the Rhine by an ancient burial mound. He dug into it and turned up the bones of prehistoric animals. He interpreted it as a sign that he must get to know nature and the world in which he lived. That, coupled with another dream in which water played a great role, made him settle for science, and so on towards medicine. Taken at its manifest level, he was right. But at another level it showed how the manifest interpretation was only the servant of a deeper process. The dream, looked at as a whole, showed him already contracted by life to dig into the long-forgotten feminine earth of the human spirit.

Yet in the beginning it was as if this life by the river Rhine externally was bent on casting all that was dark, negative, doubtful and problematical at him. He was for years an only child and had no companion to share the strange impact of life made by this uncomfortable river. His earliest memories of it seem to have been of the dead it threw up which made him face death with his eyes and senses wide open at his most impressionable years.

I myself have sat in the garden of his father's old vicarage on a bright, hot, summer day, the trees in the orchards around heavy with fruit, the scent of hay drifting like incense, and the noise of the urgent Rhine drowning the humming of the bees struggling sap-laden through the air so thick and sticky with a honeyed light of its own that they seemed to be swimming in it rather than flying through it. I should have been uplifted by it all. But I was profoundly uneasy all the time and glad to get away, wondering how so lonely a young boy as Jung could have endured so busy and fecund an earth. Yet he made his own peace on his own terms with the natural impact on his personally evolving senses. But not without sacrifice to the gods who had seemed to have prearranged it all with such profound and meticulous detail.

Already profoundly, irrevocably introverted, he was increasingly turned inward upon himself. From what I knew of my own isolation in a great natural surround, there was evidence of this for me in the fact that he was always having accidents and once narrowly escaped falling into the river. It was, he would tell me, borrowing from the vocabulary of his own theory of psychological types, all the result of the fact that he had been born with an inferior "sensation function"— an under-developed sense of the reality of his physical "here and now". Good and true as the explanation may be, there is no doubt that he was encouraged by the circumstances of his boyhood to be preoccupied, or, as my African countrymen would say, "his soul was more than ever not really in his body".

I know that what I am about to record is accounted for by the explanation Jung so often gave himself, namely that although his life outwardly was uneventful, inwardly it was overwhelmingly eventful. This picture of a person rich in inner eventfulness with a poor relation to the external world is greatly heightened by the fact that when Jung at last took time off from his urgent work to look back on his life, he was already an old man who by the most exacting standards of measurement had achieved almost too much. When he talked to one of his beginning, therefore, it was almost as if one were looking at the child through the wrong end of the telescope.

Indeed, this applied not only to his childhood but to his beginnings and progression as a young psychiatrist, and constitutes a formidable factor that has coloured and perhaps even slanted the current judgements of Jung and his work. When I met him he was already in his seventies; the shape of his major work, if not totally filled in, was clear in outline. Almost all his early contemporaries and collaborators were dead or about to vanish from the scene and the men and women who surrounded him, with a few exceptions, were much younger and without any knowledge of the pioneering Jung, let alone the boy. They were naturally inclined to see his achievement only in its most mature forms, neglecting the almost incredible flights of intuition by which he had arrived at the stage where they encountered him.

All of us have been prescribed in our valuations by a lack of knowledge of the younger Jung. The urgent need therefore is to go back to his early points of departure so that his inspired and swift intuitive vision can be consolidated and expanded. It is important to realise that most current interpretations are of the older Jung and his work in its most mature form. So however true, they must remain somewhat partial. Yet even allowing for the built-in obsolescence of our current perspectives, there is a far more fundamental cause for our difficulty if our vision of him is to be complete. Even in those few lines of his reflections devoted to his early life at Laufen, it is obvious that a great deal did happen to him also externally but did not remain in his memory because it was singularly unimportant to him.

He had been born so introverted that it would seem as if he had been only technically a child. This can in a sense be said of all children. I have always been amazed by the fact that at the moment of birth the child still belongs to all the life that has ever been and not to the moment so young in time in which we all appear so briefly. We forget that it is our own life on earth that is so painfully new. What we bring into it at birth is already as old as time, Our own progress from there on is an act of increasing separation from that organic and idiomatic antiquity of our being at our earthly beginning. To me no child at birth is so young nor so poignant and unarmed as is the boy or girl born into their own contemporary selves in adolescence. This is particularly true now that all the aids designed by a wise and infinitely experienced nature in rules and ritual of initiation for these occasions have been universally discarded by our rational selves. They have been jettisoned as an unnecessary encumbrance in a moment of plenty, and are no longer available when the need for which they were designed has re-arisen.

But in Jung, what is a natural endowment in us all seems almost to have been bestowed on him with an extra dimension and additional pull of gravity. It was almost as if something in him knew from the start that this personal birth in a contemporary idiom was irrelevant. Whatever presided over his destiny seemed to have decided that he would have to accomplish his birth into manhood in altogether another way. His birth must not exile him from this ancient water of his being but must be equipped and devoted to giving it living shape and ponderable essence on the derelict contemporary scene.

So, in a very real way, he was never young as we were and was incapable of having equals in his own time and place to keep him company. In the deepest meaning of the innocence of the image evoked by the term, he never had someone of his own kind "to play with". At school he was considered strange, odd, unpredictable and hardly ever popular with either students or teachers. That old, old atmosphere about him was felt instinctively and he was nicknamed "Father Abraham". Even this had a singular unconscious aptness, considering how Abraham himself was preoccupied with God. Abraham too was to accomplish a significant breakthrough in man's relationship with his own highest meaning on that burning Old Testament day when he abstained, at the last moment, from sacrificing his own son to the voice of his inner calling.

Something of this, I imagine, played a part which though it must not be exaggerated, was none the less real in Jung's apparent lack of concern for the psychology of children. When one considers the great emphasis of the initial Freudian approach on the rediscovery of an inevitable traumatic pattern in the child and a necessary return to a psychological infancy in the belief that it would free the maimed adult for a new fulfilment of himself, the difference in nuance in Jung's approach is most striking. Of course, his concern for the child in life was as great as any of his contemporaries. But the problem of the child, he maintained in general, had to be dealt with through the parents. He once told me that, whenever asked to help with disturbed children, he would say: "Bring me the parents and I will deal with the problems of the child through them." It was not for nothing, therefore, that he discovered, early in life, how even the companionship of other children "alienated" him from himself. It accounts for a certain bleakness and the thin wintry wind which seemed to preside and blow over the scene of his unpopulated youth. It gives one an inkling of what might have been an unendurable loneliness of spirit for anyone to have to endure to the end of their days, as he did. And he would not have been able to endure this, perhaps, had he not discovered strange companionship within himself.

It started in a Promethean instinct to have a fire of his own and to allow no-one else to tend it, as if this were a symbolic enactment of a realisation of personal awareness in himself. It was soon confirmed by his first sustained dialogue, not with other human-beings, but with something more permanent than either himself or any of the human-beings with whom he argued and talked. Awareness is nothing if it is not also a dialogue between oneself and what one feels to be "other" and greater than oneself. Inner dialogue exists between what one knows and one does not know: between what one is and what one is not. It exists between what one is called upon to be and to serve. It exists where the last horizon of a known self meets the mystery which encloses it as does the universe the earth. Indeed, one does not begin to discover oneself as an individual until such a dialogue breaks in on an hitherto undivided self and some great *forever* outside space and time and change to which we are all so irrevocably subjected, presents itself. This dialogue is a relentless process of enigmatic question and answer that is to run to the end of one's days. And that other *forever* in the beginning at all times and places has had one of its most authoritative representations in imagery evoked through stone. Stone, to the inner eye of the candidate for initiation in self-awareness, is the naturally divine in its most lasting and incorruptible physical form.

I myself have seen this awareness most movingly enacted in terms of stone by the almost vanished copper-coloured, Nilotic-cast Hottentots of my native Africa of which, after the Bushmen, they are the oldest inhabitants. So I have often watched and observed how at the ford of some river whose crossing is natural parable and allegorical material to the mind of man, or near some great tree whose presence bears witness to the seasonal changes prescribed for all in the wheeling courses of an unfolding creation, these Hottentots would, in passing, add a stone of their own to the little pile already there. When I asked them why they did this they would invariably reply that it was out of respect and gratitude to Heitse-Eibib. He, I knew, was their god-hero who came back to the day bleeding in the dawn from the wounds he had received in another victorious battle for light against the darkness of the night. It was his breath in the wind stirring the leaves of the great tree to remind these despised copper-coloured men as they sat there in the heat of the day, that he, Heitse-Eibib himself, was breathing through them and urging their spirit to rise and be on its way. These persecuted men chose stone to mark the presence of Heitse-Eibib because he himself had marked the place of his first resurrection from his first death, with stone.

So it seems to me quite natural that the first dialogue should have begun with a stone in the garden of Jung's home at Klein-Hüningen. He would sit on this stone day after day wondering whether he was the one sitting on the stone; or was he the stone that felt it was being sat upon? This problem raised by the speculation that followed was never solved. But he had no doubt that he was in some secret relationship with the stone. Also that the dialogue thus begun was in terms of a greater, more permanent and irreducible reality as represented by the stone. And it and its intimations evoked a mysterious interdependence of his own world within and the specific world without, that went on from then only to yield its answer, I believe, within hours of his death.

It is not surprising, therefore, that all his life he was especially to love stone. The moment he had broken through the wall which had separated himself and this immemorial past from the present, and so given it a truly contemporary place and form, at this moment he accomplished his own Renaissance, his own rebirth. From then on his dialogue with stone took on a more active and out-going form.

It was to be particularly so when he was about to embark on another stage in the journey within himself. He would seem compelled then to mark the exact time and place of arrival and departure by carving on stone, images and personifications of the new forces motivating him. For instance, when the death of his unique and beloved wife Emma hurled him into a totally new phase of himself and so towards a fresh encounter with the reality of his time, he took up this dialogue again and hammered and chiselled the honey-coloured stone at his lake and woodland retreat of Bollingen. He worked always with devout absorption, patient, calm, resolute, and at a certain marble measure more akin to the Olympian than the demonic element in himself to which he so often referred (using the term always of course, in its original, Classical sense).

But to return to the moment of his first intercourse with stone in the garden of his father (it was significantly always his "father's garden"). He was now launched on the way to self-discovery leading to the disconcerting realisation that not only were he and the stone a significant twosome but he was also strangely paired within as well. He appeared to himself to be two distinct persons to whom he gave the sober, empirical baptism of Personalities Number One and Number Two. The Number One personality was the awkward, inadequate, under-privileged schoolboy in his patched clothes and worn shoes, the inexperienced person that he felt himself almost to be. The Number Two personality was an old man of unchallenged authority and power, at first thought to have lived as a "manufacturer" in the eighteenth century, but later seen to have been a relatively provisional experience of an even more profound pattern than he suspected, with its origin in remotest antiquity. For all the paradoxical imagery in which it and the relationship between its two ambassadors were to be expressed, it was a relatively undifferentiated dress-rehearsal for something far more complex, ultimately to be integrated into another and much more mature personage to whom he was to give the name of the Philemon. He did this as we shall see because of a special meaning he read in the Greek myth and legend in which Philemon and his wife Baucis were the only people on earth to welcome and shelter Zeus and his winged messenger Hermes when they came down from Olympus to examine men for their piety. Number Two therefore, even in this first eighteenth-century personification, was a manifestation of the archetypal pattern of the "wise old man" who has at his disposal experience of all the life that has ever been.

Most human-beings, if they are lucky, discover him only in maturity as a resource within their natural selves. They begin by feeling they share his company in the reflection they find of him in other men in the world. Perhaps the majority of us are content to do this following others we consider wiser than ourselves, without ever acknowledging the need of turning to the original image itself and the mirror of it that we are in ourselves. It is significant testimony, therefore, to the natural antiquity of the young Jung that he discovered his "old man" within so early and kept him company so faithfully. But the Number One personality, for all its love-hate relationship with this ancient other, caused such acute tensions at times that Goethe's great cry of "Two souls, alas, are housed within my breast" might have come from Jung.

All tensions, contradictions and paradox could ultimately be contained because Number Two was, in the final analysis, a source of enrichment for the tentative schoolboy. Indeed as Jung's first immediate personification suggested with the precision of symbolism, it was a "manufacturer", a producer of the meaning which the world without so markedly failed to provide in Jung. I myself always give this element, for two reasons. a priority over other factors. Without the company, first, of this eighteenth-century old man who evolved subsequently into Philemon, Jung could not have accomplished what he did. He might indeed have been so injured by his absence as to become one of the number of casualties, proliferating at such a terrifying rate in the world today, in the battle of the individual for the meaning of his own. Instead he became a person who was to heal and so make whole fragmented human-beings.

There were to be moments, it is true, when it would appear as if Number One personality (the aspect of Jung in the world and of its immediate necessities), had taken over the whole of him. Others when Number Two overshadowed Number One to such an extent that, as a dream forewarned him later at Basle, it dwindled to a single flutter-ing light, in danger of being extinguished by gusts of a wintry wind in some titanic shadow looming over it. Yet in the main the interplay between Number One and Number Two kept Jung always in a state of balance and always brought him back to the heel of striving for fateful proportions. Asymmetric as the interplay of these two person-alities were, it was the kind of asymmetry which, as a great Zen Buddhist priest told me once in Japan, "contained the dynamic impli-cation of greater symmetry to come without which life would become petrified in one inadequate expression of itself". No wonder Jung was to tell me later with a laugh that he could not imagine a fate more awful, a fate worse than death, than a life lived in perfect balance and harmony.

Although Jung's critics, swarming particularly loud and angry like a nest of disturbed bees after his break with Freud, were to hold that this confession of being two people in one was yet more evidence of an unbalanced, if not pathologically schizoid personality, there was nothing but sanity and not a trace of the pathological in this double allotment of responsibilities within the emerging Jung. It is true that there were moments, particularly after his first reading at Basle of Nietzsche's work, when he saw how the doomed writer projects his own Number Two personality on Zarathustra and tried to raise him-self to superhuman heights. Then Jung shut the door of his mind for a long time on his "old man" out of fear that he might be a similarly morbid phenomenon. His fear did not vanish until he realised that Nietzsche's hubris had put this natural phenomenon to a morbid use and he was free to rediscover the ancient in himself in a much more meaningful and more highly differentiated form. Meanwhile, Jung had only to direct himself and his critics to two thousand years of Christianity's intense concern for the "inner man" to confound the charge in terms they could understand, as he had confounded his anxiety in his own unique way.

As far as the Number One personality is concerned, it was essential to Jung, if he was to be in the world, to face it and experience it in full measure. But only through this other Number Two personality could he be prevented from being "of" the world, in the New Testament sense, and the host he was in the Philemon sense to what the gods represented in life. This play and counterplay of his Number One and Number Two personalities, therefore, was to run through the whole of his life. He was to tell me with an unusually sad resignation that it is a pattern, though observable in every human-being, of which only very few were at all aware. Finally, I believe this activation of the pattern of the "old man" within himself started long before he was capable of forming any image of it, let alone being sufficiently aware of it to be capable of putting it into words. Apart from his own natural disposition in that direction, it was all a consequence of the extent to which his father and mother failed each other and the father, in particular, failed the son.

Jung knew at a very early age that he could derive no comfort from his parents' relationship with each other. The word love, almost from the moment of self-awareness, made him acutely uncomfortable. He was, it is true, devoted to his parents and he never doubted their devotion to him. His mother in particular, he often stressed, was extremely good to him and in the long run contributed more to his development than his father. That she was, as he would say with a tender ironical smile of remembrance, "also a bit of a witch" and had also a Number One and a Number Two personality, was to prove an advantage and helped him to honour his obligation to his own Number Two. Though he found her disconcertingly unpredictable and un- reliable, she was a great source of strength and support in his own un- confessed self, through the natural mind, as he called it, of the Number Two that dominated her being.

His father, on the other hand, though unerringly predictable, seemed to him powerless in all the areas that mattered most to Jung, and in which a father is delegated by life to exercise some of the functions which personality Number Two was evoked to assume at so unusually early an age in Jung. Even in the area of religion which happened to be the father's speciality, since he was a priest, he utterly failed his son. Unfortunately it happened to be an area of life to which

Jung was born with an absolute commitment. Almost from the start, as we shall see, he experienced what men call God as a mighty activity within himself. He experienced it with such a clarity, totality and certainty that he never himself had need of any proof in the reality of God. Moreover, from the age of three his imagination was assailed as a result of this activity by symbols and images of the most vivid and disconcerting kind. They seemed to fall like showers of shooting stars streaking through the dark on his perplexed and at times frightened senses; or, like volcanoes erupting, shook the known ground on which his mind stood and glowered with fire high in the night above him.

Yet his father in all other senses was an exceptionally good and honourable parent and there was no justification, as Jung saw it, in blaming him for failing his marriage and his son. The whole trend of the age was against him. He could hardly help being a failure to such an extraordinary son, and almost to any woman, let alone so formidable a wife. He did his best, and I find myself moved to follow the example of those pre-war Indian university students who, despite all their efforts to secure a degree, none the less felt they had achieved something which other men who had not tried likewise had not done, and indicated that something by inserting after their names in their applications for work, "B.A. (failed)". I would not hesitate to put in the lists of the university of life with all possible respect after the name of Jung's parent, the honour of "Father (failed)".

However much Jung made his peace with this failure and never bore any resentment but felt only the most heart-rending compassion for his father, it would be wrong to overlook the depth of the wound it inflicted on him. Perhaps it was this failure of his father to be a true parent to him that made it inevitable, in a boy so introverted, for nature to rush in, fill the gap, and introduce the theme of the universal "old man" long before it was normally due. Also, I believe that as a result of his failure to honour his parent, his own sense of being "father", in the much-needed worldly aspects of an immediate reality, remained under-developed to the end of his days. I think he was permanently deprived by this lack of a natural example in his childhood of what it means to be father to the man in him. Equally, perhaps, he was more influenced than he should have been by his powerful, admiring, warm, confident and strangely ambivalent mother. It was all the better, perhaps, for his ultimate development, and for us living as we do in a world where the masculine can be taken for granted but in which there is such desperate need for a rediscovery of a lost feminine self.

But in terms of Jung's Number One personality, it did create a certain imbalance.

As a result, there was in the economy of his own spirit a negative balance of exchange. I think this is one of the explanations of why he was to get on better, on the whole, with women than men. It explains, perhaps, his strange relationship with Freud as nothing else does, and also a certain archaic authoritarianism that would surge up in him at times in his dealings with other men. I believe that some of the unreliability he came to attribute to men in general was encouraged by an inability to rely, in part, on the man in himself. What was remarkable were not these upsurges but their rarity. Also rare was the fact that Jung was never tempted to hide behind the failure of his parents or behind the failures of his generation, culture, and, indeed, present-day "civilisation". He took the responsibility for all these elements within himself from an early age. He treated them as the raw material (or "base matter" as the alchemists he was to rediscover and honour as pioneers in his own field would have called it), out of which to make the philosopher's stone of his own greater being. Not the least of the greatness of his achievement is implicit in the fact that, in an age when men and their societies increasingly used the failures of parents, society and history as excuses and justifications for not being fully responsible for themselves and their reactions, he always spoke of his parents with gratitude and love, and referred repeatedly to his "dear and generous father". However sad that his father could never give him a positive light whereby to live, Jung often would go back to a moment when, restless and feverish at night, his father had walked up and down carrying him in his arms at Laufen and singing to him in a voice not only audible above the waters of the impassioned Rhine, but still clear and of value to him despite the eighty years and more between them.

It was inevitable that as a result of such a direct personal experience of all that men mean by God, such a powerful personal attack one is tempted to say, because of the density of its onslaught on his awakening awareness, Jung had questions of an unusual, urgent and original import to ask. But whenever he turned to his father, he was cruelly disappointed and dismissed with the exhortation that first he had to believe and trust; only then could he know and understand.

It seemed the wrong way round to Jung. Surely one had to experience first and then one could know and learn to understand? Belief and faith in the mind of the schoolboy were impediments to the pursuit of knowledge and understanding—a conclusion that would seem strange in so naturally an intuitive imagination where trust in what intuition inflicts on the spirit is evidence of what is to come, a report on things not yet seen but still to be observed and proved, were such a conclusion not provisional and really a symptom of the great hurt done to Jung's spirit at so early an age by the insistence of his father and the whole age on a total dogmatic loyalty to a rigidly prescribed religious belief. His father refused utterly to accept the pre-eminence of experience in Jung's approach. This, Jung suspected, was because of unacknowledged and profound doubts in his father not only about his own faith but also about its power to provide a living answer.

So, from as soon as he could remember, Jung resigned himself to the fact that he could get no help from his father. This saddened him. He was convinced that a real interchange of honest question and truthful answer between them would have helped his father too. He felt it might even have prevented him dying in a way which Jung found all the more tragic because it was the end of a living death rather than a life. Indeed, his father's death, in Jung's twenty-first year, was for him his first and most intimate demonstration of the consequences which could follow on the prevailing Christian insistence on a blind, unthinking and literal imitation of Christ.

Yet all this was redeemed in a way by one thing the father had done for the man Jung was to become which, trivial as it may have appeared to his generous soul at the time, was of an abiding polar importance in the life of the son. Nothing could have been more timely, or performed half so well a service badly needed by the boy facing this lonely personal birth through adolescence which I have defined at length before, than the father's action one morning at the foot of the Rigi in Jung's fourteenth year.

The I-Ching lays much emphasis on the importance of the small in the accomplishment of the great and implies that, in the infinite, small and great are one. It is as if the father, in giving all that it was in his power to give that morning, gave everything in terms of the fullness of life when he sent his son alone by rail up the Rigi mountain to the summit because he could not afford to buy two fares.

Few other episodes in the life of Jung move me more. Looking at his rounded life now in a way he himself never could, and as a result being more and more overawed by the absence in it of anything that can be dismissed as truly accidental, I think part of the reason I am so moved is because both father and son were united at that predestined moment as they never were at any other time in one and the same expression of greater meaning, the meaning which the Book of

Changes says, in a phrase John of Patmos could not have excelled, is that which has always existed through itself.

It was a turning point in Jung's life, As he came out on top of the Rigi he had his first glimpse of the mountain of his homeland from above. He found himself looking deep into Wilhelm Tell country, into the mythological heart of Switzerland. I myself have often stood where he stood and as a foreigner found the view almost supernaturally awe-inspiring. I can understand that for a moment he was overwhelmed not just by the beauty and scale of the externals of the scene but because it was home to him as nothing had ever been before. It roused in him a nostalgia that was a summons as on a distant bugle to some unimagined prodigal return. It was, he told me, not only a vision of the world of which his Number Two personality was so disconcerting an emissary but also, in its solemn, white, prophetic summits, dark valleys and cataclysmic gorges, a staggering visualisation of the hidden life and mind and spirit of man. It was a moment of initiation and confirmation in a great, natural temple to which he would return again and again in his imagination for a communion that was as total as it was sacred. He would say, it was the most wonderful thing ever given him by his father. And after such a gift, how relative all that Jung and all of us who write of the father have been compelled to call his failure, since, for all its inadequacy, it is the only word available.

From his remarkable mother, on the other hand, Jung received a totally different response. Part of her supported the social and spiritual conventions of the time. But the boy soon discovered that in the heart of her feminine self she was, without qualifications, at one with his Number Two personality. She supported him in an unpredictable and completely non-rational manner out of her own instincts and intuition. Not without a certain awe, Jung would refer many times to how active in her was what he came to call the "natural mind". It was a mind concerned not with ideas, moral evaluations and other ethical fall-outs of the spirit and religiosity of man. It was concerned with the world, men and what they were, deep within themselves, or what I have called to myself the "great thuses" of life. Meister Eckehart, the fourteenth-century Dominican mystic whom Jung was to study intently, somewhere called them, with far greater precision, the *istigkeit*—the "isness" of life and time.

This natural mind of his mother gave Jung no direct food for thought in concepts and ideas. But it confirmed and sustained his own inner sense of direction at all sorts of critical stages. I have already indicated how his father's failure brought his development more and more under feminine influence. But there was far more to it than that. His was above all an inspired intuitive spirit. Men whose great and besetting speciality is the world of thought and ideas for which they will fight and kill, understand intuition so little that they are inclined to mistrust it. In so far as they themselves have intuitions, they take them only to a depth which still appears to women as touching only the fringe of the reality. A young girl as a rule seems to me far more mature, intuitively, than most men at any age. Not the least of the conventional tensions between men and women have arisen from this fact. But Jung, an intuitive of genius and all the better equipped to serve his intuitions because he possessed an intellect to match them, was even more at home in this dimension of life than was his mother. He was able to share the apprehensions of her natural mind not in the partially archaic way that she experienced them, but in a totally contemporary idiom.

There were many examples, small and great, of this positive interreaction between them. But of these perhaps only one is necessary to illustrate the effect on the main theme of the evolution of the boy into the man. The first was that it was not the father in whose library shelves stood a splendidly bound edition of Goethe, but his mother who, out of sheer instinct, told him he ought to read *Faust*. The advice was timely and sent Jung to a lofty summit of his own "inscape".

Apart from the all-important fact that he was born introverted and so naturally tended to withdraw into himself, so many things had happened to the boy that he kept his inner life a secret from both his parents and his world. Indeed, if I were to review his life in conventional chronological sequence, I would have had to touch on the main causes of this long since, because one of the main incentives came from a great dream which was inflicted on him when he was little more than three years old, as well as a daytime vision some nine years later. But as this is an account of a personal experience which for me began in his old age, and so is inevitably concerned more with psychological dimensions of time and space than the more obvious and conventional level on which these great twosomes act, I am forced to turn to those moments not at their emergence but at the point, many years later, of their acquisition of meaning in the spirit of Jung. All that mattered at this point was the realisation of how his real person was growing, as it had done almost from infancy, like a pearl on the bed of the sea around a grit of secrets held inviolate within the outer shell of a mere boy doing his duty as best he could by his parents, environment and school.

Every instinct he possessed insisted that he was in possession already of facts and forms of knowledge that it would be most unwise to share with others. He knew that he was not in possession yet of the valid, properly informed and differentiated self able either to understand fully or contain all that was being inflicted from within. Nor could he defend it against a world whose values challenged or contradicted these events. But he knew all this instinctively at an early age, and had the courage, in full measure, of his, as yet, untried instincts. He seemed to know in an utterly non-conceptualised way that such secrets were in a sense holy secrets, vital for the living of an individual life uniquely his own. They were part of the living mystery whose worldly manifestations are hidden, as in all great religions, from the eyes of the generality of men and women. Only the highest of their initiates are allowed to perceive and serve. The Jews, for instance, ordained this in the holy of holies of their tabernacle. The Japanese used their shrine at Ise where the sacred mirror is screened from vulgar view by a simple white, unstained cloth hanging between columns of plain wood on which the grain of the seasons to this day are apparent like the fingerprints of God and his time. The keeping of such secrets, either collectively or religiously, is not to be confused with secrecy. Such secrets are the only forms of protection possible for experiences of the infinite and living mystery which cannot be broadcast in a manner capable of making it generally understood or saving it from popular destruction. The secrets of holiness are like seeds that need the darkness, isolation and cover of the earth to germinate unobserved before they can emerge and grow into the light of the day for which they are destined. So it was with Jung when a boy, already charged to bursting point with secret growth of an unprecedented density and power.

His Number One personality must have done its work far better than either he or his Number Two personality suspected. It is remarkable how little parents, teachers and schoolboys were aware of the volcanic world hidden from their view. Of course they had their suspicions. A teacher gave vent to them by falsely accusing Jung of plagiarism and lying when he wrote a brilliant essay. Had the teacher been worthy of his vocation he might have reappraised his judgement in observing how the boy took the punishment so unjustly inflicted on him. The natural indignation over such unfair treatment fell from Jung with unusual swiftness. A great calm came over his spirit as he discovered he was far more interested in what it was, both in him and the teacher, that had produced such a collision than he was in the pain

and injustice inflicted. The discovery of this was of immense importance to him as an act of spiritual emancipation. It proved him to be
no longer a slave to mere action and reaction as the generality of men
and their societies were. It proved him already in possession of an
acausal element in himself, and he was to put this discovery to the
most creative use later in many other ways, particularly in his parting
with Freud.

His school-fellows, too, were full of suspicion of someone they felt
they did not understand. They named him after the patriarch Abraham
and so set some four thousand years between him and them! They
liked him so little, perhaps, out of the average schoolboy's distaste of
anyone who does not conform to their norm. So one afternoon they
ambushed him on his way home from school. They had a glimpse
then of the volcanic temperament of Jung which in the future kept
them at bay. Jung seized one of them by the heels and, using him as
he was later to use a rhinoceros whip on a mob of frenzied African
dancers in Uganda, threatened the others to such effect that they all
fled. The discovery of such an aggressive temper surprised him, too,
and was at rare intervals to surprise him to the end of his days. So at
least I am told, for I never saw any trace of it myself in the man I
knew.

No-one knew the extent to which already the boy's imagination
was involved in trying to determine the meaning of things. And,
above all, the nature of the meaning of all that connected and gathered
around the name of God. Neither father nor mother knew how he
lay awake at nights in an agony of spirit over his total inability to
accept the conventional view that God was purely good and loving.
Already he accepted, as Meister Eckehart had scornfully proclaimed
in the fourteenth century, *quod erat absurdum*, that if God were good
He could be better. Jung did not doubt, it is true, that God could be
loving and a great bestower of a grace. This he, too, had experienced
after admission of the as yet undeclared vision. But he sensed there was
more to it than that. Somewhere and somehow God was terrible and
also stood in a relationship with darkness and evil, indeed perhaps had
need of them as an instrument of grace and redemption. This thought
frightened the carefully conditioned Protestant wits out of Jung.
During the three-quarters of an hour it took him to walk from his
home to school, he was, as a rule, aware of neither the time nor distance because his imagination was entirely possessed by problems of this
nature. The journey back, despite the intervention of long, concentrated school hours, was spent likewise. The dialogue within was as

alive as ever, and ready for taking up exactly where he had abandoned it when he entered the gates of the privileged Gymnasium at Basle.

Indeed, so possessed was he by speculation on problems concerned with religious material issuing out of his own nature that it came between him and the study of mathematics. He himself made little of his difficulties in his *Memories*. But he remained somewhat puzzled if not outraged by them for the rest of his life. These difficulties, I believe, were a direct consequence of the naturally profound religious nature of Jung and therefore merit far more attention than they have as yet received.

The problems started in the realm of the applied religion that we call ethics. Such statements as "If $a = b$ and $b = c$, then $a = c$" seemed terrifyingly immoral to him. The view, of course, is partly evidence of that instinctive respect he always had for "otherness" in all life, men and things, and which he held to be inviolate, even in algebraic symbols. But at heart the difficulty was more mysterious and far greater. It was due, I suspect, to the fact that he experienced mathematics at the religious level wherein, in fact, the science had its source. He entered the world of mathematics through the same door as had Pythagoras and Euclid. All these symbols and patterns which form the foundation of the great science of mathematics issued unsolicited out of him as they had done out of them and were sheer objective religious material.

For instance, there was the basis which was axiomatic and concerned with what were held as self-evident truths. But all axioms in the minds of those who first formulated them, particularly those of Pythagoras whom Jung numbered among the greatest of men, were launched more as religious statements than scientific pronouncements, however great their applied scientific potentials were to prove. To define the mathematical concepts of infinity, for instance, as that which is so great that it can be neither increased nor diminished is as good a definition of a God as one could possibly get. Jung, in his eighties, one day remarked to me that God was so great that it was utterly impossible to add or subtract from his greatness. When I called that a profound mathematical proposition he smiled. He himself later lent support to this interpretation by trying to explain algebraically the concept of the Holy Trinity. In the process he showed a firmer grasp of equations than one would have thought possible after his early struggles. But as the years went by he suspected, more and more, that each number represented an archetype of its own. There was the invention of ancient Indian philosophy of zero which said that the one divided by the nought produced infinity. This appeared to be another way of saying what the mystics proclaimed in their assertion that if God had not created the universe out of nothing he would not have created anything at all. So that the *one* as measured in mathematics against the *nothing* of the anti-one, could only produce the *infinite* as answer.

Finally, to turn to an axiom which particularly bothered Jung, namely the statement that parallel straight lines met only in infinity. It was not only a religious but a great psychological truth. The great opposites in life, man, things, or even inanimate matter, wherever body and antibody meet through their very opposition ultimately form a common transforming substance. They did steer a strange parallel and irreconcilable course until forced to join each other by some transcendental agency which is an expression of infinite meaning.

Yet with all this and much else at war within Jung, the complacent unobservant world could see in him little beyond an awkward and at times disconcerting boy. So much so that Jung repeatedly referred to his questionable popularity at school, at university and to the mistrust he seemed to arouse not so much by what he said or did as just by what he was. Small wonder that there appears to have been no single teacher or professor who really had any decisive influence on his development, or was just humanly close enough to merit acknowledgement for his ultimate reflections.

Only his mother, without any cloud of mind or ideas to dim her reactions, instinctively knew this *other* in her son; and out of instinct introduced him to *Faust*. It was as if the "witch" in her (to pursue the word in the idiom of the pre-Arthurian world wherein it had its positive meaning) recognised that there was a "Merlin" in the son in need of the protection of the magic she sensed to be in *Faust*.

The encounter that followed, as a result, was one of the most momentous of Jung's life. Although he could report on it and explain its repercussions only in terms of what he then was, the consequences continued to the end of his days and never failed to enrich his spirit. Of course, in a sense he was already a ploughed field ready for the seed of *Faust* to be sown in its soil. As a German-Swiss he was sufficiently part of the Germanic complex of European culture to be wide open for the impact of *Faust*. *Faust*, as Jacob Burckhardt observed, was fundamentally a German myth. He was, to use another Burckhardt phrase which Jung himself was to employ for a time as proxy for the term archetype, "a primordial image". But *Faust* was an image with a peculiarly German relevance. He was, of course, also a great primordial universal. But nowhere in post-Renaissance Europe, the Europe of Jung and even my own later day, was the pattern of *Faust* so active, charged and concentrated as at the heart of the German cultural complex.

One could see evidence of this, for instance, in the comparative indifference of both the Latin and English-speaking worlds, above all the English, to the theme of *Faust*. Gounod's opera, in comparison to Goethe's first and especially second book of *Faust*, is a schoolboy essay in something whose essence is really beyond his comprehension; a sort of playing with some of the late Mr Nobel's dynamite as if it were merely a Chinese cracker to explode at another second-class wedding.

The deepest English foray in the matter, Kit Marlowe's *Tragedy of Dr Faustus*, for all the wonderful lines of poetry it produced, is also by comparison almost a frolic. The level of approach is never more evident than in the stage direction, "exit devil with fireworks and crackers". Small wonder, perhaps, because the Elizabethans were still receiving so great an overflow of the fullness of Renaissance man and as a result were so rounded as to be inpervious to the tragedy of fate implicit in the cataclysmic dichotomy personified in Goethe's *Faust*. Indeed, even at this late hour the indifference of the English-speaking world to Goethe and particularly to *Faust* remains as marked as ever, and is worth examination for understanding by analogy how such a dramatised myth can mean so much to a whole people.

The indifference is there, I think, because the English have their own version of Goethe infinitely more suited for their own special needs in their incomparable Shakespeare. Their own myth is far more accurately expressed in *Hamlet* which personifies an organic problem in the culture of the English-speaking world as *Faust* does in that of the German. This Prince of Denmark is an unseen "Everyman" in the English character. Obsessed by the guilt of a mother who surrenders herself totally to the worldly aspects of the father, the man who has to deal with the world and to make his way in life, between them they neglect the need of the other and greater "father" within to such an extent that he cannot live. In other words the murder of the natural father in *Hamlet* must not be taken literally but symbolically. Deciphered, it is Hamlet's inability to be his full, mature, masculine self because of the domination of a partial aspect of his spirit, as symbolised by the mother, over the potential whole. As with all illegal acts of violence against our natural spirit, the denied, the murdered aspect will not, indeed cannot expire, and so becomes the ghost which Hamlet, and indeed we all, have taken so literally to our cost. This is an intimation an urge of life that cannot be indefinitely frustrated. As so often we get the image the wrong way round by judging it purely in terms of reflection presented to us in ourselves and others. The ghost in *life* is not an image of life after death but of spirit before birth. It is our inability to distinguish between the reflected and its reflection that makes us incapable of recognising in Hamlet's ghost a dim, phosphorescent personification of new meaning clamouring to be born. So we locate it in a dimension after death rather than the one which precedes birth.

The repercussions of such an unresolved myth are still burrowing in the foundations of the culture of the English-speaking world. Hamlet's father's ghost was *Hic et ubique*, like a mole in the ground underneath that keep of the English spirit symbolised as Elsinore. It is precisely because the spirit of the English-speaking world remains so unconsciously "female-dominated" that man has not yet been able to be his full self, unless compelled to it by some archaic motivation like war or disaster. Nor, shackled to the mother, is he capable of finding freely his own feminine self as personified by Ophelia. So he abandons her to drown in the water that is an image of human unawareness.

All the poetic imagery uttered with such power and lightning immediacy makes it clear that the damage done to Hamlet is through his own feminine aspect. Even the instrument of the symbolic murder of the greater father, his own natural royalty, is the poison which in myth, legend and history has always been regarded as a singularly feminine weapon of destruction. Moreover, it is administered through the father's ear, the means through which all the nagging Xantippes of the world instil the poison of their outraged spirit. "When the angry woman scolds", the old Zulus used to tell me, "the man who is wise closes his ears and refuses to hear or answer back."

That *Hamlet* is not just an individual myth but a collective one as well, and still active to this day, seems verified by my own observation of the relationship between men and women in the English-speaking world. In the course of the history, particularly of England, a whole people, like Hamlet, although obsessed with guilt implicit in the refusal to act on an awareness of a need to redress an obvious failure, yet does not take up the challenge immediately. The English linger with it for so long that, when at last forced into action by external circumstances, they inflict far greater damage than was originally necessary. The greater action also often proves ultimately not to have been enough. The unresolved mythological problem accordingly recommences yet another cycle of life. "Muddling through", as the

English say of themselves not without a certain inverted pride, should perhaps be called "mothering through" in the *Hamlet* sense.

Of course there remains an infinity of meanings to be read in *Hamlet*. But this much, I hope, is enough to be a bridge towards an understanding of why the drama of *Faust* could be so important to the Germans, and particularly so to Jung. Its collective import understandably escaped the boy at their first contact. He experienced it first only at a personal level. He found himself utterly absorbed by it and both uplifted and relieved for the most significant of reasons.

It was not because of *Faust* himself. "That fellow", he told me with a laugh, "made very little impression on me at my first reading. I could not guess how important he was to become, so great a bungler, such an awful amateur and fool he appeared to me. My real interest was in the devil. I hated the way Faust tricked him. I thought it unworthy both of Goethe and Faust to resort to such barefaced deceit. For although people in my world spoke a great deal about God, 'Old Nick' was hardly ever thought worthy of a mention."

And of course, Faust's Mephistopheles meant much to the boy Jung. It was proof, at last, that his own experience of darkness and evil personified in Goethe's Mephistopheles was real. The coming of Christ had abolished neither the darkness nor the devil. They existed, still active and valid as ever in life. And as in *Faust*, they played some mysterious role in what theologians call redemption, but which Jung already was beginning to regard as some sort of metamorphosis or transfiguration of individual man. Over at last was the great initial battle he had fought alone and in secret. It was a battle waged against a feeling that, in finding God's world not all light and love but also full of old night and unrepentant evil, he might be either mad or hopelessly in error. Now, however, he had the company of one of the greatest of German spirits to confirm the sanity of his awareness of darkness and evil as living elements of reality.

The comfort this gave him could never be underrated. It was true that one such victory did not mean that the long campaign was over. It had barely begun. He still had a long way to go before even the full meaning of Faust's pact with the devil burst in upon him. Later it disclosed its immense prophetic import for Germany and the world: and its collective meaning was brought into an individual focus in Goethe's drama. But already at a first reading the book had become one of his great formative experiences.

"People would ask me whether I had enjoyed *Faust*", he told me with a certain indignant bewilderment. "They might as well have asked me if I had enjoyed an earthquake which had changed a familiar scene for good. Enjoyed it, no! But it did give me a certain uncomfortable comfort."

He was to read it frequently and it was for him, as he himself put it, a pillar in the bridge of the spirit which spans the morass of world history, beginning with the Gilgamesh epic, then the Book of Changes, the Upanishads, *The Secret of the Golden Flower* (also translated from the Chinese by Wilhelm), fragments of Heraclites, and so on to the Gospel of St John, the letters of St Paul, Meister Eckehart and Dante.

The other great service rendered to Jung by his mother was less specific and spread over many formative years, often more through the atmosphere she created than by active participation. She stimulated and helped him in his interest in the non-rational, at times parapsychological, phenomena of life, so despised by the intellectual establishment of his day. The interest again came to him so naturally that the lack of curiosity in the world of science and intellect made him more aware than ever of the great divide between the natural or "country" mind, as he called it when studying medicine at Basle, and the "town" mind. He acknowledged the help science was to him in providing him with empirically established knowledge and facts. He was forever indebted to it for the discipline and method it gave to his urgent, inquiring spirit. But he was appalled by its inability to give him any real insight either into the nature of the truth it served or into material bombarding him from this preoccupied area within to which he was so singularly committed from birth.

Much as the need for concentrating on his studies at school and university had pushed his Number One personality into the foreground and driven his Number Two apparently out of sight, seen or unseen it remained at work in his imagination. So the schism between first and last, primitive and civilised, science and religion, that he saw all round him, lived on as his great preoccupation. For the moment his priority had been a re-allocation of the forces of his mind and spirit. He had learned no longer to speak to people out of his intuition alone. That in itself was a formidable step, considering how continuous an assault his own intuitive perceptions made on his attention. He accepted that he lived in a world where intuition had to be supported by facts and did all that he could to develop his empirical faculties. As a result, the difference between his mother's instinctive appreciation of the non-rational aspects of reality and his own was that he approached them also empirically. Also, as so often when some inner crisis was coming to a climax within, chance introduced the appropriate circumstance to redirect him towards his natural course. At a moment when the clash between his natural and cultivated self was at its most extreme, and he may well have been seduced into the pursuit of an orthodox medical career, three totally non-rational phenomena associated with his ageing mother burst in on him from the world. He came into his home from the garden one day to find that a bread knife had exploded inside the sideboard with the sound of a pistol shot. He extracted the knife, which was cut into four neat segments, and although no damage had been done to the sides of the bread basket or to the bread in it, an expert who examined the knife was convinced it must have been done with considerable and deliberately applied force to produce so clear-cut a result since the steel itself was flawless. Within a few days a walnut table, ninety years of age and again for the use of his mother, tore three-quarters of the surface apart with another resounding retort, despite the humid atmosphere of the room in which it was housed.

These were non-rational intrusions on his everyday reality which his natural mind just could not ignore. Then, he found that, for no obvious reason, he connected the events with a mediumistic young girl of fifteen and a half, whom he had recently met and with whom his new empirical self was determined to experiment. Why and how had both knife and table been shattered? What forces were made manifest in such a fashion? His only direct experiences of such things were from history, literature, folk-lore, and hearsay. In this area these were but two of a legion of such occurrences. And what was at work in the spirit of the young girl connected with these events to send her into a somnambulistic daylight state and to practise what were dismissed as spiritualistic phenomena? He could understand neither how her neighbours, and persons like his mother, could take so disconcerting a phenomenon for granted; nor how teachers, professors and fellow students were utterly disinterested in it.

He took it upon himself, therefore, despite the exactions of the university, to study the contents of what the girl produced in trance and in other twilight states of herself. In due course he learned, he thought, how a Number Two personality could enter a child's awareness and become an extra-territorial influence in her character, capable of an autonomy and courses of action all its own. Already he had taken his first conscious step away from the mainstream of conventional science and medicine. But he was to return to the precept and question that she induced in him again and again in later years. In her natural state she was an ordinary and simple seamstress. What then had made

her in her tranced state to be so good, confident and elegant a lady of
fashion, talking in an educated German totally alien to the dialect of
her class? One stresses here how significant it was that, in taking even
this tentative step towards his destiny, his guide was already what, for
want of a better word, one is compelled to call the abnormal and unrecognised aspect in the feminine spirit of his day. This young girl
helped to prepare Jung beyond all his own expectations to be totally
ready when the decisive catalyst appeared on the scene of his aspirations.

At the university he had left his prescribed course in psychiatry to
the last, so neglected, disdained and remote a subject was it to him and
his profession. But now he came across a book on psychiatry by
Krafft-Ebing. The psychiatric material quoted in this book, even to me
reading it in a much less inhibited day, seemed almost too startling,
too highly charged for even the strongest of Protestant stomachs to
digest. But Jung took it all without any discernible difficulties, perhaps
because it was not the case material in the book that primarily interested him. Although already strongly tempted to accept a promising
offer to practise medicine from one of his more esteemed professors,
it needed hardly more than a single sentence in the preface of Krafft-
Ebing's book to change his mind completely. It was Krafft-Ebing's
observation that madness or "psychoses are diseases of the personality".
Jung had hardly to read further. He knew at once that his future field
had to be psychiatry. There alone, he was convinced, did biology and
spirit, science and the demands of the soul, the discipline without and
the call within, have common living ground. He believed that no-one
at the university would understand so unorthodox a step. Once more
he would have to isolate himself from the generality of men. But
inwardly he had never felt happier or more confident than when he
reached this conclusion. The *two* in him were one at last.

So he ended his studies with almost everyone shaking their heads
over so strange and eccentric an act. At least, this is the impression
that he gave one. But one wonders whether everyone found it so strange
in someone already thought to be so strange, and whether far more
good wishes did not accompany him than he allowed his inverted
senses to realise? Jung, after all, throughout his life was so absorbed
in his work and the recording of it that his immense humanity could
hardly get a nose past the titanic figure of worker and writer, to get a
look in on those monumental pages. But surely the humanity of the
human being had been there for all who knew him at the university
also to savour and enjoy?

Once, in a train in Switzerland, I met a man whose father had been at Basle with Jung. He told me that according to his father, Jung was always "the life and soul" of the student fraternity to which they both belonged. I feel always compelled to remind myself of this aspect when considering the books of his youthful past. They are so closed against human warmth and immediacy, but so open and exposed to the claims of the eternal and infinite. But among the many heroic achievements of which he proved himself capable, not the least is the fact that alone, as he always was, wintry and bleak as was the scene of childhood, youth and adolescence, he never allowed those years to become a "winter of discontent". He kept a midsummer night's festival of delight aflame in himself. I find it not at all strange, therefore, that sudden as the decision was regarding his career, he celebrated it and the end of his university life by giving himself first a night at the theatre, then at the opera, followed by a journey to Germany—all just for the fun of it.

He enjoyed himself enormously, particularly at the opera, if enjoyment is the right word for an experience of such intensity. He saw a performance of *Carmen* which so impressed him that the music and theme stayed with him for days. Whatever one's own reservations about the quality of Bizet's opera, here already there was evidence that he was not, as often alleged, indifferent to music. In fact, perhaps it was intimation that music meant almost too much to him.

"I listened to music only sparingly", he would tell me, "because it made me almost unbearably sad, and upset me far too much when I had enough to be upset about already."

Even if it is not on record and the detail inaccessible, I am certain from this and all that I knew of Jung that the fun and unfailing sense of humour, the love of life for its own sheer sake, went with him also in his translation to Zürich and the staff of the Burghölzli Mental Hospital. Indeed, although he was leaving Basle and the banks of the Rhine for good, it was as if he left them on a note of music discovered for the first time in himself, to go out at last a young man on his own to the external world, as he had always been on his own in the world within.

THE VIGIL
AND THE SUMMONS

Naturally nature has so disposed me.

LEONARDO DA VINCI

Jung left Basle for Zürich as poor as ever in a worldly sense except of course that he had employment and remuneration guaranteed for the first time in his life. His baggage must have appeared extraordinarily light. Yet he travelled rich and almost overloaded in spirit, so that I always feel compelled to examine the nature of this load before accompanying him further on his dangerous journey into unexplored country.

As far as general possessions were concerned, I would put first the profound sense of history with which Basle had equipped him. It had done this not just by what he learned at the university itself or from books which he had devoured there in his spare time like food by a famished person, nor from the history extracted in his intensive reading of philosophy out of a hypersensitive and highly charged interest in the subject, but also from what the city out of itself conveyed by silent implication more eloquent even than the chosen historical word. Whenever I heard him speak on a subject I was always astounded by his knowledge of its history, just as I was by the breadth of his reading of the humanities and indeed of the literature of the world.

How he found the time to do all this among the pressures of studies, which at Swiss universities are greater than most, as well as in the midst of the proliferating demands of his inborn preoccupation and the many other calls of his family, community and life as a student, would have been a total mystery did one not know his over-riding tendency to be solitary and his natural endowment of abundant energy.

Moreover, his energies were never exhausted, not only because he was physically strong but because he followed the mainstream in himself. In this way he was unlike so many of the men and women of our time who live on the capital of their energies because they find themselves embattled against their natural selves. They do not earn new allowances of energy for themselves but merely exhaust the supply which nature had originally bestowed on them. Jung, on the contrary, seemed to generate more mental and spiritual energy for himself living, as it were, on interest and never touching the original investment of his nature. In this way both volume and value grew rapidly in an age of increasing inflation of mind and being until one almost wondered at times whether energy had not accomplished the impossible of spontaneous generation in him.

These energies enabled him to read widely in the philosophy most relevant to him, as in Kant, and further enabled him to find in its history some anticipatory support for his prevailing interest in dreams, symbols, fantasy and their mechanism. He had weighed his values in the scales of philosophy, ancient and modern, from Heraclitus to Hegel and the Schopenhauer who gave him also a scent of the contribution the Far East might make one day to his own private and personal quest. Philosophers like Heraclitus, Abelard and Kant excepted, his conclusions were not flattering to them because he found that, like theologians, they would go on delivering themselves of resounding solemnities and plausible profundities when they, as he told me once, "should have shut up and closed their big mouths until they were in possession of the facts to support their thinking".

None the less, his intensive reading of philosophy and religion had provided him with a knowledge in depth of the climate of spirit in which history unfolded. He knew the proven facts, statistics and chronological progression of external events. But more, he knew that their myths and legends were also as clouds of a forgotten dawn glory that had once been home for the spirit of a European man. Moreover he read philosophy, history and literature which breathed life into statistical fact in the original Greek and Latin. Thanks to his father, he had accepted at the age of six the necessity of mastering Latin and devoted himself to its study so ardently that still he read it at the age of eighty as if it were native to him. The Renaissance he cherished because it was the great re-awakening of the spirit in an arrested European culture, and so a fateful turning point in the life of man. Finally, his grasp of the humanities became as great as his grip on the disciplines of science. He drew inspiration from the humanists of that great awakening, seeing them as experts in the awesome business of decline and fall of great cultures and examples of how the human spirit responded creatively in such terrible moments of crisis and transition.

Above all Jung felt himself close to Erasmus, whom his contemporaries called Desiderius. As a child I preferred his original Dutch name of Geerard because, illegitimate as he may have been born, he seemed to embody, as his Dutch name implies, not only someone born of the desire of those who begat him, but also someone born out of the valid need of a whole age for someone just like him. A small proof of Jung's love for Erasmus as well as evidence of the natural priority of his spirit is that on one occasion, poor as a church mouse, at the age of nineteen, he spent money he could not spare to buy a second-hand copy of Erasmus in Latin. He was still reading it in worn leather covers when I saw him last, just before he died.

All these particular aspects of his interest in history were stimulated by the fact that history at the University of Basle in Jung's day tended to be dominated by Jacob Burckhardt, and his passionate, illuminated, eclectic grasp of it. Burckhardt still seemed to walk the university when Jung was there, with the spirit of Bachofen in close support. At that time no-one could expose themselves to history there without encountering the impact of Burckhardt's attitude to it, and in particular to his interpretation of the volcanic phenomenon of the Renaissance, the Reformation and so on to the story of Greece. Jung had reservations about Burckhardt because he could never plunge deep enough below the surface of antiquity for the young man's needs. Yet Jung did not fail to recognise that Burckhardt had plunged deeper than most so he never ignored the new perspectives of history thus made possible. I say this with some confidence not only because of Jung's many references to Burckhardt in writing and conversation, but because I am just old enough to remember the impact he made on the historical conventions even of my own day. He was my own father's favourite historian, and as a boy I read him eagerly. Even then I had an inkling of a new and utterly unique view of history which was only to be equalled by my encounter later with Acton. I elaborate on this because only a Swiss could have achieved such a view at such a time and I do not hesitate to add only a Swiss working in Basle, utterly absorbed in the cultural climate of such a city.

By this time Switzerland was already fully established in a role and character in the history of our time that was peculiarly its own. Ever since the Swiss defeat at Marignano in 1515 fighting with the forces of Milan against Francis I of France, the Swiss had totally abandoned all ambitions to become a European power. What was remarkable, too, was the fact that the abandonment was not a result of despair over defeat so much as a realisation that they had to fulfil themselves in a totally new way. It was something both praised and denounced by embattled neighbours. It was the beginning of a stubborn concept of neutrality. But, for me, it has always been neutrality with a difference. It was never a neutrality of evasion, based on a somewhat ignominious preparedness to let others fight one's own battles. It was unlike Dutch neutrality before the world wars. It was also unlike that of Sweden who, while proclaiming itself neutral, yet allowed two German divisions to cross its territory during the last European war. Swiss neutrality was a neutrality of utter commitment to a concentration on a national self and a national home and also to a defence of both, as is exemplified by the fact that all the country's manhood, between adolescence and retirement, is permanently on military call. It was if the Swiss realised how anachronistic was a purely territorial affirmation of nationhood. The frontiers which really mattered were ones of national character and spirit, and those demarcated by the right to determine a self of one's own. The Swiss, when offered a considerable extension of their German frontiers in the last century, refused. It was out of keeping with the values they had discovered in renouncing power as a principle of nationhood. Their physical shape was final. The only expansion permitted them was in the realms of the spirit, and free exchange with the nations of the world. Their powerful neighbours could invade them at any moment. Others might criticise and sneer. But for the first time in modern European history a people had come into being determined to find their increase within themselves out of their own resources of spirit and within the bounds of their self-imposed ration of enigmatic mountain earth.

This reference to the Swiss mountain earth is inescapable since the earth was an important element in the evolution of national character which followed Marignano. Living as the Swiss did among those mountains with their great heads of snow looking down on them like elder statesmen of space and time, and imposing on them great problems and uncertainties of human life from avalanche, fall of rock and flood, and so the most precarious of livelihoods, the Swiss were less inclined than others to exceed their human proportions. They tended to assess themselves as Jung had done on the Rigi in the measure and scale of the infinite and a sense of humbling wonder and mystery that these visions of unchanging heights evoke. Significantly enough, no-one has put this aspect of the Swiss relationship with his history and earth better than Jung. For instance, in an address on Paracelsus (the strange, early-sixteenth-century physician and philosopher who had a prophetic vision, however clouded, of where Jung was to stand some four hundred years later), Jung defined this with a poetic intensity which seized his pen far more strikingly than those who read him only in translation can realise. He did it on this occasion all the more graphically because from what he told me he is describing something with which he identifies an essential part of himself.

"The great peaks of the Alps", he said of Paracelsus, "rose up menacingly close, the night of the earth visibly dwarfs the well of man; threateningly alive, it holds him fast in its hollows and forces its will upon him. Here where nature is mightier than man, none escapes her influence; the chill of water, the starkness of rocks, the twisted, jutting roots of trees and precipitous cliffs, all this generates in the soul of anyone born there something that can never be extirpated, lending him that characteristically Swiss obstinacy, doggedness, stolidity and innate pride which have been interpreted in various ways, favourably as self-reliance; unfavourably as pigheadedness."

This ultimate Swiss shape, accordingly, was new in content as in form. It incorporated peacefully within itself the three main, and so often warring, cultural elements of Europe; German, French and Italian in both the Protestant and Catholic versions of those strains. They were thus the first pilot scheme of a greater united Europe. Finally, they put this neutrality not to a purely selfish use, but placed it at the service of the world in such a way that when reason and peace failed the international scene, Switzerland was there to provide some common channel of communication. Through the creation of institutions like the International Red Cross they showed their sense of a special world responsibility which their neutrality imposed on them. So that the history of the last hundred years has proved, I believe, what an indispensable instrument of humanity Swiss neutrality has been. Moreover, the Swiss produced an elite with a view of the world and history above the battle. And, by force of growing tradition, they were more and more inclined to see historic events steadily and whole rather than fitfully and in part. And nowhere in Switzerland was this more true in Jung's youth than in the city of Basle.

In a country of city states (closer to the classical definition of such a society than any other today) Basle was unique. The precious thread of historical continuity, not just Swiss but European, was firmer in Basle than anywhere else in the country. Founded more than two thousand years ago, before the birth of Christ, Basle's feeling for the past was still a living cultural element, expressing itself even in such externals as modes and institutions. I myself have often stayed in an hotel in Basle wherein three great European princes lodged more than a thousand years ago while negotiating a new treaty. Again at the city's carnival held annually to celebrate the victory of light and warmth over the ever-recurring winter of darkness and ice, one can still to this day hear the great tribal drums, beating at dawn to quicken pagan aboriginal hearts and rouse a Dionysian upsurge of senses from a year's respectable Swiss *haute bourgeois* slumber. In those days the city stood on the Rhine at the point from which the river became navigable right down to its mouth in the sea. It was therefore the nearest equivalent Switzerland possessed to a sea-port and a place through which the world came into the heart of Switzerland and from which it went forth into the world. All of these immense imponderables of history became ponderable in the charismatic historical personality of Burckhardt. And this, of course, helped to give Jung a world view of history. It gave him the historical foundation that was essential if he were to achieve the universality that I believe both he and his work have done. One only has to think how a man of genius like Freud, whose sense of history seemed to start only with Darwin, was limited if not maimed by the absence of an historical perspective capable of matching his psychological insight.

Indeed, so much history was, at first, almost too much for a young man so eager to press on into the future as was Jung. Indeed, he felt a certain relief at leaving it all behind. Zürich, at a first glance, related to the world not through the history and the intellect but through vulgar commerce. But it seemed a freer and more modern city which excited him. Yet a now invisible Basle made a city of history inviolate within his spirit and to the end of his days was there to support him, so that he was never delivered of a tangible, persistent nostalgia for the place which had so endowed him.

Yet even more important thán this wealth of history, Jung brought with him two inner experiences which were great among the many secrets around which his robust spirit had grown into early manhood. They were of immense importance to the hopes he had that his new calling would enable him to understand the cataclysmic rift that he had observed widening and deepening in the spirit of man between the religious and scientific needs of his being. Just as he had found theology and organised religion in their contemporary form bankrupt, so science too had brought no real comfort to his spirit. Yet, as he packed his bags for Zürich, poor and inadequate as they had both proved in their respective ways, the importance of bringing them back into some contemporary form of well-being, seemed greater and more urgent than ever. He knew he was leaving a city which was a privileged law and rule unto itself and considered itself enlightened compared to the "barbarians" scattered among other cities, villages, valleys and Alps of Switzerland. In particular, Basle was scornful of Zürich, with which it existed in a state of great rivalry if not emnity. Basle regarded the "city on the lake" as an ignoble opposite of itself, a place of gross and vulgar materialism.

Indeed, Jung himself felt there was a great deal of justice in the charge. He felt, I believe, that Basle somehow was closer to his own Number Two personality, as Zürich in the first instance might be nearer to his Number One. It is significant that he would refer to the Zürich of that day as "the most materialistic city in the whole of Switzerland".

He confessed that, ostensibly, he could not have gone to ground in Switzerland in a place less likely to provide the ideal human material for his purposes.

"Zürich taught me a valuable lesson", he once told me. "If you wait for ideal human material in my business, you would never start. Always you must take what is nearest to hand, no matter how unpromising, and accept it as the only and therefore the best you can do, and by sheer hard work transform it into the thing you need. You would be as surprised as I was in Zürich what can come out of the most unpromising human earth when you really try and keep at it."

Yet I wonder whether he would have reached so mature a conclusion in Zürich, had he not possessed two great secret experiences to steer his life by and so prevent himself from becoming a victim of this great rift cleaving the human spirit in two. The Chinese say that the journey of a thousand miles begins with a single step. Jung had already taken his first recognisable step when he was barely an articulate child, just over the age of three, and as a result was further on the way than even he knew or suspected when he arrived in Zürich. It was a single dream of a blinding illumination and undeniable authority, in which he went down into the earth, that great, overwhelming symbol of the everlastingly fecund and procreative feminine, and found there, deep underground, a monumental phallus set on a golden throne.

One of the outstanding characteristics of the Jung I came to know was that indifferent as his attitude was to the externals of his past, obedient as he was to the natural law of remembrance to which we are all subject and which compels us to recall before all else what we value most, his memory of his own dreams and fantasies was as circumspect, fastidious, and reliable as it was well-nigh incredible. He never forgot a detail of his encounters with the inner world in dream or fantasy that mattered to his development either in himself or his patients.

Dreams, symbols, spontaneous imagery and fantasy were permanent features of his real and natural world and, just like a guide I knew in the bush and desert of Africa who would not fail to recognise a tree, incline or dune that had marked a journey done only once some forty years before as a boy, Jung would never forget the smallest detail of significance in the dreams and fantasies and other features of his movement through this inscape of his remotest past. I would listen to him telling me, perhaps for a third time, of a dream dreamt some sixty-five years before, as children do to the retelling of a favourite story, fearful that some cherished detail might be forgotten or changed, but his accounts never varied, and even more remarkable, lost none of their original vitality in the repetition, so that one's own growing familiarity with them did not breed contempt but rather added to their meaning.

And he would tell me of this dream in a voice that even in his eighties seemed to have lost none of the awe felt at the time. The phallus, he stressed, was not only an organ of the human body because it was utterly disembodied, and had a large eye in it. Many years later he was to recognise a prototype in an illustration of a mythological deity of some long-forgotten past. This dream made such an impression on him that he could not speak of it to others until he was over sixty-five years old. This fact, when first he told me of it, made me recoil with horror that the world of nature could inflict so strange and cruel a vision in the silence and blackness of night on a young child. I was not at all surprised that he could not speak of it to his elders and betters, knowing from my own experience of a Protestant culture which closely resembled his how great an unmentionable was sex. What astounded me was that so young and unarmed a spirit could have endured alone so horrific a vision. Then I realised that nature seldom inflicts on us anything for which it does not also provide the relevant immunities. It takes not Nature but man, his slanted societies and savage intellectualism, to force us to bear the unbearable. Somehow Jung took the dream upon himself alone, great as was the burden for a child to carry. For from then on in his mind he could never be confronted with the conception of God, of his father, or the world, without the dream of the phallus presenting itself, as if to say, "That which you see may be well and true. But look and beware, I also am here and I too have a meaning that is not in these reckonings."

None of this prevented the dream from becoming a master compass of his spirit, almost an automatic pilot keeping his life on course. This dream like the later dream of a burial mound on the banks of the Rhine, which intervened in so timely a fashion to correct his course at the University of Basle, seemed to ordain clearly too that his main interests would have to be, as it were, underground. Far below the solid surface of things he would find the greatest creative energies.

It was in this collaboration of male creativeness of which the phallus was the image, and the great feminine elements represented by the earth, that his destiny would be found. From then on the dreaming process had become increasingly important to him, whatever his incapacity for decoding its secret intent. He told me how, more and more, dreams and visions at crucial moments in life came to keep him on his way. But the real parallel, the other great secret equal to this first dream, was a vision. It also was another terrible imposition from within. He saw the cathedral of Basle, on a day of unblemished sun, shattered by divine excrement which dropped from a golden throne on high in a bright blue sky.

Once again I recoiled at the apparent brutality of the way nature inflicted this vision on a boy only twelve years old, and at the refinement of the cruelty of its timing. Heaven knows, life at school for Jung was difficult enough. There were not just the agonising difficulties of being poor and looked down upon, and in any case by nature the odd child out in a school like the Gymnasium, full of the richest and socially most privileged children in the city. There were troubles at home and troubles within, and yet for once he had left school on this particular afternoon oddly contented and reassured to the point of exultation. But as he came out of the wide gates of his school, just opposite the vast cathedral, to see the blue of the steep-angled roof all a-glitter against the blue of a sky without remnant of cloud, filled with such rare feelings of well-being and confidence that God was there on high, well in command of the universe and all below for the best in the best possible of moments, this vision struck like lightning and entered his mind with imagery full of unmistakable physical detail. Even to this day such a vision could hardly be the favourite intrusion on the privacy of imaginations. But in the nineteenth century of Jung's Switzerland, its impact must have been of a ferocity incomprehensible to us today.

Yet in the years I have lived with Jung's account of these two great secret experiences, this aspect of their intrusion has been redeemed for me by the realisation of how indispensable they were to what I call to myself the great necessities of his being and of life. The first dream, in terms of these necessities, seems to me the only thing that could have protected the chosen flesh and blood of Jung against corruption from its purpose by the values of an outworn and spent world, and ensured that it should already be firmly in position in Jung's imagination before external values could solicit him for themselves. Only such an impact at so virgin a moment could give a dream the authority that would make all other influences by comparison powerless and so hold the needed emerging spirit safe in its keeping.

This second secret vision years later also seemed justified in the same way. It is true that one is forced never to forget how such visions were abhorred by orthodox intellectual and religious establishments. This is the only means whereby one can realise the inborn courage which allowed the young Jung to admit them to himself and hold on to them. It is our only certain intimation that something in him already knew that the vision, too, was a continuation of the dreaming process possibly even more imperative than the dream itself.

I say this because it seems that there is an important difference between the two processes. The dream, I believe, is part of the unconscious made accessible to our waking selves in sleep; a potential form as it were of conscious unconsciousness. The vision is an illumination from the unconscious so charged and powerful that it breaks with startling clarity through the watchful barriers of our awakened mind to become a dream experience in a fully conscious state. Somehow, Jung knew this. Or rather, he allowed it to know more for him than his upbringing allowed him to know for himself. So both vision and dream could, with extraordinary accuracy, combine to keep his imagination in its natural way against the trend of the entire age.

Not surprisingly, with no conscious precedent to guide him, there was a stage when the sense of direction into which his imagination was being impelled was taken literally. This is why he had believed that his most ardent wish at Basle was to become an archaeologist. It was years before he realised that the latent meaning of this urge was archaeology of a sort—but not in the physical world. It was archaeology of the mind aimed at uncovering, amid the ruins of the modern spirit, the foundations of the authentic city of the soul. This had once stood four-square and complete against chaos and old night, before the coming of the Word in the beginning and that trumpet moment when the first spirit delivered itself saying, "Let there be light. And there was light."

One is humbled by the protective power of the inborn intuitions which joined dream and vision to keep Jung on course, despite the ridicule and disapproval heaped on him. He was enabled to maintain his interest in all sorts of phenomena beyond the pale of respectable knowledge and investigation.

"I was", he told me at one of our earliest meetings, "often amazed to the point of despair at the presumption of the organised knowledge and discipline of my day and their common attitude of all-knowing-ness which I encountered everywhere among men in command of religions, and scientific and philosophic heights. I was enraged by their lack of ordinary, natural, healthy curiosity in what they did not know. And also by their instant dismissal as irrelevant of what seemed to me to be pointers towards increased knowledge and new areas for investigation."

I was prompted to tell him how moved I had always been by the Bushmen of my native country, because they gave out the feeling of belonging to life and time and nature. They had no doubt of being known in full wherever they went. Whereas in this world and this war from which I had just come, I had a feeling that, for all our pose of all-knowing, we ourselves had utterly lost this feeling of being known.

Jung slapped his great hand on his knee and said, "That is precisely what I felt as a student. I started out in life with the feeling of utterly belonging. I had a most wonderful sense of participation in the beauty and wonder of my surroundings. Then I found myself pushed by the life of my time in a direction where the feeling seemed to vanish over the horizon and be permanently lost. And I knew that somehow, however necessary that separation might be, it must not be allowed to last. If this sense of separation was to have any meaning, I had to live life in such a way that one day I was reunited with the sense of that all-belonging that I had had in the beginning."

Even more remarkable for me than the intuition which led Jung so unerringly in the direction of this "other archaeology", was his knowledge that it could not be done by intuition alone. Already in his first years as a medical student at Basle he was reprimanding himself, "I must stop talking to others out of my intuition. I must talk more out of facts. Somehow, somewhere, I must find the facts to match my intuition."

Although this has been implied in the account of his student years, it is of necessity re-stated here, clear-cut in his own words, because the conclusion it expresses was a turning point not just for himself but for his time. It was a brave, moving and truly evolutionary example.

I myself have known an unusually large number of intuitive people. I have been absorbed in the workings of many intuitive imaginations in history, art and literature in the world, from the Old Testament prophets; Heraclitus and Goethe, to soldiers, bookmakers and gamblers who just follow their hunches in war, on roulette tables and on race-courses.

I have known remarkable soldiers who, with no dire uncertainties of war to exercise their gift of intuition, cannot wait today for night to come for some casino to open, desperate for a game of chance as any alcoholic for a drink in a pub not yet open. For the great peril of the intuitive always is that having hunches is a whole-time occupation. They tend not to stay with any single intuition, however great. No sooner have they had an intuition full of promise of new increase than they move on to the next, because intuition after all is their speciality, and it is almost as if the joy of just having the hunch is satisfaction enough for them.

But Jung had a quality that only the great intuitive possesses. He felt bound to stand fast in his hunches and not move on until he had proved their validity. No matter how far forward his hunch pitched him in time, he brought it back into the heat and dust of a common day and worked his way back to it empirically with all the conscientiousness and thoroughness of a Swiss watchmaker, fitting together a new and infinitely complex timepiece.

That made the charge of "mysticism" commonly hurled at him so preposterous. For instance, he worked through 67,000 dreams with his patients and helpers before even attempting to theorise about them. He avoided theorising and only did so when the necessity of doing so was imposed on him by facts. All his life he remained as in love with facts as he had been born in love with intuition.

One of his earliest hunches was that this dream he had had as a child, and his vision of the shattering of the great cathedral at Basle, were somehow interconnected. He thought also they had a great deal to do with a mortal split in the Western European spirit which manifested itself outwardly in the increasing conflict between science and religion. Himself the son of a minister, the offshoot of a long line of parsons, with a bishop or two thrown into the lineage and far, far back some progenitor involved in the dubious pursuit of perfidious alchemy, his interest in religion had been encouraged by his inner and outer environment to be even more profound than his interest in the science to which he was apprenticed and in whose discipline he was so highly schooled.

Yet intuitively he was convinced that the division was as unnecessary as it was lethal. Both, after all, were dedicated ostensibly to the pursuit of the same truth. He expressed the dilemma in words to me which are as real and applicable now as they were in those broad ample 'nineties of the last century of a Switzerland still secure in its own long summer of the mind with the harvest still to come. "In religion, even as a medical student", he said, "I found that I had utterly missed the factor of empiricism. In science I found a total absence of considerations of meaning. Something had gone terribly wrong to bring about such impoverishment and I was frightened for all of us."

The interdependence of the two is implicit in this observation, and it was a clear indication of how much more pre-prepared Jung was than he realised for the call to Zürich. From the day that he arrived at so firm a conclusion it was inevitable that sooner or later he would make it clear to all that for the first time in history meaning could only be restored to religion by enabling it to become a living experience for all men. At the same time it was only by a re-dedication of science also to the service of meaning that religion could receive an essential empiricism and the two be joined in an overall purpose. Since science and its method dealt with what was demonstrable, Jung intuitively had perceived what was inadequate in its approach. Once he started his medical training he had only to apply his naturally acute powers of perception to see what was lacking. But it was another matter with religion. There his conclusion was the result of a long and painful growth of awareness which had started with the first dream at the age of three. Today one can trace from that remote point with an extraordinary wealth of detail the acceleration in the mind of an increasingly isolated boy, the irrevocable estrangement from all that was religiously acceptable to him. Finally, reality broke in with the vision Jung had of the shattering of Basle cathedral.

Taken literally, of course, the vision was either blasphemous (and it has been denounced accordingly) or comic, and I have heard it raise a kind of laughter that has left me dismayed for the laughers. But if taken impersonally as a dream accurately decoded, then the message of the vision was plain to Jung from the moment he admitted it to himself after running in vain for shelter to his father's vicarage. Excrement is an image of food which has fulfilled its function of feeding the body that has consumed it and is, therefore, expelled from it as waste. What the vision would seem to be telling Jung, and us, is that whatever the Christian church (as represented by the great cathedral on a hill. overlooking the Rhine) has given as food to the religious spirit of men in the past, it has exhausted its powers of nourishment. In that shape and form it has served its purpose and ceased to be a source of living religious experience. As remarkable as the content of the vision itself was the effect on Jung when once he accepted it in full, after struggling against recognition of the detail for some days and nights. His relief and joy at allowing himself, at last, to think the unthinkable was almost indescribable. The effect and meaning stayed with him always. It was, he told me, the unfailing source from which he drew his courage for a future in which he had to face even greater unthinkables into his reckoning. Provided he always obeyed what he took to be the will of God, no matter how incomprehensible what was inflicted unsolicited on him from within, he would have the power to pursue it with the comfort of unimagined grace that such obedience conferred.

Indeed, the feeling of relief after yielding to the vision of the shattered cathedral was so great in the months that followed that he longed for his parents, particularly his father, to share it, but knew that any effort to share his vision would fail.

Few of us to this day recognise the imperative of courage in the life of the imagination and how it alone can make us free from fear and open to the fullness of reality. Its "cliffs of fall, frightful, sheer, no-man-fathomed" demand a heart as brave as that of any soldier going into battle or any mountaineer pioneering a new way up Everest. Only those who have never hung over the cataclysmic abyss of their own spirit hold such exercises of the imagination to be cheap. So from that moment on, it was inevitable that Jung's choice of a profession could never be partial. It could only be the way on which he had decided because he hoped so ardently that along it, those divided ends, these estranged opposites of his day, were active and could be enabled to meet. When one considers how easily he could have become the doctor, for which he had trained so long and followed a vocation for which he was exceptionally endowed, or again why he did not turn philosopher, or priest, to which natural preoccupations the dreams and visions inflicted on him showed him also to be inclined, one can only make a respectful obeisance to the power and clarity of his intuition. Just as the instinct of the physicist was compelling men to explore the nature and tensions of the nuclear atom as a gateway into the mystery of matter, similarly Jung was propelled into walking an untrodden way towards the meaning of which the science and religion of his day appeared so deprived. He turned, again instinctively, to the tensions and disturbances of the rejected and despised atoms of humanity locked out from the so-called normality of life in the lunatic asylums of his day.

So on the 12th December, of the year 1900, Jung reported for work at the great Burghölzli Mental Hospital situated on a woodland fringe of Zürich. That he did so at the beginning of our desperate century seems to me another of those coincidences of timing in his life. It is almost as if the symmetry of meaning wanted to demonstrate thereby that a new era was beginning also in the mind of man.

It was in this same year wherein Freud had published *The Interpretation of Dreams*. Many years later, when Freud died, Jung used the term "epoch-making" to describe this work. One might add that it was also an epoch-shattering work. It would be hard to say which area of the great Victorian world, still so sure of itself and its values, was the more outraged by Freud. Was it science, philosophy, religion, or all the complex vested interests of mind, morals and conventions of the entrenched apparently idealistic, yet rationally conditioned spirit of the time? Almost every level of educated society felt itself insulted. Much of what was hypocritical and Pharasaic could no longer plead ignorance as an excuse in the new court of law of the spirit that Freud's findings constituted. The gloomy Dean Swift once remarked that you could tell a man of genius by the number of dunces gathered against him. If the dim-witted, ignoble and ill-informed were the only impediments in these matters, the bearer of new truths would find his work far easier. Unfortunately it is the opposition of the intelligent, honourable and public-spirited men who should be the first to welcome the pioneer who usually make his task so difficult. Fear of change and an over-compensated certainty of being in the right outlaws any doubt of their evaluations. One could perhaps better have measured the originality of Freud's achievement by reason of the numbers of the highly intelligent, well-informed men who instantly mobilised to attack him. Their resistance was evident and understandable. The world of appearances in which they had their self-importance and which their minds and imaginations had served as the only permanent and worthwhile dimension of reality, was suddenly shown to be merely one aspect of reality and a rather shallow one at that. Ironically enough, the time was fast coming when even this first historic penetration of Freud into an "unconscious" in man (or "subconscious" as it was first called) was to be seen for the mere prospector's shaft that it really was, sunk just deep enough beneath the skin of appearances to prove that there was a wealth of meaning to be mined from below.

But at the beginning of this century it was more than any establishment could take. Most impossible of all was Freud's concept that sex was the greatest driving force in this underworld. Sex had been savagely repressed in Victorian man, after some two thousand years of either total denigration or at the best lofty condescension and patronising tolerance from the Christian heights of European culture. The implications of Freud's findings, moreover, were all the harder to bear because they made highly respected values of ethics, behaviour, knowledge and science, the villains of their own history. They implied that mental sickness, derangement and disorder of the spirit could originate in the wilful repressions of age-old instincts in man. Nor was

Freud's revelation of disturbances in the human spirit caused by sub-conscious forces the only portent of decline, and fall and change. The suspect German concept of a *zeitgeist*, a specific of spirit universally valid in a given moment of time, now appeared to have a far greater meaning than our rationally orientated world was prepared to concede.

Similar portents were gathering everywhere in fields other than those of science and religion, like that vortex of crows which Vincent van Gogh, in whom a sense of prophetic unrest was already present as a fever in his urgent brush, painted into several of his most discon-certing landscapes of a Provence yellow with the corn of some last rich summer of spirit, fulfilled but never to recur. The world of physics, too, was already poised for a breakthrough into that universe in reverse, which is the atom. Einstein was about to announce his theory of relativity, which was to end a Newtonian era which had served science so well but had in its turn spent all its provisional energies. A total transformation of the scientist's view of the laws of the universe and the role of space and time in it, and life, was about to take its place. In literature and art, omens of undreamed-of tensions and cataclysmic conflicts were appearing at an even more terrifying rate. Patterns of society and culture which had once appeared so authoritative and stable were being challenged, strained and either irrevocably changed and changing, or in the process of being destroyed.

Jung himself had read the portents as accurately in art and literature as he had in science and religion. The natural processes of examination of his own self and his time, encouraged by Goethe and Goethe's *Faust*, were followed by his encounter with Nietzsche who, too, had been a brilliant, if outrageously controversial professor at Basle. Unfortunately, like *Faust*, Nietzsche's *Also Sprach Zarathustra* failed to have the significance for the English-speaking world which it possessed, and still possesses, for the complex of German culture. But the loudest warning of all, perhaps, was sounded by the volcanic eruption in literature of Dostoievsky. It is significant because Russia herself was to be overwhelmed by revolution as France had been before her. And there was Dostoievsky suddenly laying bare with the surgical precision of genius the terrifying anatomy of the modern spirit deprived of the pale idealistic Pre-Raphaelite beauty in which the European world had tried hard to cover it. His authenticity and authority were so singularly unquestionable because they were rooted in an act of participation by the whole self in all he wrote. He was not just an artist but a man exposed and engaged in totality. He was as humble in his tiny allotment of strength and nobility as he was naked and unashamed in his confession of a powerless involvement with an unsolicited, unilluminated, instinctive self which carried him almost to the point of personal dissolution. It was a terrifying view into chaos ahead on the modern road. As Hermann Hesse, to his everlasting credit, was one of the first to note, "The unconscious of a whole continent and age has made of itself poetry in the nightmare of a single prophetic dreamer and issued in his awful blood-curdling scream in Dostoievsky's *Brothers Karamazov*."

Indeed, so prophetic, accurate and vast was this nightmare vision of the future evoked by Dostoievsky that the world has not yet arrived at its horizon, just as the consequences of the slant of mind and heart that produced the French Revolution are far from over. The world is still moving through the Dostoievskian area of disaster and horror and the phase of the Grand Inquisitor—the visionary anticipation of Stalin and his kind, as well as of all else that he evoked. Indeed, in the last Karamazov dream there is, as a road sign at nightfall warning of dangerous incline on a steep pass ahead, the appearance of a desperately thin, under-nourished young woman, standing with empty breasts and a famished young child in her arms against a wintry setting of ice and snow, pleading to a deaf world for nourishment for the child. For me it is as accurate and frightening an image as it is possible to find of the present state of the lost soul of man not only of Jung's generation but all over the world today.

Yet Jung had no need of Dostoievsky at this time. *Zarathustra*, written years before *Crime and Punishment* and the rest, had already been almost too much for him. Its impact was profound more because of the unfathomable depths of unexplored forces in man that it revealed than because of the unhuman heights to which Nietzsche aspired. All that Jung had inherited so richly of the values of the earth protected him against any temptation to emulate this soaring vision of "superman" which Nietzsche evoked and which was already present like a virus incubating at the heart of the German nation which had produced him. Grateful as Jung was to Nietzsche for this new perspective in depth, he saw the disproportion, the pathological morbidity in Nietzsche so clearly that he slammed the door firmly on the primordial spirit which Zarathustra represented in such perilous excess. The door was not to be opened again for a number of fateful years during which Jung devoted all he had of heart, mind, passion, and thoroughness to his new calling as a psychiatrist at the Burghölzli hospital.

To this day the Burghölzli is one of the great mental hospitals of the world. It is impossible to visit it and not be moved by what is done there with compassion, imagination and dedication for those who have found it impossible to endure the world on the exacting terms that we who live in it not only endure, but encourage and maintain. But it is not so exceptional today as it was on December 12th, of the year 1900, when Jung first arrived there. Under the remarkable Eugen Bleuler it had acquired a great European reputation, and Jung never ceased to stress how much his own development owed to Bleuler. Over and over again when accused of ingratitude to Freud and betrayal of the Freudian school of which he was popularly regarded as a graduate, he would assert, not without indignation, that he was never of the school of Freud.

"Eugen Bleuler and Pierre Janet were my teachers", he would tell me, and stress that to Bleuler in particular he had always felt grateful for the encouragement he gave him as a young man and for the example he set of total respect for his vocation as a psychiatrist. Above all, Jung felt indebted to the exacting methods of observation in all forms of hallucination and derangement that he acquired from him. His own work was destined to take him far away from the world of psychiatry. But the method of accurate, unflinching observation that he acquired from Bleuler at the Burghölzli never failed to keep him company.

"He helped me more than I can say", he told me, "in dealing with the totally unanticipated and the unknown."

Yet Jung could not have acquired this much had he not arrived at the Burghölzli prepared to give it and its methods every conceivable chance within himself. He went partly as a result of the alarm set ringing in himself by Nietzsche's example, with the door firmly shut on his Number Two personality which since boyhood had had the disconcerting knack of intrusion into his daily round. Therefore Jung could say for the first time since that moment without stain in the beginning at Laufen on the Rhine some twenty-three years before, his life appeared to have taken on an undivided reality. He surrendered himself entirely to what was best in his Number One and entered the world of so-called normal men like someone, as he put it later, entering a monastery dedicated to the commonplace. His interest in all those strange, non-rational phenomena, the dark, unexplored areas of the spirit which his Number Two was already bringing to his attention, was to be put firmly behind him. He was henceforth determined to be, he declared, "all intention, consciousness, duty and responsibility". For six months he locked himself within the limits set by the Burghölzli to get to know the life and spirit of the asylum. Yet with incredible thoroughness he found time, among other things, to read through some fifty volumes of the *Allgemeine Zeitschrift für Psychiatrie* right from its beginning.

However, unseen and locked out as it was, his Number Two, firmly in keeping of those master secrets of his of dream and vision, remained a force in being. Indeed the fact that its subtle magnetic attraction beneath the surface of the activities of the young psychiatrist was still very much alive, seems to be apparent both in the motive for this self-imposed incarceration, and the consequences of his half-year of monastic dedication to the world of appearance and unending routine. The motive stemmed from a firm belief implicit in him after his reading of Krafft-Ebing; namely, that delusion and hallucination could not be just dismissed as symptoms of a disease of personality. Somehow, somewhere, there must be an important human significance. He wanted desperately to know how the human mind reacted to the sight of its own destruction. And as he moved through the wards so full of people who had either rejected, or been deprived of, normality, he was increasingly tormented by the question; what really takes place within the mentally ill?

He was amazed how little this question and all it implied bothered his colleagues. Consequently, he found himself observing them almost as much as their patients, and he began to suspect that there might be some strange interdependence between what passed for "normal" and what was condemned as "abnormal". He began to suspect that there could be a pathological element in what paraded so confidently as "normality" around him. The conviction grew that no knowledge of the problem confronting him would be complete which did not include the study of both. So, at the end of some six months, the vow was not broken so much as absolved by some inner dispensation of the rule of truth. His life at the Burghölzli ceased to be monastic and took on increasingly the nature of an apprenticeship to something immeasurably greater to come.

In the Arthurian age with its Round Table, legends and stories which had been one of the great formative influences of Jung's imagination as a boy, these years of vigil at the Burghölzli would have corresponded to the long night of the initiation of the Esquire into Knighthood. Then would come the day in which the Knight could set out on his first chivalrous errand as armed in spirit as he would be properly equipped and horsed, in the world without. That is why I have felt compelled to call this chapter of Jung's life one of vigil and summons.

And this heraldic parallel is all the more accurate because the summons was from the imperilled feminine to whose service the original knight was pledged. For this Jung had already been rehearsed, as it were, by his meeting with that young girl near Basle who, though born to a modest station in life, had the possibilities of grandeur and nobility locked up in her, so that in moments of trance they became articulate in the most impeccable and elegant German. This experience, I have no doubt, was beside him from the start, and as some veiled emissary of his primordial self guided him on an untravelled road with a will all the firmer because of a return of relish to his spirit which he had lost in his dutiful beginning.

However exalted the great in spirit may appear to those who regard them from without, inwardly the only certain mark of their stature is the measure of their own sense of inadequacy before the problems which confront them and the humble, tentative and hypersensitive nature of their approach. So from then on Jung turned to all this discredited human material in the Burghölzli not as someone who knew any of the answers for them, or for himself. He turned to them as someone hoping to learn some of the answers from them. Unlike his colleagues, he no longer set himself alone or apart from his inmates. He did not regard himself as a repository of the final and absolute concept of sanity. He went to work conscious of agonising conflicts in himself between two apparently irreconcilable poles of the spirit which he had experienced ever since early childhood, when his first great dream locked him out with such apparent brutality from the total feeling he had had as he lay in the beginning in his pram in the garden of the vicarage on the banks of the Rhine, that everything was utterly wonderful. He now approached the community of the mentally disturbed increasingly as someone who was a mere acolyte in what St Paul called "the priesthood of the suffering".

Encouraged only by an as yet unproved intuition that if somehow, somewhere, he could find an intimation of the causes of all that suffering and a hint of its meaning, he would come to some understanding both of his own conflict and that of that deep and increasingly dangerous split in the contemporary spirit which either kept him awake or appeared as a nightmare in his sleep. It was almost as if in derangement and suffering there was an unlived meaning, crying out for attention to its need for being allowed to live in the life both of the sufferer and his society. But how did it come about? Perhaps it was due, in part, to the fact that his time, and their time too, were both "out of joint". But unlike Hamlet, he did not curse the fate to which he was born.

His one concern was what could he, Jung, do to set it right and give life back "the readiness that was all".

He was certain now that mental disturbances and even the most profound derangement of the human personality were not mere diseases of the mind. They were, like dreams and visions, human behaviour with a human meaning; but a meaning that was in code. If only he could break the code and transcribe it into a contemporary idiom, making it accessible to himself and others, much of the problem would be solved. In all this he was much closer to the patients than to his own profession, which, set against the lack of curiosity of his colleagues, isolated him once more. He was as alone as he had been at Basle. He could not make his peace with the blindness of the assumption that there was no sense to be found in the condition of the patients. Nor with the conviction that what was needed was yet more doses of the prescriptions of normality, the very approach which had failed the sufferers and had played no small part in the shattering of their person- alities. Therefore, much as the Burghölzli taught him method, it would be wrong to imply that he did not find it lacking in insight. He marvelled at the fact that his colleagues looked on the symptoms of derangement as if they were the disease itself and remained utterly disinterested in the content to which the symptom tried in vain to direct their attention. Consequently the less could Jung feel himself secure in what passed for normality. So, for all his training in a great scientific discipline and his own increasingly well-adapted social personality, he felt more involved with the sick than with the col- leagues who administered to them. How right he was in this, and how much he gained thereby, was ultimately evident in the fact that these lost souls so rejected by the normality of his time were forever re- membered each in his or her own disinherited right. In his old age at Bollingen, they figured as "fairy-tale" characters in his recollections of the emotions and labour of that time. He could say then with assurance that the men and women who had given him most in life were not persons whom the world considered great (and of whom he had met more than most), but the unrecognised and unacknowledged and forever anonymous of his own day.

There was, for instance, the case of a woman who had been declared totally insane. To the end of his days, Jung still spoke of her with animation as if all that had happened only the day before. She would make remarks like, "I am the Lorelei". The doctors would take this as conclusive evidence of her insanity. But Jung, so he told me, thought immediately, there must be some reason why she called herself the

Lorelei. What can it possibly be? He went on to recite the lines of Heine's poem to himself until he realised that already he had her clue in the opening line: *Ich weiss nicht, was soll es bedeuten*—I do not know what it can possibly mean. Obviously the woman was not so mad that she had not registered with some despair how these lines described precisely what the great specialists thought of her and her condition. She would reiterate the remark, "I am Socrates' deputy", which appeared even more meaningless to Jung's colleagues. But following the same instinct and using the same sort of mental procedure that was soon to become part of an established method, Jung concluded that this woman was telling him, like Socrates' deputy, that she was falsely accused and that this label of insanity was wrongfully applied to her, encouraging a growing suspicion that there could be few forms of madness so absolute as not to have some longing for new sanity concealed within them. Most remarkable of all, she would declare extremities of the seemingly absurd like, "I am plum cake on a cornmeal bottom", or, "Naples and I between us must supply the world with spaghetti". Such remarks raised many an amused if not derisive smile, even more alarming than those smiled since over Jung's vision of the shattered cathedral. But to Jung they were the most significant of all her utterances, seemingly evidence of some law of creative compensation still at work in a profoundly troubled spirit. It was as if behind the dark, opaque screen of derangement, there stood another woman longing to join in the natural life of her time.

Over the years Jung spent many hours with her. I was impressed at how great must have been his compassion for her and, judging by the clarity and warmth with which he remembered her in his own old age, how fond of her he had become. He came to her too late to cure her, but he told me that he learned more from her than from any of his colleagues. She was to provide, also, an indication of how fundamentally Jung's and Freud's characters differed and how it was inevitable that they could not long continue together. When, after eight years at the Burghölzli, Jung took Freud to see her, Freud declared after a curt expression of at most perfunctory interest, that he could not understand how Jung could have spent so much time with such "a disagreeable and unattractive old woman", a remark which both surprised and shocked Jung.

Jung was now convinced that the fault of not understanding the deranged lay with the psychiatrists and their failure to realise that, in derangement, there was embedded something fundamental to man. As a result he went to work with the whole of himself thrown into the task of understanding the estranged, averted, wounded personalities confronting him. He committed himself to as total an act of participation as possible. No fantasy, statement, gesture or remark was any longer dismissed as meaningless. It was treated as if somewhere in Jung himself it could have a particle of meaning, recognisable in terms of "reality" as he knew it.

He told me that when faced with persons who had not uttered a word for years, he would refuse to accept defeat. Watching them closely when he saw some frowning, or other, expression appear on their faces, or even just an unwarranted gesture accomplished with their hands, he would repeat as best he could the expression and gesture himself, trying to think at the same time of the first thing his act of imitation brought to mind. He would then put it in words to the patient and was amazed how often, thereby, he established contact. The silence was broken and in time a dialogue was established that led to a cure more often than he had dared to hope for: and certainly at a rate that the Burghölzli had never experienced. All of this, of course, needed not only confidence—for how could anyone have been confident in so strange and unexplored a region? It needed moral courage of the highest order.

I think always of a case he discussed once at length with me. It is referred to in many of his writings and was described in detail during a series of seminars in London organised, between the wars, by Hugh Crichton-Miller, who was one of the first psychiatrists of distinction and originality to recognise Jung's work in England. The case for me has been of singular importance not only because of what it taught me of the texture of spirit of the younger Jung but also for what it revealed of the origin and nature of moral necessity in the spirit of man. In this case, far from merely being a pragmatic expedient of man and his societies, an imperative pattern seems to be exposed as if it were a basic element in the nature and structure of the universe itself. However provisional and imperfect a particular ethical pattern in a specific culture may be, however relative its historical significance, and however constant the need for scrupulously reappraising and changing it, none the less it does represent one of the great, natural, indestructible necessities of life, time and the universe without which no society, culture or individual life can achieve any given state of meaning. It has seemed so to me at least from that day on which Jung, in the deep, sonorous voice that rose up in him whenever he was speaking of anything that had particular meaning for him, first told me the story. It is as if I see a reflection deep within the life of man of all the universe has of law to keep sun, moon, planets and stars on their appointed courses. Without such precondition of law and order, both stars and men would be thrown into disorder wherein all would be shattered in a collision of irresistibles—great and small, with equal and opposite immovables.

Inevitably, therefore, this story was of a moral disorder. Inevitably, too, it challenged Jung's own moral order within. He had not been at the Burghölzli long when he was presented with a woman who was classified as schizophrenic and given a poor diagnosis for cure. Jung put all he knew of fantasy, dreams and his new evolving "word-association system" into his encounter with this woman. In essence, the woman's immovable depression was a consequence of the fact that, while deeply in love with a socially desirable man, she had yet married another. She had two children by her unloved husband. Then, five years after the marriage, she learnt that her first love probably would have returned her own. This knowledge plunged her into a profound depression. She lived in a district where the water was notoriously impure. Yet while bathing her children one night, she allowed her young girl, who was her favourite, to sip up the bath water from her sponge without attempting to stop her. What is more she gave her little son impure water to drink, although there was pure spring water kept for drinking. As a result the young daughter died of typhoid, although the son was not affected. It was clear to Jung from all he learnt that the woman, unconsciously, by deed of omission or active participation, was accomplice to the fact of murder of her daughter and the attempted murder of her son. Obviously she was not schizophrenic but was weighed down with the burden of both guilt and outrage of natural law. What was he to do?

He had no precedent to guide him. He knew he could not consult his colleagues. He had to solve the problem on his own with the chances, judging by the assumptions of his time, that if he faced this profoundly disturbed woman in front of him with exposure of her guilt, it might shatter her, as well as ruin his career. And it was as if within what was in the best of senses a deeply committed Protestant self, there fell a summons like one of the greatest New Testament exhortations: "Know the truth and the truth shall make you free."

Jung confronted the woman with the truth and in two weeks he was able to discharge her. Moreover, even then, he did not refer to his unorthodox method and its success to his colleagues. It was the first intimation to him that the task of healing depends basically on an element in the relationship between the healer and the sick. This relationship was sacred. Whatever success or failure might be implicit in its undertaking, it belonged more to life and the mystery of creation than the psychiatrist who had been midwife to the occasion. So Jung kept the woman's secret to himself as rigorously as a priest keeps knowledge gained fron confession. Seeing how much his age believed in judgement and how great was its capacity for moral condemnation he concluded, with compassion, as rare then as it was moving, that life had sufficiently judged and punished the woman. Life could only gain by taking her back to atone for an offence against natural law so that she could live in the world again as she had been unable to before. She must use the load of her guilt as if it were a transformer of whatever negation should come her way.

This story wa₃ soon to be followed by another encounter that Jung had, not with a patient but with a woman who came to him out of her own accord. She arrived at his office one morning, refused to give her name and was to walk out of it and Jung's life without ever revealing it. Knowing Jung, I am certain that if he had thought the name important he would somehow have elicited it from her. But the fact that she was so obviously in desperate need of help was enough for him. She admitted only that she was a doctor and went on to confess that many years before she had killed her best friend in order to marry her present husband. The murder was never discovered and in due course she married the man and had a daughter by him. Consciously she had no moral compunction over what she had done. Such unease as there was appears to have been felt by nature, and the atmosphere of the murder communicated itself to all around her through the damage it had done to her own inner personality and changed the climate of her spirit accordingly. First, her husband died soon after the marriage. Their daughter grew up estranged from her, and ultimately vanished without trace from her life. Her friends one after the other abandoned her, and soon even the animals she loved appeared to be afraid of her. She loved riding but had to give it up because the horses she had hitherto managed so well became nervous, shied and ultimately she was thrown by one of her favourite mounts. She was left only with her dogs and clung to them. Then her favourite dog too had to be destroyed. Finally she could bear this exile from life and nature no longer, and came to Jung to confess. After the confession she left, and he was to see and hear of her no more. But the vision of the woman and her total, unsupportable alienation from life and nature inflicted on her by the murder stayed with him to the end. He found it of such importance that he selected it from thousands of human encounters for special mention in his autobiography. There he observes that though one could keep such things secret in oneself, one could not prevent life from knowledge of it. The consequences of the murder one had done to oneself in the process found expression in the subsequent unease, estrangement and even disasters in the world without. "And sometimes it seems as if even animals and plants 'know' ", he added.

And I extract this incident from many others because, when he first mentioned this case to me one bitter winter at Ascona, it added new meaning as so often to my experience of Africa. I told him that it reminded me of a primitive people I knew in the interior of Africa. They believed that there was no secret so small that nature sooner or later would not extract. They held in particular that if a person had been guilty of some great natural evil, even the grasses would accuse him of it in the sound they made against his feet as he went walking through them. They had told me a story which everyone among them accepted as an empirical fact. A man had murdered a woman unobserved in a dark wood in circumstances that were incapable of detection. He had buried her deep in the ground and covered the place with leaves and strewn grass. Yet as he walked home a small bird appeared on the branch of a tree in front of him saying, "You are the killer of 'Nshalalla' " (the woman's name). He tried again and again to kill the bird, but in vain. It kept him company to the edge of the village where all could hear him accused of the crime. And, I added, perhaps unnecessarily, that for this people, judging by their myths and stories, a bird always represented as they put it, "the thing which they could not have thought of for themselves."

I went on to add how impressed I had been, ever since the war, during my explorations of bush and desert, by the extent to which one's own most secret intent for being there, seemed to make itself known to beast, bird and even plants around one. This feeling always was like something imposed on me objectively. I had found, for instance, that when I moved through the bush to all appearances dressed and equipped in the same manner as for many weeks, always carrying the same gun, the atmosphere and behaviour of all around me changed subtly on those days when I had to shoot buck or bird for food. I told Jung that this was not only my experience but also that of many of the most perceptive of the great hunters, primitive as well as European, that I had known. And of course, as so often, there was confirmation in Shakespeare, and I quoted *Macbeth*:

"Stones have been known to move and trees to speak;
Augures and understood relations have

By Maggot-Pies and choughs and rooks brought forth,
The secret'st man of blood."

Jung looked at me and said quietly and rather sadly, "And even so, they go on denying the reality of the collective unconscious."

Through encounters with disturbed and deranged personalities such as these elaborated here, and others in numbers far too great for inclusion but greater than even he could record in the profusion of lectures, seminars, books, essays, letters and other writings that fell from him in the course of his long years like leaves of a great maple set on fire by some Fall of time, Jung came to the conclusion that every human being had a story, or to put it in its most evolved form, a myth of his own. It was as ironic and devastating to him at the beginning of the century as it should be today even more so to us, who persist in the same error, that the word "myth" in common usage was the label applied to what the rationalist in command of the day dismissed as illusion, non-existent, apocryphal, or some other of the proliferating breed of reductive words which the cerebral norms of our time produce for denying the existence of any invisible and non-conceptual forms of reality. Yet one has only to read Jung's stories of his encounters with patients in hospital and private consulting room to realise that one is in the presence of a new phenomenon in the life of our time.

It is perhaps understandable that the literal-minded object-obsessed scientist does not see the obvious significance of the myth. But he cannot continue to ignore their proven therapeutic importance. Nor can the artist and the free-ranging spirit of any imaginative individual go on failing to recognise that these accounts contain matter charged with material of illumination and transfiguration. It would seem clear that they are the nearest modern equivalent to the parables used to such Metanoic effect in the New Testament, and in their Far Eastern kinsfolk. For they are used as creatively in the stories which are the milestones on the road of Zen and constitute the organic precedents which took the place of the dogma, metaphysics and theology in the religious development of Japan.

Like the parables, all these stories and case histories of Jung are packed with the seeds of new meaning. No-one can take them with good faith into his own imagination and remain unchanged. And none of us, particularly those engaged in the business of story-telling, can fail to realise that ultimately, from what we have experienced of the story in ourselves and throughout its evolution from myth, legend,

dream and fairy-tale into its most sophisticated present-day form, th,
known or unknown, we have derived meaning from it.

But to return to the matter as he put it to me first. He said that he
had learned from the start how in every disturbance of the personality,
even its most extreme psychotic form of schizophrenia (or dementia-
praecox as it was then commonly called), one could discern the
elements of a personal story. That story was the personality's most
precious possession. And the person could only be cured or healed by
the psychiatrist getting hold of the story. That was the secret key to
unlock the door which barred reality in all its dimensions both within
and without from entering the personality and transforming it. More,
he held that the story not only contained an account of the particular
hurt, rejection or trauma (as other men were hastening to call it),
but the potential of wholesome development of the personality. This
arrest of the personality in one profound unconscious timeless moment
of itself which was called "psychosis" was due, he would assert,
because the development of the person's own story had been interrupted. All movement of the spirit and a sense of beginning and ending
had been taken away from it and the story, like the sun in the midst of
Joshua's battle against the Philistines, suddenly stood still.

"The hell of the mad", he once told me, "is that not only has time
suddenly ceased to exist for them but some memory of what it and its
seasons once meant to them remains to remind them of the fact that it
is no longer there."

He was rapidly learning from the nature of some specific hallucination, delusion, psychosis or neurosis, how a personal story was clamouring to be carried on and to be lived. Even more, he recognised
from what his own dreams meant to him how dreams were an essential part of the evolution of the story. But none of these things, he
stressed, were ever there just for the asking. They could be discovered
only by a constantly reiterated, truthful, and face-to-face encounter
between patient and psychiatrist. Already he was beginning to see
psychiatry in terms of a dialogue at the deepest level between his own
outer–inner self, and the patient. Without such an interchange in which
both the reality of the psychiatrist and deprivation of reality of the
patient faced each other openly as problems to each other, the vital
secret remained hidden.

And it is of importance to realise that here, already, there was firmly
established at foundation level a vital difference of approach to that of
Freud. Symbolised in its simplest and most direct form, in Jung's
consulting room both he and patient sat opposite each other as two

human beings joined in mutual consultation over an interdependent problem directed to a resolution that was important to both. Whereas with Freud and his followers the patient lay stretched out on a couch and the psychiatrist sat invisibly behind the patient listening to what was told, rarely taking part, and in the end delivering judgement according to a preconceived rule on what had been so impersonally revealed.

Moreover Jung did not regard the story and the secrecy which he had to extract for the purposes of healing to be his own. Since it was to him so great a point of departure it was to become, also, one of the most precious of the patients' possessions. Its extraction was justifiable only because he needed it for the destruction of the inner barrier, whether thrown up by injury or neglect in the world without, or self-inflicted from within. Once this provisional demolition task was done, he held with passion that the sooner the story was returned to the patient for private and personal keeping, the better.

It is, therefore, of the utmost importance to realise the clear limits he set to the uses of what we call understanding. He never confused understanding and knowledge nor made it dependent on knowing. Knowledge and observation obviously played a great role in the process but understanding for him was far more than knowing.

"Nothing worse could happen to one than to be completely understood", he told me once with a twinkle of mischief and an acute glance. "One would be instantly deprived of one's personal *raison d'être* if one were. I'd hate it myself. I learnt very early on at the Burghölzli how hurtful it could be to my patients to give them a feeling that I knew and understood them better than they did themselves."

The only creative and helpful form of knowledge and understanding, he would elaborate, was one that grew naturally out of a process of respectful interchange as of two clouded and mutually searching souls. There was a way of understanding, he discovered, which came out of respect for the mystery of the other human being. No two persons or cases were alike. It is true that a psychiatrist had to have a method as a kind of compass. But there were as many exceptions to the rules almost as there were cases, and each case had to be treated on its own merits. Even when he felt convinced he knew the solution to a person's problem, it was not for him to proclaim it but rather to hold it back and use it only in so far as it helped to lead the patient to recognise it for himself. Once the patient discovered it, the sooner the transfigurative knowledge was handed over to him the better. And when the psychiatrist forgot it himself that was even better still! But always the beginning and the end was the reclamation of the personal story and then surrendering it with honour to the patient whose inalienable property it was.

This was a clear indication of how through all the vicissitudes of learning at school and university, of study in an approach alien to him, and adapting himself to the world which at the most only half of himself took seriously, Jung had never lost an innate reverence for the reality of all things great or small, and his respect for their "otherness". Indeed, this respect was part of his native love of proportion and a vital element in balancing the profound commitment of his total self-in his encounter with the sick; and the resultant capacity for discerning and understanding the problems of his patients long before they did.

As far as this problem of understanding itself is concerned, it is of such importance that it needs reassessment in a contemporary manner to rescue it from the half-truths which have been worn thin by constant use and degenerated into unheeded sentimentalities. I quote, therefore, something that Jung wrote about understanding in the modern way. It was written as far back as 1915 during the first World War, when Jung himself was almost overwhelmed by the problems of understanding his own secret self. This was a long letter to Hans Schmid, who was himself a psychotherapist, friend and pupil who had helped Jung a great deal in his work on the psychology of types. Jung could write to him on the subject as to few others without fear of being misunderstood. Although the letter was written after he left the Burghölzli, I can only quote here what seems relevant and synchronised with the rapidly evolving psychologist at the Burghölzli.

"Understanding is a fearful binding power", he wrote. "At times it can be a veritable murder of the soul as soon as it flattens out vitally important differences. The core of the individual is a mystery of life which is 'snuffed out' when it is grasped. That is why symbols want to remain mysterious. They are not so merely because what is at the bottom of them cannot be clearly apprehended . . . All understanding, in general, which is a conformity with general points of view, has the diabolical element in it that kills. It is a wrenching of another life out of its own course, forcing it into a strange one in which it cannot live . . . True understanding seems to me to be one which does not understand, yet lives and works . . . We should bless our blindness to the mysteries of others, for it shields us from devilish deeds of violence. We should be connivers at our own mysteries. But veil our eyes chastely before the mystery of the other. So far as being unable to understand himself he does not need the 'understanding' of others."

And characteristically, Jung sums it all up in one of his own dreams never previously understood.

"I was standing in my garden", he recounted. "And had dug open a rich spring of water that gushed forth. Then I had to dig another deep hole, where I collected all the water and conducted it back into the depths of the earth."

This dream was a rounded definition of Jung's approach to others. In particular it was the essence of what he evolved as an instrument of healing in the Burghölzli. It was as if the scientist, dreamer, visionary, and artist, the subject of the mighty activity within himself which he had, in adolescence, termed God, had all joined forces. This enabled him to receive the secret symbolic meaning of the personal story in the sick confronting him. But, once having received it, he returned it finally (like the water in the dream to the earth) to the eternally hidden feminine in the human personality for reconception, protected gestation and rebirth.

In this connection he once told me a story which I have not found recorded in any of his writings. I had dropped in at Zürich on my way back to England from Africa as had become almost a matter of routine since our first meeting. Apart from wanting to see him I wanted to ask his permission to dedicate a book to him. In the process I told him that it was about the first people of South Africa, their stories and the meaning that the stories possessed for them as well as for me, and could possess, I hoped also for the world. I remember how keen his attention became when I told him how difficult it had been to get the Bushmen concerned to tell me their stories. I was as always at that moment amazed by Jung's capacity for listening when he himself was constantly almost bursting at the seams with things to say. One had only to put a worthwhile question to him to release a flood, not out of any egotistical source but purely from the constant fountain inflow of new perceptions and fresh inspiration as well as information and wisdom stored up in him as in a reservoir built against a great drought.

In this regard he always made me think of Bach, whose *Kunst der Fugue*, the last of his works, was for me a kind of compendium of revelations to all the composer had written before. Perhaps surprisingly for someone accused of indifference to music, Jung had listened and relistened to its twenty fugues and canons with great care and out of a feeling that it could tell him more of the nature of music than any other composition.

Bach was approached by a young admirer one day and asked, "But, Papa Bach, how do you manage to think of all these new tunes?"

"My dear fellow", Bach is said to have answered, according to my version, "I have no need to think of them. I have the greatest difficulty not to step on them when I get out of bed in the morning."

Jung, I believe, could have said the same about his own work, so that I never ceased to find it extraordinary that in conversation he always remained the best of listeners.

On this occasion, before telling me his own story, he interrupted my account only once with the question, "And those resistances to telling you their stories, what did you do about them?"

I explained how baffled and even hurt I had felt about the refusal of this desert people to telling me their stories; all the more because they had lied to me and had said they did not know what I meant by "stories". They said that they were only poor old Bushmen who had never heard of such things. Yet I knew from the history of my own family, who had been in contact with them for some three centuries, that they were perhaps the greatest story-tellers Africa had ever known. I remember how happily Jung laughed when I went on to tell him about an old Bushman grandmother in this regard. I had gone to her one evening because I had heard a young hunter, who was my favourite companion, whisper to his youngest brother to take a tortoise they had just found as a present to his grandmother, saying that she would undoubtedly reward him by telling him a story. Immediately I decided that I would be there to hear the story. But when the moment came and the old lady was eating the great delicacy, which a tortoise baked in its shell was to them all, with the young children gathered round her, no story was told and only the most trivial of polite exchanges put in its place.

I protested, "But, grandmother, I thought you were going to tell us all a story tonight?"

"Excuse me please," the old lady replied. "I am utterly deaf."

"It is true what she says", all the others who by now had joined the children loyally came to her support. "She is very deaf and cannot hear what you say."

"You see," the old lady hastened to add. "You must listen to what they say. I am very deaf and cannot hear what you say."

Of course I joined in the laughter and was moved because suddenly I saw how the motive behind the "resistances" and what I called "lying" was justified. I realised that the story was their most precious possession and that they were protecting it as best they could. They knew how dangerous it was to let a foreigner, above all a white foreigner, in on the secret of their stories. He might destroy them, either by making fun of them or using them against them. I was aware at the same time of something allegorical in the moment. It was an illustration of how we Europeans have destroyed primitive societies and also even other more sophisticated cultures, by taking away or rejecting the story which was the seed and essence of their history and both their present and future. Even with the best of motives, as in the sudden imposition of our version of Christianity on primitive societies, we had been thieves and killers of some aboriginal story. And so we had deprived them of both their past and their present meaning and purpose. I told Jung that I had realised that without a story of its own no culture, society, or personality could survive. So I tried no more to get stories from them. Happily the time came when somehow I had proved that I could be trusted, and they of their own accord told me stories. When they saw how honoured and delighted I was by this, they themselves appeared to find a new meaning and pleasure almost in delivering their myths and legends to me.

To my amazement, Jung thanked me in a manner almost over-whelming even for someone who possessed good manners in the depth the French call *politesse de cœur*. These resistances, he said, were so like those that he encountered in the society of the sick at the Burghölzli. He had to learn to respect those resistances because they too had a meaning. Either they were a sign that the sick were not yet ready for the dialogue that was psychological analysis; or that they should never be disturbed behind these barriers because the "cure" might be worse than the illness. And how right, he added, that the grandmother should have been such a bastion of protection of the story! Only the wise and eternally feminine in life knew how vital secrecy and reticence were in these matters. They knew it out of the experience of creation in the heart of themselves. They knew that it was only in the dark, calm and silence within the walls of the womb that the vulnerable, defenceless living cell of new being could be conceived and receive its impulse to grow. All the time he had been listening to me, he had found himself thinking back to one of his earliest cases at the Burghölzli. She was a comparatively young woman, he said, and sent to the asylum as insane. After a considerable effort he got her to tell him one of her dreams. From that moment on the dreaming process in her and the interchange between them accelerated and intensified. She progressed as a result at such a pace, and found a new sense of reality and meaning and the courage to test both again in the city from which she had come, that he was prepared to let her go from the asylum months before he had expected to be able to do so.

On the morning on which she had to go, she came to see him for the last time.

"Are you not feeling nervous about going home today?' he asked her.

"Of course I am, what do you think!" she replied with a spirit that surprised him.

"Did you by any chance dream again last night?" he ventured again.

"Yes, I did," she answered, paused and then added, "And it's no use badgering me, because for once I'm not going to tell you what it was."

"I cannot tell you how moved I was", Jung now told me. "You see at last the dream, the story, was her own again. At once I discharged her."

And as if to emphasise how great a meaning there was in this experience not just for Jung, and through him for myself, but for life as a whole as well, the relevant coincidence to render it as it were beyond doubt was inflicted on me a decade after Jung's death.

I had cause to go to the Burghölzli and ask the director if he would allow me to go through the records of Jung's early case histories in his archives. He produced a mass of folders suitably dressed in the colour of the Swiss military uniform, for they dealt with conduct in the field of battle of human life for meaning. As I read through them I was impressed how Jung, even before his meeting with Freud, was using dream analysis in his own natural comprehensive and un-slanted way. Then suddenly I was reading through a case history that seemed familiar, and soon realised I was reading the clinical abbreviation of this story Jung had told me at length.

When I came to the last sentence, the answer to the final question put to the patient about her dream, "Yes, I dreamt. And for once I'm not going to tell you what it was", I saw, in Jung's own hand the one word *Entlassen*. The idiomatic translation of the word is "discharged". But the idiom does less than justice to the meaning implicit in the German which means "let go". For that had been the whole purpose of the exercise in healing that had just taken place. That which had been so disastrously held back in the feminine personality had suddenly been set free and let go.

Jung's handwriting to the end was strangely youthful. It never seemed to me to change in character but only grew larger as his eyesight became less clear. But I had never seen it younger than in his recording of these final exchanges. Indeed, the manner of the writing of *Entlassen* across the yellowing page seemed in itself excited, flowing and streaming almost like a banner in a wind of morning.

The dream as a result had long before become like a sword in his hand to cut away real from unreal, illusion from truth, and the weapon itself, once the preliminary battle was over, was surrendered to the patient for future use. Some of his most spectacular successes were accomplished almost entirely in terms of a dream process both in himself and his patients. Indeed, one of his most cherished recollections was of a woman who came to him listless, depressed, without sense of purpose and yet left him some two weeks later restored to her own full self almost entirely because he told her of a dream he had had about her.

I could multiply the examples because I have read other case histories of Jung, now dusty and unthumbed in their folders in the archives of this hospital where he broke the code of derangement, established contact, and brought back to the world men and women who had appeared lost to it forever, and certainly would have been lost a few years before he had begun to work there. But this should be enough to show how Jung came to the conclusion which still rang out like a bell announcing the day when he told me of it more than half a century later.

"I learned there", he told me, "that only the physician who feels himself deeply affected by his patients could heal. It works only when the doctor speaks out of the centre of his own psyche so provisionally called 'normal' to the sick psyche before him that he can hope to heal." He paused, and then added that maxim straight from what was central to the practice of healing at those ancient places of mystery like Epidaurus: "In the end, only the wounded physician heals. And even he, in the last analysis, cannot heal beyond the extent to which he had healed himself."

He had to accept, however humiliating to his own "sanity" and "normality", that he could take no-one further than he had taken himself. Nothing was more dangerous to the sick than expecting of them qualities that the psychiatrist had been incapable of realising in himself. Indeed, that was as much a problem beyond the walls of the Burghölzli as it was inside it. One fundamental problem of the life of his day, as it is even more so in our own, is that individuals, as well as their societies, are continually expecting of others standards that they themselves cannot attain. The favourite yet lethal game was being high-minded in the lives of others so that one evaded the necessity for being so in one's own. The pretentions, confusions and damage done thereby is great and led only too often to the increasingly overcrowded mental asylums of today.

It was at the Burghölzli that Jung first evolved his own method mentioned before, the word-association test, which is being rediscovered and put to greater use in current schools of psychiatry. Jung made it an instrument for charting out suppressed and secret areas of injury not only to the mentally disturbed but also in so-called normal men and women. It was an amplification of a known psychological test adapted by Francis Galton, a cousin of Darwin, to evaluate degrees of intelligence. Galton would put one of some hundred key words to a person and an observer with a stop-watch noted the seconds taken to produce a reply. But so little value was obtained from the method that it was abandoned. Jung, however, reintroduced it with important modifications. When the person took longer than usual to produce the first word that came to his mind, Jung would question him about the hesitation and his associations with the word. Observing also how often certain words quickened an unaccustomed emotion in the person's response, he would note it carefully and explore that area as well in a process of more specific question and answer. There was a day, for instance, where the word "horse" put to someone was followed by a reaction of over a minute's silence. Subsequent discussion revealed a story of great emotion about a horse that had once bolted with the patient, caused an accident, and had had other dramatic consequences which the patient had, he thought, completely forgotten. From this and other similar experiments, more and more accurate and embracing, it became obvious to Jung that in human beings there was a repressed area wherein they tended to bury experiences too painful to be remembered or too hurtful and damaging to be remembered. Out of this work he reintroduced the word complex in current vocabulary to describe areas of hidden experience and suppressed hurt, critical for the emancipation and development of the personality. This term complex is on everyone's lips today and yet even now, very few people who use it know that they owe its present use to Jung. Indeed, in his experience at the Burghölzli so far-ranging did he find this mechanism in the spirit of men that his own psychological approach for a while went under the name of "complex psychology".

I have mentioned the association test here not just for its chronological relevance but because it demonstrates both how thoroughly empirical and how inventive was Jung's approach. It is important because he was soon to be branded a "mystic", and the adjective "mystical" (which I know from bitter experience is often an equivalent of "mistical") was to follow him to the end of his days and so prevented many people from examining the evidence of his work. I myself needed no reminder of the abuse of the term in this regard, seeing how I had been guilty myself of accepting the charge before the war. Few, if any of us, know what mystical experience really is, being incapable of it ourselves. The experience itself in any case occurs relatively rarely and even then only in the rarest of spirits. Had Jung's critics known, even vicariously, by reading a truthful history of the mystics and their writings, they might have realised the painful reality and demanding consequence of mystical experience. Jung, in his own writing, never pronounced on that area of himself. He steadfastly confined himself in print to what his intuitive self had proved, observed and established objectively; an exercise in discipline all the more remarkable considering how much he himself was afflicted by so uncomfortable a gift.

That alone should have given his accusers an inkling of how much the psychology of man itself is a form of inherited history of all the life that has ever been. It is a history more objective and compelling than any written by man about himself because it carries within itself, without moral partiality or slant of judgement, all that has been proved true and enduring in the evolution of life on earth. In history many things have been wrongly and falsely interpreted. But within itself there is nothing but truth, naked and unashamed, battered into shape on the anvil of the battle for survival and for a sense of the meaning of life. Perhaps, too, in an anticipation of a dimly apprehended transformation awaiting it in the future. However abhorrent its contents to the provisional manifestations of life on earth, history knows no falsehood. Wordless history is implanted in the soul of man, accessible only in the contents of the symbols issuing from it, which give unassailable truth.

Of course, Jung's intuition was always in a hurry and made great exactions on his scientific discipline. In a sense he was like a rider always needing all he had of skill and power to prevent a high-spirited, swift and easily provoked racehorse from bolting. He found it essential, therefore, as soon as he had reached a phase in his work which appeared established with relevant objective proof, to put the results and his conclusions into written form and move on. As early as 1904 he established a laboratory for experimental pathology and drew a number of notable American associates to it. He also produced his important paper on the "Psychological Diagnosis of Facts" in 1905. He already had eight other papers and essays all of scientific note and full of evidence of originality and impending change in the approach that he had first encountered in the reading of Krafft-Ebing. Accordingly, when he came to do battle on Freud's behalf in 1906, he already possessed a considerable reputation on his own. Most important of all, the more experience he had of the pathologically abnormal at the Burghölzli, and great as his interest in that area of work was, he became more and more interested in what was considered a lesser phenomenon, that of neurosis.

He was already uncovering in the depths of his most pathologically psychotic patients patterns that seemed to him to be non-personal. They seemed to belong more to the mythological past and the history of the mind and spirit of man, than to the present. This, together with what he was learning from neurosis (held to be a "purely imaginary" illness of a neurotic) gave him a conviction that psychology must be freed from identification with the pathological and given a much wider and greater relevance in the world without. In this regard his conviction was all the stronger because his experience at the Burghölzli suggested that unless he had a psychological framework that was valid for humanity as a whole, its pathological confinement to mental hospitals would never work for the patients there in the way that was expected. It was as if through the phenomenon of neurosis encountered in normal man he was at last on the track of the original cause of the rift which had exercised his imagination so disturbingly over the years. The world of the so-called normal, he suspected, was even more in need of healing than the abnormal, not least of all because it was in command of the day. He was amazed that a world which moved to instant concern and succour of a person with broken limbs could be so blind and indifferent to the suffering manifesting itself as "neurosis". This seemed to Jung to be far graver, more painful and considerably more difficult to heal than any shattered bone. He knew this much with all the greater certainty because news of his success in treating the mentally ill in the Burghölzli had spread to the outer world.

Already his stature had been recognised in a world singularly impervious to recognising the sort of incomparable originator that he was. He was appointed professor of Psychology (*Privatdozent*) at the University of Zürich in 1905. But even more significant, people thought to be normal and inflicted with this "imaginary disturbance" called neurosis came to consult him in increasing numbers. After some eight years at the Burghölzli the demands of his private practice were to grow greatly. Consequently his own inner focus shifted from the pathological to the so-called normal man, which meant that he was to leave the Burghölzli for good.

I say "so-called normal", because by this time normality had become

for Jung an unreal abstraction. He had been through the most disturbing encounters with personalities who walked in the world of men
with authority, success and an air of unassailable moral integrity. Some
of these most "normal" people had come to him as patients. He had,
in many cases, been so appalled by the abnormality lying underneath
the worldly attitude that he refused to treat them. He knew that any
attempt at healing could release vast forces of abnormality already
mobilised beneath "appearances" and so overwhelm them. This latent
abnormality in the "normal" he recognised as one of the deepest pit-
falls on his road, and he taught himself to respect the precarious balance
between "normal" and "abnormal". If in any case he had the slightest
hint from dreams and fantasies that an encounter with the deeper self
would shatter them irrevocably, that the cure would be worse than
the sickness, he would withdraw from the relevant case as creatively
and as soon as possible.

Much as his belief in an analytical approach had broadened, he
realised it was only for those who came to it because they felt themselves in the New Testament sense "poor in spirit", and suspected
those who wanted to take to it straight away as a means for healing
others. It was not surprising that the statistical abstract called "normal"
was like the average rainfall which, in my own arid part of Africa, is
the rain that never falls!

Perhaps only one more fact needs evaluation here. Asked how many
of all the people who came to him had been healed, he replied that
once he had made a rough assessment. He thought that one third of
the vast number had not been healed, a third had been partially healed,
and a third entirely. He added that the middle category was the most
significant and the least conclusive. He was constantly amazed how
persons included in it saw the meaning of what they had learned
in their work with him only years later. Consequently the healed
could be far greater than he, in his most conservative of estimates,
had calculated. In any case, he emphasised, only the most naive of
attitudes assumed that the analytical process was aimed at resolving
the problems of life. In essence life was problematical, and men
derived their purpose from living it as if in answer to the problem it
posed.

"I myself", he told me once, "have never encountered a difficulty
that was not also truly the difficulty of myself."

The most that a psychiatrist could do was to encourage an honest
attempt at living in the patient, giving him or her at most what they
had of resources within themselves. Analysis was nothing if, because

of it, life did not become also a process of self-analysis and self-synthesis
to be continued to the end of their days.

Once asked then which people he had found most difficult to heal,
he had answered instantly, "Habitual liars and intellectuals". I myself
thought this negative association of liars and intellectuals so interesting
that I asked him why he had bracketed them together. He implied that
the association was not arbitrary. He did not despise the intellect. How
could one possibly denigrate what was one of the most important
attributes of the human spirit? When he used the word intellectual he
had in view a person guilty of "intellectualism", attributing a final
omnipotence to the intellect which the whole history of man and in
particular the scorched, disordered scene of our day proved that it did
not possess. Perhaps he should have called the person he had in mind
an "intellectualist" rather than intellectual, I suggested. But, in the
sense as amplified to me, Jung maintained that the intellectualist was
also, by constant deeds of omission, a kind of habitual liar. He was
untrue to other equally important and valid aspects of himself. He
tended to lead a highly compartmentalised existence, creating concepts
to shield him from reality. As fast as they were challenged he invented
new ones to take their place. This made another "ism" which, like all
the others so abundant already, spoilt by excess a faculty of vital importance. Jung explained with some dismay how he observed this intellectualist's success in identifying intellect with spirit. Spirit was so
much greater because it included all the feeling values as well as other
non-rational sources of awareness in man. What had happened to the
passion of the spirit, he once asked rhetorically of me, that it should
have declined into an arid exercise of intellect alone? And what of the
effect on consciousness that it should be held as equivalent only of that
which is capable of verbal articulation? Look, he said, and see how the
spirit of the West had been impoverished and become sick in a vital
area of itself. To correct all that in his patients was as common as it
was a difficult task. He was appalled by the numbers of persons too
that Western civilisation was turning out as mass producers of "concepts" for their whole-time occupation. The amount of thinking for
thinking's sake without any obligation to the rest of the personality
was one of the causes of our profound collectively pathological dis-
sociations from our past. Given no sense of the dependence of our
future on an honest historical assessment of ourselves and our cultures,
the loss was almost total. The myth or story, he added, which as I had
discovered for myself in the desert of Africa, was vital to the well-
being of man. Such a dissociation in the consciousness of men was

generally fateful. It was the overture to forms of psychosis that were the most difficult of all to heal. And alas, not only individuals so dissociated went mad but whole societies, cultures, and civilisations out of the same self-inflicted psychological partialities, likewise became demented. Had we not just been through two world wars to prove how demented our civilisation could be?

It was not surprising, therefore, that one problem connected with the most profound dissociation of all pursued him to the end: the dichotomy described today as schizophrenia. It was, he found, the most difficult of all to heal in individuals, not least because it was supported by a similar tendency to dichotomy in the spirit of an entire civilisation backed up as it were by all that was negative in the twentieth-century *zeitgeist*. So, in a sense, schizophrenia was incapable of cure without healing at the same time the mass of humanity and cultural pressures rallied unconsciously behind it. Even so, he had had his successes after what seemed to him a disproportionate effort, since it demanded from him so great a concentration that he hardly had time or energy left for others, let alone for himself. But there were countless others, lost in a world which seemed increasingly cold, impersonal and fundamentally mythological, ruled over by unknown powers against which a man fought from within in vain. He was to confess that he never clearly discovered what caused the severest forms of this particular sickness of spirit. In one of the last of his utterances just before he died, he suggested that there could be pathological forms of schizophrenia that might have a physical origin in some undiscovered mutation in the chromosomes and genes of the individual— thereby demonstrating conclusively that, dedicated as he was to psychology and the world within, he had never been so fanatically. He had always remained open to the claims and validity of the physical and the external as well. Yet he stood firm and proved in his practice that many more cases than were imagined, condemned as incurable forms of the disturbance, could be made whole again by applied analytical psychology.

It was in some such fullness of an awareness of phenomena such as these that he turned his back on the Burghölzli and took to work again on his own in the world pulled in a direction which even he had not anticipated and which demanded so much attention that by 1913, just before the outbreak of the first World War, he was to resign his professorship as well.

ERRANT AND ADVENTURE

Le chemin longue de la queste et l'aventiure

FROISSART'S KNIGHT

Meanwhile, Freud had come to play a considerable role and to make, both in a positive and a negative sense, an immense contribution to Jung's future. Yet I have deliberately not dealt with Jung's relationship with Freud before, because in essense it seemed to me least concerned with Jung's time at the Burghölzli. It belonged far more to the wider world of analytical psychology as a whole, full of important implications not only for its own but also for Jung's personal development. Jung had read Freud's *Interpretation of Dreams* on its publication in 1900 but it does not appear to have made much impression on him then. He re-read it nearly three years later and immediately saw how there were links between Freud and what he was trying to do. For instance, his own word-association method was revealing areas of hurt in men of which they were unaware. Freud's concept of an unconscious at work in the mind of man, and therefore a source of mental disturbance, made immediate sense to Jung. Above all, he was struck and excited by the importance Freud attached to dreams and so restored to honour a process which the rationalism of western Europe had either forgotten or dismissed as some idle old wives' matter, too ridiculous for serious consideration.

This, of course, was not surprising in one who had had his first great dream when he was barely three and so had quite naturally assumed that something imposed upon him from within in such a way had a natural meaning, and had continued against the trend of the world and his own education to cherish and go by them accordingly. It was remarkable to me, going through some of his own case histories at the Burghölzli, both before and after his encounter with Freud, how from the beginning he was using the dreams of his patients as an instrument of healing and using them, moreover, in a comprehensive sense alien to the arbitrary method that Freud was to develop.

Yet Freud, in this particular work, was also truly on the scent of a new truth. He was also much more advanced on the trail than anyone else; so Jung warmed to him instantly. He recognised that a great iron gate shut, for centuries, on the inquiring spirit of man had now been swung open again. That for him, I believe, remained Freud's greatest achievement. Jung's debt to Freud in this regard was unqualified, and he was to stress repeatedly to the end of his days that "Freud, by his evaluation of dreams, discovered an avenue to the unconscious which had hitherto existed only as a philosophic postulate, and so put back in the hand of man a vital instrument which had appeared irretrievably lost."

He wrote to Freud at once to tell him of his appreciation and gratitude. However, in one sense the discovery of Freud was not entirely welcome to him. Jung was busy writing a paper as passport to a new academic career. He knew how Freud was reviled and unaccepted in the academic world of his time and how damaging any openly acknowledged support of Freud's theories would be to him. Considering that unaided, through his word-association method he had already arrived at many of Freud's own conclusions, it would have been only too easy, and morally plausible, to present his paper without reference to Freud. He refused to do so. I mention it here not so much because it demonstrates Jung's moral courage, but also his dedication to truth, since these, I believe, are demonstrated beyond doubt by his earlier life, but for the reason that his decision was to reveal how alive and active his excluded Number Two personality had remained. It was the first clear intimation for years that his Number Two, far from being content as a mere force in being, was preparing to assume a much more differentiated role in his future development.

In the midst of this temptation, like "a clear voice in my ear", he told me, his Number Two warned him that not to mention Freud would be cheating and that he could not "base his life on a lie".

From that moment, he became quite openly a supporter of Freud, and though warned by two eminent German professors of the danger to his career which his partisanship of Freud constituted, he continued to defend him. Even more, despite the fact that from the beginning he had doubts of his own about some of Freud's assumptions, he did what he could in private to broaden what appeared to be too narrow an approach in Freud. They began to correspond regularly and in 1907 he and his wife visited Freud in Vienna where at their first meeting the two men talked for thirteen hours without a break. Although Jung emerged from the marathon session with mixed feelings, an association began which meant more to him, I suspect, than any other ever did. Up to the day of his death, he never completely made his peace with the pain inflicted on him both by the association and the parting with Freud. The matter, therefore, needs closer examination.

The need that Jung and Freud had of each other, I believe, was far more in a human and psychological dimension than a scientific one. Their scientific need of each other could have been met, and perhaps more fruitfully fulfilled, by exchange of letters and findings than in terms of a friendship between two natures so fundamentally unalike. No-one could ever regret the association because of its consequences for psychology as a whole. But these consequences cannot be properly understood unless one tries to see the association clearly for what it was and so rescue it from the miserable and humiliating partisan interpretations to which it has been sacrificed.

To begin with, Freud, although he was already a firmly established influence in science, was still a controversial figure. He was assailed to the most despicable extremes of which even that quarrelsome world had proved itself capable, seeing that it was so unaccustomed by exaction of its partial masculine disciplines to the emotional realities of life that a young girl of four could almost be held up to it as a model of maturity for self-correction. Freud had committed the Promethean sin of recovering a great, transforming truth and, like Prometheus, he was being punished for it by the gods of his own world. He had found this gateway of dreams into an unconscious region in the spirit of man. He had performed the Odyssean task, as Homer puts it, of "pointing the way to the gates of the sun and to the land of dreams".

By reason of his work and an inner compulsion of his own, he concentrated on one of the most neglected and cruelly repressed areas in European man; the attitude to sex. In doing this he was taking on at least some two thousand years of Christian history: and a great deal of Old Testament man as well. Even in this permissive day one is amazed that civilisation (in so far as it is an attempt at Christianity) has never attempted to evolve a truly Christian attitude to the role of sex in the life of man, and continues to sweep its natural claims under a carpet of narrow ethical assumption. In its place it raises a lofty, Gothic concept of the relationship between man and woman, based most inadequately on only a few foundation stones. First, one solitary utterance by Christ, used out of context with His all-embracing and predominant value of love for which, indeed, He was crucified. And then some of the lesser utterances of St Paul. I doubt if anyone could love St Paul more than I do. Yet I have always been appalled by St Paul's attitude to sex and women. He was in a large measure responsible for organised Christianity's lack of recognition of the sexual values of the spirit, and its profound dismissal of the importance both of the woman in life and in the spirit of man. This was a tendency already encouraged in the Old Testament and its dedication to a masculine patriarchal concept of God.

I have discussed at some length the impact of all this on European history and on my own particular life. But some reiteration is necessary. Despite the Romantic revival and that great dynamic and living example of the search of the feminine presented by all who joined in the quest of the Holy Grail, this rejection of the feminine, and the suppression of sex, reached its most omnipotent height in the Victorian era. Although this age carries an English label, "Victorianism", it was spiritually in charge of culture from Cape Wrath to the littoral of the Mediterranean, the Urals of Russia, extending to the remote Pacific coast and across to the New World of the Americas.

Freud cannot be properly understood if not set against this background. Only then can he be seen as a long overdue and scientifically informed reaction against this repression. That was both his originality and strength, as well as his weakness. He and we have all reached a point where mere reaction to history and events is not enough. This was demonstrated beyond doubt on a cross in Palestine some two thousand years ago. Something new was needed. But although the new was implicit in Freud's reaction, it was also imprisoned in it. Men, alas, tend to make either a god or a devil of what they and their society need most. Freud after his great initial breakthrough into the underworld in man, installed sex there as a kind of god together with some of the most infantile aspects of which human imagination is capable. He did this moreover in the context of Austria, in particular of Vienna, where in many regards, and particularly that of sex, man was freer than elsewhere.

And there, I believe, we come to the basic difference and point of departure in the characters of Jung and Freud, which made it impossible for them to remain friends. Jung, exposed to the same inadequacy of European culture in its far more severe Protestant context in Switzerland, was not content just to react to it. The temptation must have been great after his first great dream of a phallus enthroned on gold to be slanted towards a literal interpretation of the dream event and himself become sex-obsessed. Yet he reacted in a way that was totally new in the spirit of modern man.

Even as a child Jung was never interested in just reacting to circumstances and events. He was committed as if from birth to their transformation into something that was greater than either their cause or their effect. In contemplating not only what had happened to him but also what had happened in the history of man, Jung did not fail to note, as his beloved Heraclitus had done centuries before Christ, this perennial tendency of men and their societies to swing over into their opposite. Heraclitus called it Enantiodromia. But Jung himself, by instinct, would have no part of it. This great initial calm, which one has already observed in him on the occasion when an obtuse master at school accused and punished him unfairly for lying over an essay, descended on his spirit. He decided that it was of prime importance first to discover the causes of these violent pendulum swings in time and human personality. Only then could he consider the reconciliation or transcendence of the two already insinuating itself into his treatment of the sick and also his view of his work in the future. Sex, however important, was only part of the story. From there arose his first great and ineradicable difference with Freud. To illustrate it at its most immediate and simple level, he could no more see a great Gothic spire, soaring above the finest of medieval cathedral achievements, as merely a phallic symbol, than mistake a horse for a mule.

Great as was the instinctive rage of the world over Freud's sudden exposition of the shallowness and hypocrisy of the assumptions by which it had lived, it was to become reconciled far sooner to Freud than to Jung. By implication Freud nourished an historic appetite for a change that was merely the opposite of what had preceded the historic pattern to which it was only too well conditioned. Jung already was arriving at something far more original and difficult to understand. Indeed the moment was fast approaching when both the world and the Freudians were to join forces in denouncing Jung with greater ferocity than anything that Freud had had to endure. And Jung had no champion of stature to rally to him at that moment of crisis, as he had rallied to Freud.

The fundamental difference in the two men was already clear in their attitudes to fantasies, symbols and dreams. For Freud, fantasy always appeared to have an infantile, wishful and sexual origin. Dreams were a highly censored process which disguised man's unconscious promptings from his socially respectable self. The symbol was merely a metaphoric and almost literal expression of totality. Freud held that the message of the symbols, because of their very nature, was absolute and unchanging; for instance, that the appearance of an umbrella in all dreams had a phallic significance for all, however much some might protest they thought of it more as a shield against rain or sun. He held, Old-Testament stern, that it was for the psychiatrist to determine their meaning and inform, or perhaps more accurately impose them on the disturbed personality.

Jung saw the symbols in the classical and far more meaningful role,

issuing unsolicited, like lightning, or passing like meteors through the
darkness of man's unawareness. However much the person who experienced them could participate in giving them a specific form, their
contents and importance came from an as yet uncharted region of the
spirit. For Jung they were beyond any intellectual grasp and also were
sources of great transfigurative new meaning. Among the dynamic
forces in the spirit of man that he was to explore, they were to remain
for him, forever, among the greatest. He was certain that the decline
and fall of meaning in the world around him was due in no small
measure to modern man's increasing inability to guide his life by the
symbol. The significance of the imagery of the symbol in the life of
the person who experienced it could not be imposed from without.
It had to take into account that person's associations with it. As for
dreams, they were the most precious and inalienable possession of the
dreamer in that they were vital elements towards the progression of
his story, or myth. They had to be accepted too without reservation
by the psychiatrist. Any person who laid hands, however well inten-
tioned, to grasp the dreams of another was violating the first principle
of healing. Even misinterpreting dreams submitted by the dreamer,
Jung found, could be crippling to the task of healing unless the error
was honestly confessed as soon as it was discovered and the future
course steered as on a compass of the associations of the dreamer with
the detail of the dream. On the whole Jung preferred to leave the
dreamer as much as possible to his own dreaming self, and whatever
it was that dreamt through him. If the dreamer could honour the forgotten language of himself and life within himself, Jung believed half
the battle was won.

With such differences it was not at all remarkable that Freud and
Jung should part company. It was only surprising that they should
have succeeded in being friends for so long. That was only possible,
I believe, because their human need of each other at that moment in
time was even greater than the vocational necessities of their lives.

First Freud, in spite of the fact that adherents to his cause were increasing daily, never had anyone of his own stature to stand beside
him. Even Adler, who was to differ violently with Freud later and
strike out on his own with a psychological view based on the hypothesis of an inborn urge for power in man, and who stood head and
shoulders above the rest of Freud's supporters, could not give the
strength to Freud that Jung did. Adler, as Jung himself told me, was
always a sidelight, although not an unimportant one. Freud was always
the exponent of a real new view.

Sensitive, imaginative and exposed as Freud was to scorn and mis-interpretation, Jung came to his support at a moment when he needed it most and gave him a feeling of confirmation and confidence that he had not had before. Profoundly concerned in the future of psycho-logical science, Freud was, in a symbolic sense, badly in need of an heir and successor to carry on his work. It was one of the indicators of Freud's stature that he was as concerned for the future as he was for the past and the present. It soon seemed to him that Jung was born to be his successor. Before long he talked of Jung as his "son", and others referred to him as "crown prince".

Embarrassed as he was by these appellations, I believe Jung at first was not altogether displeased by them. I have tried to show how already Jung had suffered from the lack of a father in the world. The place in the human spirit reserved so significantly for the fathers of this world was still vacant in Jung. The need for its occupation in the world of psychiatry where he was outwardly and inwardly alone was great. Whatever Jung's protestations, my own personal belief is that Freud moved in, occupied that place, and was made welcome there during a number of vitally formative years for them both. And out of this great need for each other, they completely overlooked their essential differences not only of character but in their respective approaches to psychology.

What was it in Freud, one wonders, that made him overlook Jung's reiteration, with increasing urgency, of "Man's need for the eternal truth of myth?" And seeing that even after Freud's authority had already become questionable to him, what of Jung's description of himself to Freud as of a man "sitting precariously on the fence be-tween the Dionysian and Apollonian", and one, moreover, who "could not muster a grain of courage to promote ethics in public, let alone from the psychological point of view?" What of Jung's emphasis that "Two thousand years of Christianity had to be replaced by something equivalent?" And, in addition, the great poetic statement of a funda-mental element in Jung's spirit: "An ethical fraternity with its mythical nothing is a pure vacuum and can never evoke in man the slightest trace of that age-old animal power which drives the migrating bird across the sea."

Here, and in far too many other instances, was unmistakable evi-dence of a spirit which Jung saw as only part of an infinitely greater whole, and not an end in itself. Yet Freud, who was doing his utmost to explain everything in terms of a science where method and theory were one, ignored all this in Jung for years. Jung, equally, suppressed his reservations about Freud and his reductive attitude of "nothing but"—a term derived from William James's statement in *Pragmatism*: "What is higher, is explained by what is lower and treated for ever as a case of 'nothing but'—nothing but something else of an inferior sort."

So great was Jung's psychological need of Freud's authority that, where he ventured to challenge him as he did over Freud's dogmatic declamation of "the omnipotence of the idea", he instantly retracted when Freud hit back. Jung apologised as if he had been guilty of some heinous offence instead of merely having delivered himself of an honest expression of opinion. Similarly, their profound differences over the meaning of symbols and complexes, particularly the Oedipus complex, so basic to Freud's teaching, were mutually held back almost until the moment of the parting of their ways.

Jung, of course, was convinced that the Oedipus symbolism and its role in the imagination could not be taken literally as did Freud. He was certain it was not there to protect man, literally, against sexual incest. For him it was there as a protection, a portentous warning to prevent "psychological incest" between parents and children. It expressed how vital it was for man's increase that children and parents scrupulously should respect their differences of personalities and needs, and so be freed from spiritual and psychological bondage to live lives of their own. Though to my knowledge, neither Freud nor Jung stressed it, I believe that perhaps the most important aspect in the Oedipus legend has been overlooked, namely the fact that the incest took place *without* mother and son knowing their true relationship. In other words, as always, Fate struck through lack of self-awareness which the "not knowing" in the myth symbolises.

This element would reinforce Jung's symbolic interpretations, that the myth was directed at a psychological emancipation of the son from the mother and a rebirth of himself into his own individual role in life. More, he saw the myth in its ultimate resolution as a union of the individual with his highest creative meaning and so it was, essentially, a religious signpost. He had only to look round him, reconsider all that he had observed at the Burghölzli and in his own consulting room to realise how, despite this profound inbuilt system of warning symbolised in the Oedipus story, the extent of psychological incest in the life of his time was so great, as it remains today. Despite Oedipus, Theresias, Freud and Jung, the world is still full of parents who attempt to live their own lives through their children. Daughters take their fathers' unlived self on themselves, to the extreme even of assuming his unfulfilled sexual self as their own. Sons react in the same way with their mothers.

In a very real sense too, Freud's preoccupation with sex and Oedipus in his psychology was a consequence of the projection of a profound problem of his own on to the life of his time. He himself had an archaic concept of the relationship of man and woman, parents and children, re-affirmed by the extent to which he had become a mere opposite of what had gone before. It is indeed strange that he never seemed to ask himself why he took so obsessive an interest in sex. His interest in the father–son relationship and his insistence on the fact that Oedipus had "wished the father dead" are striking evidence of this. He wanted a "son" himself who would carry on his, the father's work, even to the extent of sacrificing his own life—a modern version of Abraham's Old Testament urge to sacrifice his son Isaac to his God. Freud had already fainted twice when Jung had dared to imply his opposition to the viewpoint in regard to the "death wish" that the son was supposed to have towards the father. Both the facts and details are on record and in no need of amplification. But there is a possibly important fact that has been overlooked. Taken literally, of course, this death wish is sheer nonsense, and was so particularly in Jung's regard. But taken symbolically, it is full of meaning since it is the image of the son's legitimate striving to be psychologically free of the father. So, when Freud suspected Jung of such a secret wish (to the extent of fainting twice) he revealed of course how much Jung had come to mean to him as a "son". But perhaps most important of all, he revealed also that, on an archaic level, he was already experiencing an intuition that Jung longed to be rid of his symbolic "father" and so abolish Freud's psychological hold over him, if only to defeat Freud's unconscious wish to make Jung live his future for him.

How dangerously far the symbolic confusion between the two men had gone, appropriately came to light through a dream of Jung's. The interpreting of each other's dreams was one of the main bonds between the two at the time—a bond whose strength it is almost impossible to appreciate fully today, when all psychiatrists have been trained by others and have trusted colleagues to guide them and help them. Both these men, however, had come into the world of an, as yet, untested unconscious without guides and on their own. They had only each other for confession of their dreams and their interpretations. Jung, already, through this means had relieved Freud of a painful neurotic affliction. So, on the rare occasions when they were together they continued to submit their dreams to each other. However, there did come a moment when Jung confessed that he had lied to Freud. He had done it because he still needed Freud. This had occurred in the course of the interpretation of the dream that Jung had just given to Freud to explain. The detail of this particular dream which produced the lie is irrelevant. All that matters is that Jung knew that Freud, whom he had come to know very well, would be pleased only by an answer from him (Jung) which revealed a "latent death wish" of some kind. So Jung produced one. He said the death wish was directed at his wife and sister-in-law. He did this because for him it was the most devastatingly absurd and unreal illustration he could imagine. But even to this day I find it a harsh revelation of how crippling and unreal his relationship with Freud had become that he could betray in words, however momentarily and for an ulterior purpose, someone he loved as much as he did his wife.

The two men happened to be on their lecture tour of America at the time, and this dream also possessed an importance of a different kind. The dream was set in what Jung insisted on calling "my house", and he would always utter the "my" with an unusually emotive emphasis that what the house represented was his and no-one else's, not even Freud's, and something for which he would and indeed did unimagined battle. It was a large house of many compartments, two storeys high and with a deep cellar underneath. Although the year was only 1909, the dream foreshadowed Jung's future uncovering layers in the unconscious of man, with the rediscovery of perhaps the deepest of universal contemporary truths—the world of the collective unconscious. Combined with the uncharacteristic lie, which Freud's spell over him compelled him to utter, the dream seemed to show unerringly how doomed their association already was, and in what a totally diverging direction Jung's spirit was moving. He told me that from then on all his doubts about Freud's increasingly doctrinaire concept of psychoanalysis, his emphasis on sex, raised to the metaphysical heights of psycho-sexuality, came to the boil. The long concealed differences between them emerged into the open.

As often in these things, the immediate cause in itself was slight. It came about over a single incident in a long dream that Freud had brought to him.

"I told him", Jung explained to me, speaking like a person for whom the pain inflicted, however far back, was still so real that it sought relief in being discussed, "that there was an aspect of his dream about which I needed more information. In particular I had to have his associations with the dream if I were to be of any help to him. To my amazement he told me he couldn't possibly do this. When I asked him why not,

Freud answered, 'It would be bad for my authority.' And in that moment something snapped in me. I knew that if a man cared more for his authority than for the truth I could no longer go down the same road with him. An irrevocable break between us from there on was just a matter of time. But in reality it had started in the doubts I had had many years before, but had suppressed out of respect for the many great services Freud had rendered me in particular, and psychology in general."

I asked him, "Could you possibly tell me what that aspect of the dream was which Freud would not reveal to you?"

Jung looked at me with severity, and said curtly, "That is a professional secret."

Begged on television many years later to disclose the nature of the dreams Freud brought to him for interpretation, Jung refused even more resolutely, declaring firmly that there were after all such things as professional confidences. When told that this reservation need no longer be allowed to hold since Freud had been dead for many years, Jung answered with great warmth and dignity of feeling, "Yes! But these regards last longer than a lifetime."

Complex, long and painful as was this growth of differences in their contribution to modern psychology they can be simply stated, without over-simplification. Freud had discovered a comparatively narrow and special area of the unconscious of man which one could call the "personal unconscious". Jung went deeper, to uncover below what one might call a racial or historical unconscious, leading finally to the greatest area of all which he called the "collective unconscious".

"I found", he would tell me in a voice which seemed to have lost none of the original reverence of the observation, "that the more I looked into my own spirit and the spirit of my patients, I saw stretched out before me an infinitive objective mystery within as great and wonderful as a sky full of stars spread out above us on a clear and moonless winter's night."

This, he stressed, was neither a merely subjective world nor one just of suppressed instincts, infantile urgings too painful and inconvenient for human-beings to allow their admission into consciousness. It was this "inscape" of Hopkins, empirically rediscovered, this immense world of utmost objective reality within, charged with the experience of the whole of past life and all the possibilities of life that can ever be, arranged in patterns of energy, and complete with an infinite sense of direction—a kind of inbuilt radar and homing device particularly its own.

Yet nearly three years more were to pass before the final break. That it took so long was in no sense caused by their mutual need of each other. This had already come to an end. It was due almost entirely to the respect and affection that the two men had come to feel for each other. This was the real substance of the tragedy of their ultimate separation. Their letters to each other at this period, particularly Freud's, made touching and often moving reading.

In his effort to understand a nature so different from his own and to erase their differences, Freud summoned up all he had of Old Testament patriarchal benevolence within himself for someone he considered as a son. The patronage implicit in this approach could no longer have helped and in a sense was incidental. Jung himself had already accepted the inevitability of the break. He was writing his first major work, *Psychology of the Unconscious,** which was to reveal an attitude to symbols, dreams, myths and the unconscious, so at odds with Freud's that he knew nothing would stop Freud from disowning him the moment he became aware of it. Jung's wife tried in vain to comfort him, assuring him that Freud would understand in the end. And he himself made a major effort to avert the break as late as 1912 by writing Freud a very carefully worded, placating letter on their Oedipus differences, trying desperately to make himself not just humanly but scientifically understood. Yet even the over-stretched words reveal an underlying certainty of impending separation. So tormented was Jung by the prospect that for two months he could not go on writing the fatal book.

He may not have succeeded in doing so had it not been for a dream. As always in the past when he had reached an apparently insoluble crisis in his life, the appropriate dreams came to his aid. He was fond of saying, "He who looks outwardly, dreams. But he who looks within, awakes." Because his attention was directed outwardly towards Freud, he dreamt; and through the dreaming was compelled to look within and to awake to his own self, and to a greatly extended view of his role and life. All that is important for understanding the future course of events is that the image which represented Freud in this dream was a peevish Austrian Customs official, old-fashioned and out of date, trying to control as it were the exports and imports of the spirit. There could be no doubt that the image stood for Freud and his spent professional role in Jung's life. This image possessed a certain poetic justice, however ironic, seeing how much importance Freud

* *Wandlungen und Symbole der Libido.* Retitled in the revised edition, 1956, *Symbols of Transformation.*

attached to a mechanism of censorship in dream material, and how one of the main differences between him and Jung was that the dream, for Jung, was no façade, hiding the truth from the dreamer, but an urgent summons of unrealised being and meaning for recognition.

Other aspects of the dream pointed to the way Jung had to go in the future and need examination in detail, and in a manner I believe was not appreciated at the time even by Jung. But first, it is important to realise that by this time Jung, out of his need for a father, and his need for authority and the uncertainty of his capacity to walk alone in this new field of science, had done great violence to himself. Of all wounds, self-inflicted ones go deepest. They are the most difficult to heal, the hardest to forgive, and their scars are impossible to conceal. This self-inflicted wound hurt Jung to the end of his days, all the more because he would have given everything he possessed—except his integrity—to have had real male companionship of Freud's quality with him on the stormy road he was to take. He was perhaps most of all hurt because, apart from respect for what Freud had done, he also had become devoted to him.

I think, however, that hurt as he was by isolation and the sustained attack on him by Freud's followers which drove him to hit back hard himself, he behaved with great dignity. The recollection of the respect and love of Freud would flare up, in the long years of controversy, and give him the necessary calm. I know it from the way he spoke to me about Freud, and also from the facts of his life. For instance, after the last war, with the help of his most distinguished male collaborator, Dr C. A. Meier, who was later to occupy his old Chair of Psychology at the National University of Zürich, he tried hard but in vain to establish an institute in Zürich where all genuine modern investigations into psychology would be studied and taught—including of course, Freud.

All his friends were aware of the paradox of the experience with Freud in him and were influenced by his own positive attitude towards it. I hope Freud realised it to an extent that would have brought comfort also to his sorely tried, battered, pioneering and finally cruelly exiled self. I find confirmation of the fact that when the Nazi explosion threatened Freud's life in Vienna, it was not to fellow Freudians in London but a distinguished pioneer of Jungian psychology in Britain, and also a friend of mine, that Freud's family turned for help. Dr E. A. (Eddie) Bennet, a close friend of Jung and his family, helped to organise Freud's escape, found a home and organised a welcome for him in Hampstead in London. On the day that Freud arrived in London, Jung and Bennet were attending a psychological conference in Oxford. In the course of the morning session the news of his safe arrival came by telegram. Bennet and Jung immediately decided to send him the warmest of telegrams of welcome. The secretary of the conference found this so strange a procedure in regard to someone held to be Jung's greatest opponent that he was uncertain and hesitated. When Jung heard at lunch-time that the telegram had not yet gone, he was, Eddie Bennet told me, more angry than he had ever seen him. He ordered the telegram's immediate dispatch. So perhaps for both men, however much pain was endured, somewhere in the deeps of themselves, error was absolved and tragedy redeemed. Yet unless one understands the extent and complexity of the injury done, the consequence of separation cannot be fully comprehended.

Important, therefore, to realise that this partially explored fringe of the collective unconscious which led to the break with Freud, was something that evolved directly out of Jung's role as a pioneer. Jung never ceased to impress on all who came to him that no-one should ever attempt psychiatry unless he himself had gone through an analysis in terms of what he now called analytical psychology. He insisted on this as a fundamental for many reasons. For instance, he knew now for certain that psychiatry only worked if the psychiatrist himself, too, was affected by the plight of the patient. He knew also how in various ways a psychiatrist could become over-identified with his patient, as well as the other way round. These states Jung called "transference" (from patient to doctor) and "counter transference" (from psychiatrist to patient). Further, Jung knew how contact with the unconscious forces that disturbed the patient could call into violent being unknown elements in the psychiatrist, to such an extent that the psychiatrist in the process could come to need help as much as the patient. The psychiatrist's only protection against all this was by getting to know his own "unknown" self as deeply as possible. So Jung insisted on a thorough three years' analysis as an indispensable preparation for the would-be psychiatrist. In addition, he warned even the most experienced psychiatrists of the need to have a "father" or "mother confessor" to help them out of the subjective entanglement with the problems of their patients which he knew so well from experience were bound to occur.

One recognises not only the practical import but the overwhelming wisdom and the disconcerting psychological implications of all this for Jung. He was the first in his own field and had none of these complex prerequisites to help him on his way. I believe this is one of the more unmistakable marks of Jung's and Freud's genius—that they reached this vital stage in their work without any example of other men to help them. For brief periods they were able to confide in each other and interpret each other's dreams. But this was of diminishing value because their approach to dreams and their interpretation widened with increasing swiftness.

To me it is miraculous that Jung could have got so far and retained not just his sanity but maintained his appetite for pressing on with this exacting voyage of uncomfortable discovery. The measure of his achievement in this regard is the fact that for some twelve years now he had the unconscious material of thousands of deranged, neurotic and disturbed persons thrust on him, with no-one to help him. As a result, the activation of his own unknown self in terms of the laws of the dynamics of the as yet undiscovered collective unconscious must have assumed titanic proportions. Besides, had he not since the age of three been assailed enough with strange, inexplicable and horrific material from within to make this demonic acceleration by contact with the disturbances of others as unnecessary as it was dangerous?

Indeed, he told me that the burden was so great, even in a physical sense, that he would have been incapable of enduring it had he not been born with so robust a constitution. Yet perhaps he would not have succeeded in this had it not been for the dreaming process and all that it evoked of symbol and fantasy; and also for his great natural trust in what had been naturally imposed on him, and a certainty that there was great meaning in it. So one is not surprised that, in the greatest crisis yet, the dreaming process remained an archangelic constant in him, protecting himself against confusion and error. The second half of this dream was striking confirmation of this and showed up clearly how harmful had become Jung's self-subjection to Freud and his theories, leading him to a definite point of reference in the map of his past to redirect his path.

This half of the dream, therefore, needs particular examination. It was set in Italy, and reminded him of the Basle which was history to him, thereby indicating that it was his own kind of Italy that was the setting of his dream. And what precisely was this Italy? It was pre-eminently that of the Dante and his Beatrice he loved so well, of Petrarch and his Laura, and the scene altogether of the Renaissance, the great rebirth of the Western spirit, as he knew it from Burckhardt's remarkable study of the event. The dream indeed made it clear from the outset that it had to do with rebirth and renewal. The sun was at its zenith and it was the zenith too of the seasons which we call summer. The noon-day sun was blazing and the light fierce and sharp on the city. The shops were closing, the crowds of people streaming towards their homes. Clearly the business of the spirit was over for the moment, not only for him but also for the seasons.

It was the hour the primitive people in my part of the world call dead; the mid-day hour when men, animals and trees lose their shadows, become unreal and ghost-like. Ghosts who, as I suggested earlier on in reference to *Hamlet* and *Faust*, do not portray the uneasy dead but prefigure life as yet to come. It was the moment in which the Chinese say that midnight is being born. There is no doubt that this is a dream not only about rebirth but about renewal made desperately urgent, because another fall of night in the spirit of man is on its way. At this moment of climax inevitably too the relevant natural compensation of spirit was called into life. A knight appeared in full armour of chain mail—how significant an element this detail is too, seeing that the armour to come was to be evolved as it were by the human spirit in chains out of its links of chain, with the living spirit of the past seeking the liberating truth for itself. Over the armour fell a white tunic on which was woven front and back—that is in the future as in the past—a large red cross which delineates the four quarters of the circle cardinal to the rounding or totality of life. Apparently the dreamer in Jung gathered that the knight had appeared regularly thus for centuries in the land of rebirth at the precise hour when midnight was being conceived as its counter, and yet no-one of the great crowd present had ever taken notice of him.

Unlike the customs official which had done proxy for Freud in the dream mentioned, which foretold the end of his hold on Jung, but not described in detail, this knight was no peevish, debilitated person, exercising an outmoded control on the frontiers of awareness, but full of life and reality to such an extent that the image obsessed Jung's imagination for a long time. In fact, he was never to forget it. He knew the moment he awoke that the knight belonged to the twelfth century, the age wherein alchemy was to begin an important role in European imagination, and above all the hour which witnessed the emergence of the dynamic transfigurative theme of the quest of the Holy Grail. Dreamt only some two years before the world war, what, I have often asked myself, could have described the state of spirit of the Western world more accurately than the symbolism of this dream?

I have stressed how, as a boy, Jung had read Froissart, Mallory and their Germanic and Wagnerian equivalents on the Holy Grail, and how profound an impact they had made on him. Wagner's *Parsifal* was one of his favourite pieces of music, and the world of the knights of the

Holy Grail, ever since the age of fifteen, had been his world in the deepest sense. He took this dream as a sign that his whole being was seeking something still unknown and far beyond any Freudian concept; something that might bring back meaning to the increasing meaninglessness of the life of his time. Obviously that was true for Jung on a personal level. But for me it has always had also a deeper, universal significance, not sufficiently brought out in his *Memories, Dreams, Reflections*. It not only describes, in the imagery of a universal symbolism, exactly the nature of Jung's future role in life, accurate even to the extent to which the world would fail to recognise both it and him. But it shows also how his work would be a turning point in history and time. Achieved in the context of our lean and hungry era, it would provide us with the means of defeating a new invasion of darkness which was already beginning to attack the human spirit, despite the apparent brightness of our day. Essentially Jung's was an heraldic and knightly spirit in the most modern of idioms. In this dream something of him appears to be charged with the task of finding something that could contain and unify the divided, imperilled spirit of modern man.

I remembered when we discussed this my own agony as a child when I came to the moment in Mallory when the dying Arthur compelled a reluctant Sir Bedivere to return to the waters the great Excalibur—wherein its image had been born. The sword which itself in its extraction from stone, the stone the medieval heart had become, represented so evocatively the awareness of man in action on his quest for wholeness symbolised by the Holy Grail. I was haunted for years by the dismay that the great order of the Round Table had been dispersed and no longer had a Royal Centre around which it could reassemble. It was as if this dispersal and defeat and death of Arthur reflected the dispersal of what was best in the Western spirit and the arrest of its essential quest, story or myth, whatever name served the imagination best of him who reconsidered it, and explained the fragmented and splintered mass formations that had ever since tried to usurp its place. And it was for me, when I encountered this dream of Jung and considered how he proceeded from there, as if the ancient Arthurian call had gone out loud and clear again and Merlin, who had preceded and tutored Arthur, and all the magic of life which had been buried deep with him in his wound for so long had been unsealed. Through Jung the order of a reassembly of all we had of awareness left of this most authentic, specific and urgent quest of Western man was there once more for all to hear and help in the making of a new Round Table for the nourishment of a truly modern spirit. That for me to this day is the real symbolic content of this dream and is confirmed by the fact that Jung told me the only reason which stopped him from going on to work on the theme of the Holy Grail with the same psychological detail as he was to do on other historical parallels—as, for instance, that of alchemy, and as would have appeared the logical issue of such a dream and his associations with it—was that his wife Emma was making it her own special study. Somewhere in Emma Jung's remote ancestral background there was a family legend of a knight of her own kin who had failed the Quest, and she felt called upon to set the failure to right. The moment her special duties as mother to five children were discharged she began a vast, imaginative research into the origin and meaning of the legend. Consequently Jung felt that he had to respect her sense of responsibility and not intrude upon her theme of unique meaning.

It is one of the most striking as well as deeply moving testimonies of the formidable innocence of responsibility, more effective by far than any self-conscious sophistication of it, by which he, his friends and fellow workers brought to understanding and transforming, in contemporary terms, the unfamiliar historical. New material now began to rise like a great flood, yet they all committed themselves whole-heartedly to whatever seemed special in it to themselves. Jung began his own special inquiries in a humble and even humiliating way. He started with a painful reassessment of all that had led up to the parting of the way with Freud.

Jung had been impressed by the fact that invariably among the many people who swarmed to him as patients, he found at the core of their neurosis a sense of insecurity. This unease coincided with a loss of faith; a loss of the quintessential requisites of personal religious experience. He found that he seldom succeeded in what for want of a better word is called "a cure", without enabling the patient to recover his lost capacity for religious experience. Subsequently a purely psychiatric approach to the problems of life could no longer satisfy him. In any case he had always been aware of the vitally interdependent roles of science and religion. The interest of psychiatry itself compelled him to know that it was not enough to reassemble the fragments of the shattered spirit among the men and women of his day and put them together into some sort of working order. He had at the same time to restore to them a sense of overall direction, a feeling of meaning. The process of reassembly, the re-integration itself indeed, was impossible without bringing back to his patients a feeling that they were instruments of meaning, however remote.

Healing the sick without a re-quickening of religion, as he put it to me, was "just not on". He used the word "heal" in the sense of "making whole". This indivisible concept of life was symbolised by the finding of the Holy Grail, the transcendental vessel (*graille* was an old Provencal word for a vessel) wherein the spirit, with all its apparent self-contradictions, could be poured and contained.

This approach made Jung an inspired healer in the ancient, classical sense, and inevitably compelled him to reach out in his work more and more towards grasping what greater end healing itself served. Even more urgent than the work of trying to heal became the search for what constituted the "wholeness" that was the condition of "holiness". As if from the moment of his first glimpse of this vast unconscious objective within, he saw the mentally deranged, and even the least disturbed of his patients, afflicted with the sickness of an entire age and culture. He saw us all, as it were, as guinea-pigs in a vast laboratory of Time. And he knew that the only valid answers could be answers extracted under the knife of the great vivisectionist of "meaning".

Jung no longer looked for the answer vicariously through the neuroses and mental sufferings of others. More and more he looked into his own deeply wounded self and into the impact of all history upon his own life, mind, and imagination. We are all compelled to be "mirrors" to one another of unknown, unacknowledged aspects in ourselves. The mote in our neighbour's eye is invariably a reflection of the beam in our own. From our own normality we look out upon the abnormalities in asylums and clinics. But they are a magnification of something similar in ourselves. The suffering there is something experienced on behalf of us all, pleading for recognition as a reflection both of inadequacies and possibilities of new being in us and the life of our time. It was Jung's greatness that he did not hesitate to use his experience as a psychologist as a mirror for himself. He set himself the task of knowing the averted face of his own nature reflected in this mirror. Accordingly no physician has taken the task of healing more seriously than he did. He was, in all this, quite alone. He lost Freud, the one man that could have been his peer. He was denounced and abandoned by most of his former colleagues. He had to face, alone, the unknown in this unconscious universe to which he had been brought. He was bombarded by symbols and images demanding that he should return with them from whatever fathomless depths they had come. Not only were his nights troubled with the strangest dreams but his days were made terrible with visions that shattered his calm at the most unlikely moments. He could not tell when and where and how a normal hour would not suddenly be deprived of light because of what he came to call "an invasion", or "intrusion" from this other unconscious where Freud's examples, and even his own past work, were of no help. He found himself turning to the child in himself as if instinct, too, was exhorting him to become like the child which the New Testament exhortation makes imperative. In this way he hoped to emerge from darkness into the light of which the Kingdom of Heaven is the supreme image. He went back to his early years when he had had a passion for playing with blocks and stones. It seemed absurd at his age, and for a man already so distinguished in worldly terms. But he accepted the instinct implicitly and began to gather stones on the lake shore by his house at Küsnacht and build miniature villages with them. He became a most impressive example of how the human capacity for achieving new meaning depends on our readiness to let life (in a sense) make fools of us.

I remember how impressed he was when I told him of a Stone-Age mythology in the deserts of Africa. There, the god-hero was always being made to look foolish in terms of his future self. Foolishness, simplicity, naivety almost to the point of Dostoievsky's concept of "idiocy", these Africans stressed, was a divinely inspired state and had to be served as such. So, through some such sort of god-given foolishness he was led too to a rediscovery and a visual continuation in stone of the dialogue started with stone long before in a vicarage garden on the banks of the Rhine. Despite the eyebrows that must have been raised at so mature and big a man playing childish games with such concentration and zeal, in the process he regained an inner certainty that he was on his own way again. This way he had always wanted to go in order to discover his own story or myth and, through that discovery, the relevant myth of his own time. From the moment of the completion of his first model village in lakeside stone (the houses huddled, as Anatole France once had observed of a French hamlet, "like chickens around a hen"), and the church itself, after great inner resistances, dedicated around an altar of a special lakeside reddish stone carved into the required shape by wind and water and time, Jung found himself at last in the right dimension for errant and adventure.

Even so, in order not to lose all identity, he had to remind himself over and over again of such everyday realities as that his name was Carl Gustav Jung; that he was a doctor of medicine; a psychiatrist of growing reputation; a man of standing in the everyday world; and that he lived at 228 Seestrasse, Küsnacht, Zürich, in a house on which was carved in the stone above the entrance, a saying that the Romans had borrowed from the Greeks, "Called or not called, God shall be there". Above all, Jung would reiterate constantly to himself that he was married to a woman he loved called Emma Rauschenbach, and had five children by her, and so on and on, turning these repetitive patterns of everyday recollections into exercises of discipline so that he should not be swept away from his present reality and down into the cataclysmic depths of his mind. Even these numbered footholds on everyday reality were soon significantly reduced by resignation of his professorship in 1913. His mind, so under attack, had no space or energy left for academic teaching. Indeed, for some years it had not the space even for scientific literature, and once his *Psychology of the Unconscious* was safely published, he had no heart or mind for writing. All was needed for this earthquake and eruption of spirit within himself.

He told me that suddenly he would see visions of a great tide of blood coming up over Europe from the north. It rose higher and higher until it lapped at the rim of the Alps like flood waters at the top of a dam. And in this vast swollen tide of blood was a porridge of mangled corpses and torn-off limbs until he could almost cry aloud at the horror of it. This particular vision with even more enigmatic variations in dreams was inflicted on him many times. It made no sense to him at all.

"So unaware was I at that moment", he told me, "that I did not seem to have noticed that this vision invariably came to me when I was travelling by train in the direction of my wife's home near Schaffhausen, which is on the German frontier. Therefore I overlooked one key to its significance as an image of a warning not only of private and universal peril but also a foreshadowing of its macrocosmic manifestation in the first World War . . ."

By the end of 1913 these pressures summoning him from a great new objective within were so many, and so great, that he could no longer ignore them. Although he recognised in the dreams and fantasies psychological material and patterns that he had encountered only in the most schizoid and psychotic of his patients, he felt he had to accept them also as part of himself. How could he pretend to cure others when he failed to recognise similar aspects in himself and so deal with them? He felt he owed it even more to his patients than himself not to shirk such fantastic issues. No-one could possibly know better than he the dangers of succumbing to such dark forces. He had seen defeat of this kind too often. Yet the feeling that he would be doing it for others as much as himself sustained him in his choice.

So, on the afternoon of December 12 of that year, 1913, sitting in his chair at his desk, he made one of the bravest decisions, I believe, ever recorded in the history of the human spirit. He committed himself absolutely to this equinoxial urge from within and in doing so apparently subordinating reason to unreason, and risking the sacrifice even of sanity to insanity. But he had always wanted to know how the human spirit would behave if deprived of all preconditioning and left entirely to itself. He had an intuition that no real beginning would be possible unless he had some experience of what mind and imagination did if allowed to act naturally and freely on their own. And he was about to find out in a way which a world which does not recognise the reality of "these mountains of the mind and their cliffs of fall, frightful, sheer, no-man-fathomed" of which Manley Hopkins had spoken, cannot measure. His whole spirit must have reeled with an inverted vertigo and horror of what he was about to do.

He put it to me once, without hint of laughter. "I said to myself, 'Well Jung, here you go.' And it was as if the ground literally gave way under me and I let myself drop."

That was the greatest of his many moments of truth, and so far did he fall and so unfamiliar and frightening was the material that he found as a result, that there were many moments when indeed it looked as if insanity might have overcome sanity. He told me how, for instance, just before the outbreak of the 1914–18 war he was summoned to address a meeting of British scientists in Scotland. He debated long and anxiously with himself whether he should go.

"I had to face seriously the chance of being called mad", he told me. "I argued with myself day after day whether it would be right to go. Whether, by going, I might not spread among a world audience what could be a mental contagion in myself. But I went, despite my doubts, delivered my paper and on the way back, in Holland, heard that the war had broken out . . . Tragic as it was, I felt immensely relieved in the sense that it came as some sort of cosmic explanation of the terrible visions of tides of blood that had been inflicted on me. It confirmed a feeling that nothing that had happened to me was not, in a sense, also happening to the life of my time. More than ever, therefore, I felt urged to investigate the link between the two levels of experience."

New as this confrontation was in the terms of the life of his and our day, there were parallels in world history, art and literature that help our own understanding of what happened. One thinks of course of Dante who, "mid-way through life found himself in a dark wood". Jung himself at that moment was approaching the half-way mark of his own life. He was in a season of himself to which Dante's metaphor was precisely applicable. Dante too had to go down into a netherworld to its uttermost depths. Only Dante's task was easier because he was, in a sense, supported by one of the most highly organised systems of religion the world has ever seen. The vast establishment of the Holy Church maintained a belief that the terrible world of the Divine Comedy did exist, and such events as Dante described were the facts of life. Without detracting for a moment from the quality of a poet of genius, Dante's imagination was following a way comprehensible not only to his peers, but in keeping with the religious tradition of his day. Yet this journey of Jung's, too, was essentially a Dante-esque journey, although the vehicle was not poetry and the object scientific, however religious in intent. Dante moreover had as an overall guide and protector his love of a woman whose face, once seen when a boy in the streets of Florence, changed the course of his whole life. All that this woman and this face evoked in him grew into a love that was total, universal, and outside space and time. It became a power in his spirit that made Dante always feel firmly directed and safe. As a result, even at moments when Virgil, who was Dante's immediate guide on the descent into hell, was full of fear, yet Dante could declare without a tremor of doubt, "I have no fear because there is a noble lady in Heaven who takes care of me."

All these, of course, are quintessential elements in the classical pattern of confrontation in so cosmic an order. Men in other idioms and contexts of civilisation and culture have been compelled to confront unknown aspects of themselves and their societies. They have been compelled to go down into their own deeps in order to rescue life from arrested aspects of itself which would lead only to disaster and death. And always, by dispensation of life, some feminine spirit from within their nature has been presented. Some messenger of love beyond the boundaries of appearances and knowledge has been summoned to act as guide. There was the example of Ariadne who provided Theseus with the golden thread which brought him out of the labyrinth in Crete after he had killed the beast which devoured the youth and beauty of Athens—the gleaming city—which had so nearly been deprived of the renewal and greater future self of which its youth and beauty were the image. And up to the present, with rare exceptions like that of Dante, the male spirit tended to abandon the feminine soul which had guided him so well and had served its purpose. It was left, forgotten and isolated on a rock-like aspect of itself in a sea of unknowing—even as Ariadne was left in an Aegean of her own tears over her betrayal. The same basic theme is reiterated when all the re-discovered feminine values of Greece, at its noblest, had joined the masculine of the Roman that was in the European spirit in order to bring about the immense flowering of being in the Renaissance. But these were rejected in the Reformation that followed. Leonardo da Vinci, so obsessed himself by the importance of the feminine in man that even his sexual instincts were transformed accordingly, gave this Ariadne pattern of redemption and abandonment by the masculine spirit its most authoritative visual expression yet in that heart-rending painting *The Virgin on the Rocks*, so prophetic of what was to come.

"You see", Jung was to say to me many years later, of this painting, "there is the eternally feminine soul of man where it belongs in the dark feminine earth. See how tenderly and confidently the Virgin holds in her arms the child—our greater future self. But make no mistake, da Vinci saw her there not only in her Christian role but also joined to her pagan aboriginal version. That is why the painting is so meaningful. She is not just Mary, the Mother of Jesus. She is also the feminine soul of man, the everlasting Ariadne. Her immediate uses fulfilled, she is forgotten and abandoned on the rocks ... Rediscovered, as she was briefly in the Renaissance, da Vinci's prophetic self already foresaw that she was about to be abandoned again. The wonder is that unlike Ariadne, the Virgin is not in tears. She is content, confident and un-resentful because she is also the love that endureth and beareth all things even beyond faith and hope. She knows that, in the end, the child will grow and all shall be well."

Jung, because the law of life in these matters is as timeless as it is impartial, also was guided in this going down by a spirit that was essentially feminine. But it was shattering proof of his originality and measure of his greatness that he came to this feminine spirit, in a way unknown to man before him. It is easy enough, after all, for the imag-ination of a man to follow a beautiful feminine face and form. But the feminine spirits that led Jung on his first essays were not beautiful at all. We have seen one representative already described by Freud as a "disagreeable and unpleasant old woman". And she was by no means the only one. There was long before that his own mother, whose in-fluence, as we have seen, outweighed that of his father. She was formidable and by no means cosy. As Blake said of Milton and his *Paradise Lost*, she too was "of the devil's party without knowing it". It was Jung's mother whose unconscious interest and sympathy for the aspects of reality as symbolised by the devil prompted her to give the boy Jung *Faust* to read. This turned out to be of much benefit to Jung, for it enabled him to enlarge its meaning in this deeper journey into himself.

Already as a student his eyes had been turned in the direction of what wandered beyond the boundaries of the intellectual interests of his day by that young woman who in ordinary life was of modest station but capable in trance-like moments of grand pronouncement in the manner of exalted ladies of the world of fashion. In his work at the Burghölzli and in his private practice, women held his interest in a way that no man ever did. It is no accident that in looking back just before his death, almost all the cases he discusses in his autobiography as being of special interest and importance for his development, were women. Nothing could make it clearer that the rejected feminine concerned him even more than the rejected masculine and evoked his powers of mind and imagination most powerfully.

It is not surprising therefore that his gigantic Dante-esque journey began by a pursuit of the fantasies of an American lady with the totally unmythical name of Miss Miller; and yet in its lack of singularity so appropriate, as she represented also "Miss Every-woman". Her personal conscious self was ultimately lost in the flood waters of an invasion from her unconscious. Yet, following the apparently dubious trail of this Miss Miller into an underworld of her own, Jung entered a labyrinth of mythology and history and came to write *The Psychology of the Unconscious*—the book which had finally caused Freud and his followers to break with Jung. This book already presupposed the existence of the as yet unexplored world of the collective unconscious, and the need for recognising its reality and activity. It might appear to be no more than a force in actuality and being, but in this work Jung already assumes its existence is an a-priori fact—together with the vital necessity of rediscovering it as a force in the life of man since his beginning. The urgent need to restore its living continuity up to our own time was increasingly laid bare. In particular this freed the myth of the heroic in the imagination of man from its archaic chains, and left it free and proportionate for a new lease of meaning and life in the modern world. No wonder that, as a personification of the symbolic given a life to live symbolically and not according the symbol, Freud and his followers were profoundly affronted.

That a frail, fanciful, feminine spirit could combine to lead rational man to any meaningful intent, of course, made no sense to anyone at the time. It also made Jung more suspect than ever. In a sense that was as understandable as it was inevitable. There was no exact parallel to confirm the validity of this approach in history nor even in the mythologies, legends and modern literature of the world. There were only hints and intimations of the worth of what Jung was attempting to do in the long neglected dream world and fairy-tales, dismissed by the grown-up world as food fit only to still the increasing hunger of children.

Fairy-tale ground is parable earth. Fairy tales, like the parables of the New Testament, are charged with the seeds of new being. The parable which spoke of the stone that the builders rejected becoming the stone of the building to come is rooted in the same earth as this story of Cinderella. Jung's imagination was obsessed with the Cinderella aspects of both mind and spirit. His nature predetermined that his truest seeking would follow the greatest of all our rejections, which is that of the feminine and which is made visible as a magic mirror in the metanoic story of Cinderella. There the beauty that serves as a symbol of the highest feminine values is disfigured by the ashes of burnt-out fires of the world of her suppressors. She wears the rags and tatters that are the uniform of rejection of the lowly, working figure unrecognised and despised in some sordid kitchen of life.

Already, in the course of his work in his asylum and even more in his vast private practice, Jung had rescued many a Cinderella spirit from some ignominious and dishonoured state and transformed it into a personality once more capable of walking, enlarged and reintegrated, in its own path. But even in this recognition there is a foreshadowing of a gift of perception, amounting almost to a power of divination not present in any of the prescriptions we have inherited in this regard. Jung clearly had both the capacity to see and also to act as a catalyst of transubstantiation and transformation which are the magic the godmother possessed in the parable of Cinderella. Like the godmother, he could recognise beauty in its ragged and tattered state long before it became obvious at the ball. This was his own special genius. It sets him apart and ahead of any others who have ventured into this enigmatic region.

It is easy enough to recognise the beauty of Cinderella transformed at the ball. It is easy enough, with the benefit of hindsight, to denounce the iniquity of her rejection. But only Jung, in our day, possessed this extraordinary capacity to see in advance beyond the dirt, the triviality and even the banality of appearances, and make it his most immediate and urgent task to reveal the vast potential of beauty suppressed and hidden underneath.

The achievement was all the more remarkable because this pattern of rejection has so much history to it. It seems to have been part of the mechanism of the spirit of man since the beginning of time. One searches in vain for a venture in which both the masculine and feminine values, both the man and the woman, have been honoured in their full proportions and each allowed their unimpeded role in life. The history of civilisation appears to be a sorry, one-sided history of domination by man. One can, of course, point to brief moments of matriarchy where an archaic, suffocating femininity produced another disastrous imbalance of spirit which has presided over our destinies. But almost invariably the basic cultural pattern has been the work of man. Whole areas of history are darkened by the ignorance of men of the truth that they can only create through the feminine in their own natures. Similarly they procreate in the world without through woman. As the spirit of Dante glowed in all that was evoked in him by the face of Beatrice, so, significantly, the most creative moments in history have come about when the imagination of man was alive to the reality of the warm, loving, caring values of his feminine self. The height of Heaven to which Dante's spirit ascended corresponded exactly to the depths of Hell and Purgatory through which the thread of his own feminine nature safely led him.

This truth in the dimension of the civilisation wherein the European spirit has its roots, however displaced its appearance today, is illustrated in its most striking manner by the difference between Greek and Roman cultures. Both have their origin in one and the same story or myth which, joined to the Hebraic theme as set out in the Bible, was to provide the greatest formative values of the complex of the western spirit. Both Greek and Roman cultures had a common point of departure in the Trojan War. This represents the struggle to establish what role the feminine is to play in the life of man. The Helen about whom the war was fought is, possibly, the first non-biological stage beyond Eve, and introduces the evolution of a fundamental image reflecting man's profound inner dependence on the feminine and his need to give it a value uniquely its own in the law and order of his being. But it is essentially a war fought in the external world about the feminine in her external role. Helen is fundamentally only a masculine reflection of the feminine, and the war is waged between men about the role that she is to be allowed to play in their lives. Helen herself, the woman as woman, is never consulted. She is taken for granted with such unawareness that tragedy, not surprisingly, overtakes almost everyone involved in the war, victors as well as vanquished.

What adds even more to the significance is that the battle takes place between two groups of men who appear to have been born of two opposite psychological types. This is a division in the human spirit which seems to run like a great rift in mother earth herself, from the beginning of time to this day. It compelled some men to be born what Jung came to call "extraverted" whereas others were "introverted".

Some belonged to the Classical approach to reality; others to the Romantic. One had an Apollonian attitude inevitably dedicated to the light of reason and an urge for shape, form and the fashioning of all things with regard to law, order and precision, so as, ultimately, to contain and preserve all with the greatest possible symmetry. The other had a Dionysian urge, committed more to movement, change and the abiding rhythm of things: the dance of the stars and their constellations, and the swell in the swinging sea. It was concerned not so much with the how and why of reality but with a total involvement in the feeling and tide of emotions, impatient with any barriers of mind and spirit that would impede their onward movement. So one is profoundly committed to the world without and, naturally, is represented by an expeditionary force that crosses the sea in black ships to do battle on the great plain of Troy under the foredoomed Agamemnon. The other is the natural, romantic, Dionysian way which has already done violence to the world of law and order by snatching away its highest feminine value, Helen of Menelaus, from her lawful husband, and manifesting its introverted spirit by taking refuge within the great walls of Troy, an image of spirit seeking protection from within. The Trojans lose the war. They lose it not because their approach is less real or lacks courage but because it is less aware than that of their opponents. The difference in awareness being symbolised by the Greek ingenuity in inventing their Trojan Horse and the inferior awareness of the Trojans by their failure to see through the device. There again is another emphasis on how dearly man pays for his lack of awareness and how it is always, as in the Oedipus story, through his lack of awareness that Fate is compelled to punish him with tragedy.

Out of this protracted war two journeys emerge, allegories, as it were, of the essential quest in the spirit of man. Indeed it is as if in the story of these journeys we have the original blueprint of the spirit that was to make Greece, and its opposite that was to build Rome. The Greek allegory is contained in the voyage of Odysseus and his followers. Why Odysseus, seeing that he was by no means the greatest of the heroes who fought on the great plains of Troy? He is instinctively chosen, perhaps, because he represented the hero in his legitimate, individual and most diversified proportions more accurately than any other. Others had more courage and strength; were more compulsive and dedicated warriors, or wiser and more experienced as was Old Nestor. But Odysseus had all of these qualities and none in excess. All aspects were subject to his awareness of reality, and an intelligence acute enough for him to be referred to as the fox. His advice was constantly sought, and it was he who ultimately thought up the fatal Wooden Horse, and he is obviously chosen for being so many-sided and individual without hubris. Most important of all, perhaps, he was an island prince from Ithaca where a beautiful, loyal feminine self, Penelope, awaited him.

This island is an image of supreme symbolic importance. This Jung had already suspected from his own fantasies as a boy when he walked from home to school on the banks of the Rhine, imagining a narrow isthmus of rock rising out of the river and transforming it in his fantasy into an island by cutting a canal between it and the mainland so that he could safely build a fortified city of his own upon it. The imagined island was an image of a unique self in man, where a singular totality of the mighty activity he had called God as a child, could be experienced. This piece of land surrounded by water was a symbol of the ultimate in Jung's seeking, as it was the ultimate too of Odysseus. So the whole *Odyssey*, when read, is a supreme symbolic representation of the most meaningful adventure of the spirit of which individual man is capable. Every stage of Odysseus's journey back to fulfilment with Penelope in his island self represents faithfully the most ancient search of humanity, as in the *Pilgrim's Progress*, or the life of some Sanyassim taking to the road in Hindu India towards the resolution and transfiguration of life which, in Christianity, is called salvation. John Donne, the great Elizabethan poet, was only partially right when he wrote: "No man is an island to himself, we are all part of the main." Every man is, as Odysseus knew, an island to himself joined to others by a main, but a main that is not land but sea. It is not surprising that one of Dante's most significant encounters in the underworld of his *Divine Comedy* was with the spirit of Odysseus, an encounter which exposes in a great poetic statement how Odysseus felt he had failed not in the completion of his own journey, which was so truly fulfilled, but in failing to make the collective values of his age, as represented by his men, his own. Hence these lines resounding still like a call to cavalry on a trumpet at dawn:

"Brothers", I said, "who now have reached the West
By conquering a hundred thousand dangers,

Deny not to that little span of life—
The brief allotment of your waking hours
That yet remains to you—experience
Of that unpeopled world behind the sunset.
Consider from what noble seed you spring:
You were created not to live like beasts,
But for pursuit of virtue and of knowledge!"*

As for Penelope, she is perhaps the greatest personification yet of the soul constant in man provided he endures to the true end in his search to rejoin her. It is precisely because this journey of Odysseus and his reunion with the eternal feminine that is Penelope, is the blueprint of the Greek story that made Greece, I believe, more creative than Rome.

That this is not a subjective reading of the *Odyssey* is proved, I believe, by the fact that Samuel Butler was so impressed by the feminine element in the *Odyssey* that he was convinced it was written by a woman in revenge for what seemed to him the caricature of femininity that men had made of woman in Helen. He travelled all over the Aegean in Odysseus's wake and spent a small fortune trying to prove that the *Odyssey* was a woman's answer to the Man's conception of "woman" deployed in the *Iliad*. Of course, literally, he was wrong in this. But he was right in the sense that the *Odyssey* was conceived of all that was best in the fundamentally feminine psyche of man.

How different the Roman blueprint which, too, is a prescribed voyage. It is the painful, warring, bloody journey of another individual, Aeneas. From the beginning the mark of an unmistakable inadequacy, it seems, is fatally placed upon him. With Troy in flames and himself in danger of capture by the Greeks, he has an opportunity of rescuing either the wife he loves, or his old father Anchises, from death. He rescues his old father, carrying him out on his back. He leaves his wife to the Greeks and is forever commended for his choice. But from that moment on the Roman spirit is hampered because it is made to carry an ancient father on its back to the end. Moreover Aeneas rejects the feminine not just once but twice. He leaves Dido of Carthage, who succoured, protected and re-equipped him, desolate behind him to commit suicide over so ungrateful an abandonment. Aeneas sails on, obsessed with one purpose, to re-establish a great city, far greater than the Ilium left behind in ashes. But he did this with such a violent swing over into the fatal opposite, namely reconstructing it

* From *The Divine Comedy*, translated by Lawrence Grant White. New York, Pantheon Books, 1948.

in the totally extraverted form that was to become the model for the Roman empire. Of course, the achievements of this empire too were to be so considerable that to this day one can still detect all over Europe an almost unbearable nostalgia for Rome at its best. And yet it never measured up to Greece, so that one understands why Cicero felt compelled to warn the Romans when they set out to conquer Greece that they would only succeed in vanquishing that which would in turn vanquish them. Athens, not Rome, still seems to me to be the incomparable lighthouse of the spirit. It presupposes the vital honouring, in equal proportions, of the masculine and feminine in being that we have betrayed in our own Western history. It was this which Jung was setting out to rediscover and restore to the sterile, unprocreative spirit of my day.

Greece, and not Rome, was the natural earth of Jung's mind also. It is significant that, with all his immense interest in antiquity, he never went to it, although he went twice to Ravenna; and once on a visit to Pompeii. Once, out of an inner sense of uncompleted historical duty, he went to a travel agency to buy a ticket for Rome. But he was overcome by an attack of fainting at the ticket counter and never went. It was, I believe, too partial a place for him to endure, although he obviously had other reasons for not going as well which he has expressed at length in print. But he knew, even then, as we should know more clearly now, that we are caught up in another Roman moment of decline and fall in the spirit of man, wherein worship of the material and subservience to the value of power has driven the feminine and its accompanying love, out of life. The rebirth of the lost feminine principle and its reliance on love as the only true transformer of inadequacy and imprecision of spirit, is as urgent today as it was two thousand years ago on the first Christmas Day in the Roman colony of Palestine. Day by day the life of the individual is increasingly threatened by a proliferation of collective values and worldly power. The State, like the city of Rome, is taking the place of God in man.

I have elaborated on this illustration for it is one of the few to which I have access in some proved, historical detail. All other realisations of the feminine in man, however they continue to dazzle and amaze us, are brief and exceptional moments in the history of our societies and mind. They are the result of unusually questioning and inspirational phases of religion and art, that are as short as they are bright. But even when man was joined to all that is feminine in himself, another kind of rejection of the feminine was still at work in volcanic and unknown areas within him and in the life of his time. It was these areas that Jung was to uncover. But he still had to earn the right of so fateful a discovery by the most harsh of journeys, and the most painful of apprenticeships in a new deep of himself.

As Jung "let go" and fell abysmally, he landed in an area of his spirit so dark and deep that it was as if he stood where the source of all life gushes out as a fountain of blood, red as the fire which later he was compelled to paint. Aspects of the Western spirit that he and the world had long assumed dead were rediscovered alive and in a personified form. This included his own primitive aboriginal self, magnetic and full of meaning in a re-assumption of a feeling of belonging to an endless process of birth, death and rebirth. Within days, he had again, and of most immediate personal relevance, one of his greatest dreams. He rediscovered in it the personification of his cultural heroic self in the great Siegfried, of German mythology, whom, to his horror, he had to kill. But once awake, and capable of analysing the dream, it was plain how symbolic was the call to kill in the dream. The death to be inflicted on Siegfried was to enable him to be reborn in another dimension. Siegfried had represented too archaic a concept of the heroic in man. He was not at all the illuminated modern one that Jung's imagination was pursuing. He represented the German hubris whose maxim was "where there's a will there's a way". Siegfried was the central figure in a drama of wilful, rationalistic man trying to impose himself, as were the Germans, on the entire worldly scene—the process so evident ever since the rise of Brandenburg into Prussia and the Prussian domination of the entire German scene. It was this precisely which had so disturbed Burckhardt that when the news of the crowning of the first Kaiser Wilhelm at Versailles after the Franco-Prussian War reached him, he remarked sadly, "That is the doom of Germany." He should have added that it could be the doom of Western man as well, unless he mended his spirit.

Somehow this process had to be stopped and changed, both on the collective and individual level—as the theme of the killing and rebirth in Jung's dreams. Above all, Jung had the clarity and honesty of spirit to recognise that Siegfried's hubris had also been his own. In a sense he had been wilful towards all this strange new material coming at him. His own attitude had to become more humble and accepting than he had allowed it to be. As a result, he came not in a dream of sleep but most significantly, as in that initial vision of God and the Cathedral of Basle, to a revelation, in his own daylight imagination, which is perhaps a first great portent of sanity and ultimate wholeness in the long Odyssean voyage of himself, and as such it deserves closer examination.

Jung had, of course, long ceased to rely purely on dream material for his advancement. He had taught himself to give an unimagined freedom to his imagination to go wherever it had to go on this late descent into his own netherworld. One day he went deeper than before, so deep that he might have been in the land of the dead, until he discovered on a steep slope of rock two figures, an old man with a white beard, and a beautiful young girl. He went nearer and saw that they also had a black serpent with them which immediately took a great liking to Jung. Jung said the old man called himself Elijah. He was, perhaps, another personification of the "wise old man" in the human spirit. The girl, who called herself Salome, was blind. This was a visualisation of the feminine element in man that Jung was to name the "anima" in his future delineations of the patterns in the objective world of the collective unconscious. The snake, since it appeared in many an heroic myth as counterpart of the hero, was a symbolic confirmation of the fact that the dream was concerned with a healing and mythological content. It is possible that Jung somewhere else may have gone into this encounter in greater detail and interpreted its meaning fully. If so I am unaware of it. Finding this encounter, as I do, of critical concern to his future development, as well as of great importance to the life of our time, I cannot leave it where Jung casually abandons it in his *Memories, Dreams, Reflections*.

Up to this moment Jung had not hesitated to relate the mythological to the personal in his own life. Indeed, we have seen that, only a few days before in the dream wherein Siegfried was killed, he felt compelled to rebuke himself by admitting his own personal responsibility in the dream. It was necessary to realise what Siegfried represented in the German spirit and the *weltanschauung* of the day. But Jung's duty was only half done if he did not identify also with the message so poignantly and fiercely directed at himself. This he had done all along. But Salome was no less a mythological character than Siegfried. In many ways she was more meaningful since she was not Germanic, but an emanation of the whole Greek, Hebraic, Roman and near-Eastern complex of culture that was Western. Above all she was a feminine figure of whom there had been a notable scarcity in Jung's dreams and fantasies up to the present. It is true that there was an early portent in the dream figure of a young girl and a dove, image of the Holy Spirit, in an Italian Renaissance setting. Here the girl was not only clearsighted but had embraced Jung tenderly, as if to say "Whatever happens, I shall be there at the end, for I, child that I am, am mother of your future self." But that apart there was, so far as I know, no visualisation of the feminine until this profound encounter with Salome.

I would have thought that his own personal associations with Salome, therefore, were as important as were those with Siegfried. Moreover Jung had repeatedly warned that to have such encounters and not to draw from them the necessary lesson for one's own life is as dangerous as it is unethical. But here for some undisclosed reason, he is uncharacteristically curt and reticent. One cannot avoid asking oneself, therefore, what the encounter meant to him personally? And as he does not provide the answer, one must try to do so as best one can. For I, too, believe that what happens to us on a mythological level must be considered also in its impact on our miserable selves.

As far as the Old Man and the Snake are concerned the answer is not over-difficult. In Jung the ancient called Elijah is the reappearance of his long suppressed Number Two personality in a much more mature and dynamic form than before. Indeed, I feel this to be proved by the fact that Jung's imagination seized instantly on Elijah and he evolved another and even greater ancient out of it. He took all the experience of this pattern in the Ka of the long mythological years of ancient Egypt—the Egyptian period lasted twice as long as our own Christian culture has done—and with Elijah made it join its Biblical and Classical evolution to become Philemon, the host of the gods, who accompanies Jung from then on to his end. This Egyptian experience, I believe, was necessary for the wholeness of this pattern in Jung of the "ancient of Days"—it was not called Elijah for nothing. Elijah appeared to stress that the ancient, in the Old Testament form, still had a tendency to fly off the earth—as Elijah had done in a fiery chariot. An aspect was attempting to go straight up to Heaven and so bypass the agonising renewal through death which is indispensable to our transformation. That this is not over-fanciful seems clear. There are references that Jung made later in his letters that are not without a certain dismissive irony of the "curious flight" of Elijah. But the Egyptian experience, the Ka, is a far earlier one possessing a *gravitas* that the Elijah aspect lacked. This *gravitas* was necessary for the concept to become the "greater personification" that Jung called Philemon. In fact, Philemon imposed himself on Jung with so charged a vision as being an old man, with kingfisher blue wings, the horns of a bull, and four keys in hand, that he was compelled to paint and repaint him.

Henceforth Philemon accompanied him as an archangelic guide throughout his journey, as Virgil had been for Dante. He represented superior insight to Jung and we shall find him in due course honoured, calmly and authoritatively installed in the tower that Jung was to build in his house of stone at Bollingen on the upper shores of Lake Zürich. From him, Jung says, he was to learn real psychic objectivity. It was Philemon who taught Jung that what he had regarded as his own thoughts were not only his own. They were also objective events within him. He was not their creator but observer and, at most, guardian and pilot in the world without.

All this had the most creative consequences for Jung. So too had the serpent. The serpent not only proved that he had re-established contact with his deepest instinctual self, because that is the image the much persecuted and reviled snake has been compelled to bear. Yet, if considered with all the positive and compensatory associations attached to the snake, as, for instance, its closeness to, and in, the earth, Jung stood there in the presence of vital elements that would assist in healing the rift within himself and within his time. These latter associations explain why a snake to this day is curled, as a badge of healing, around the Hippocratic staff of medicine.

But what of Salome? Jung confesses that he considered her in all her Biblical and other aspects. But he does not say what they were. He only hints at the fact that she is an image of *Eros*, the principle of the love and feeling values of life. Then he abandons her. The next time there is any reference to the feminine in himself it is to the dubious image of a sophisticated lady patient of his, highly endowed but pathological, who tries to persuade him that this encounter with the unconscious is an artistic engagement and that he is not a scientist so much as an artist. The gap between Salome and this other insidious feminine sophisticate is too wide even for a spirit as great as Jung's to have straddled unaided and alone. The need for there to have been a bridge between these two stages is only too self-evident.

One can believe that it is no accident that Salome was young, beautiful *and* blind. And no idle chance that she was called Salome. It is true, as Jung says, that such relationships appear frequently in the history of sages in their old age, such as the dancing girl in the life of Lao-Tzu. Salome as we know was a dancing girl too, and the story and the legends surrounding her are so familiar that Jung could not have failed to see the obvious personal associations involved. For him to say that Salome was blind because the anima is incapable of seeing, is really the unconscious way of confessing that he himself could not see the meaning of Salome.

For the anima, this feminine in man, as he himself has shown us so many times, is full of potential womanly vision uniquely her own since she personifies all the experience of the feminine in the life of man. One has only to consider the life of Dante and the role of Beatrice (who was his anima), to see how far from blind this aspect can be. How could Dante safely have accomplished his journey down into hell and up again to Heaven without her, for all the expertise of his Number Two, his Philemon, the Virgil in those subliminal regions of the spirit.

One is compelled to remember that it was Jung's original gift of genius that up to now he had allowed the rejected, despised, deprived and persecuted feminine in life to be his guide. It had done its work accurately and so well that it had brought him as far as it could without fatally wounding him, as it itself had been hurt. It is indeed as if in the vision of Salome, all that had guided his past is saying to him, "Look at that girl. That is what life has done to her. It has denied us her own feminine vision and so deprived us of meaning. That is what is wrong with your so-called civilisation. That is the wrong so great that even *you* have been maimed likewise. We can do no more now. You know now what the trouble is and knowing it, you ignore it at your peril."

Jung, being the man he was, could not have overlooked the fact that it was Salome who demanded, and received on a platter, the head of John the Baptist, the foreteller of the coming of Christ. In doing that of course she *was* psychologically blind. She was failing her own feminine role in life by making it impossible for the renewal of life and realisation of a divine self in man—a selfhood which Jung stresses and re-stresses—Christ was the most dynamic and complete living example as well as the most transfigurative symbol accessible to the western spirit. But Salome failed history and her own positive feminine self because of a Roman man-dominated partiality of spirit. Even in history she was the spoilt daughter of a powerful Roman Pro-Consul, exercising her feminine pull on the father in the most negative and archaic way. What therefore in this encounter is Salome telling Jung and us? Perhaps that Jung's own feminine self, though possessing the beauty which is the image of her creative potential for man, is far too immature either for his or for her age? Too immature also for their mutual good? Indeed so immature is she as to be blind enough, in her position of natural power, to prevent him from realising in himself his own vision of individual totality and selfhood.

It is the moment of the greatest danger in Jung's encounter with his unconscious. This danger, which accompanies all opportunities of renewal to such an extent that the ancient Chinese symbolic ideogram for "crisis" and "opportunity" are the same. So there is this urgent warning implicit in the blindness of Salome. It suggests that unless she is made to see, Jung's own venture is doomed, despite the healing presence of the snake, and the protective wisdom of Philemon. Jung, I believe, unaided and alone as he had been in his protracted self-analysis (something which he had stressed throughout his psychiatric years was far too dangerous to be permitted in the careers of others who followed the same vocation), clearly had come to a point where not only could he go no further without help from someone else, but also he was in danger of failing in the task he had set himself. The deranged feminine had done its work. Now a guide of a positive and integrated feminine self, with eyes wide open and alerted, was needed.

Yet it is significant that though there is a great deal more to be heard about Philemon and his role, there is no more mention of Salome, except for one casual mention some two years later, as someone still blind. Thereafter she vanishes forever. And when Jung resumes the theme of his feminine self again, it shows her to be in a state of increasing maturity and, finally, so fulfilled and resolved that he himself can declare that he has no need of any further personification or imaginary dialogues with her. That this was possible is probably due to the fact that a fine and illuminated feminine instrument was beside him to externalise Salome for him and take over the role of a conscious feminine guide. There was at hand a true feminine mirror without trace of error or falsehood beside him to reflect the feminine nature so blind and hidden in himself. Moreover she was a mirror, as it were, of his own making. For her Jung had been the Moses who had led her to a promised land which he had not yet been allowed to enter himself.

Jung had always stressed that, after Freud had disowned him, all his friends and colleagues had abandoned him, except Riklin and Maeder. He meant by this that all the men he valued, except those two, forsook him. He does not stress that, in fact, all the women around him stood fast. Not a single one of them, of any consequence, abandoned him on the march or even fell out of step. They were the nucleus of what was to become one of the most remarkable groups of gifted women ever assembled round a single man, however great. I was to meet and become friends with a number of them and was profoundly impressed by their quality as well as their unwavering support to Jung. But at this blind, Salome moment in himself, there were two who stood out above the rest.

First, of course, there was his own beautiful and extraordinarily gifted wife, Emma. Engaged as she was at this moment, however, not only with bringing up a family of five, but wife also to a great man involved in the battle of a lifetime with himself, she hardly had the space either of time or mind to give Jung the kind of help that he needed at this point. Nor did she possess, as yet, the necessary qualifications. She had never been a patient of Jung's, nor indeed of any other man.

Happily, however, there was another woman who was a close friend and possessed all the necessary qualifications. She was Toni Wolff, with whom my wife studied and worked in Zürich. She is not mentioned in Jung's *Memories*, and one understands the omission in measure, because the book is a record only of quintessence. Jung's own personal relationships are deliberately not a part of it. Jung's gift inflicted a special form of loneliness in him that was a part of an over-whelming compulsion to serve a cause of universal meaning. The cause always had to come before men and women. Yet from what I know of such people both in my own life and history, I find it remark-able that, being so heavily burdened with historic occasion and responsibility before life and time, Jung yet gave so freely and gener-ously of himself to family, friends and fellow sufferers. He himself was keenly aware of the sacrifice demanded of him in terms of human relationships. Talking to me he once compared himself to a man com-mitted to fight on a desperate battlefield. Friends and companions were shot down all round him. Yet he was not allowed to pause to nurse their wounds as he longed to do, but had to move on deeper into the battle, if it were ever to be won.

In his autobiography, concerned with the cause and the battle, there is no pretence that it is also a full account of his life. It is, as the title implies, memories, dreams and reflections—a session of a great old soldier remembering the battles he has fought. His own wife is barely mentioned and his feelings over her death, of which I have a moving record in a long letter he wrote me, are not admitted. There is not even the barest reference to the woman who went with him all the way on this stage of his journey. With so many other associations of great distinction that are not referred to, perhaps one should not be surprised by this omission. Yet I, for one, feel compelled to mention Toni Wolff in enough detail to explain the significance of her role to Jung at this critical moment. It is all the more necessary because, how-ever much I understand and sympathise with it, there is still what I find to be reprehensible silence about her among the persons who are alive and knew her. They behave as if she did not render the particular service that she did to Jung, and therefore to psychology. One of the most notable among the exceptions has been Dr C. A. Meier who has seen to it that Toni Wolff's written contributions to psychology are preserved, collected, properly edited and published, so that her distinguished record in this regard, at least, is secure.

But of the woman herself little that is authoritative and authentic is said, and less still is known, to those who have come to carry on the work of Jung. All that is left is gossip and speculation which as always tends to be negative in these regards and does less than justice to a noble story. The situation is made more obscure by the fact that Jung burnt all his letters to Toni Wolff and all her letters to him, so that history forever lacks their witness to how they, the immediate trinity of Emma, Jung himself, and Toni Wolff, conducted with such honesty, courage and dignity what, at any time, must be the most difficult of relationships, but at that Victorian–Edwardian hour almost unendurably so. One knows of course all the excuses for the silence because those who knew Jung at this period were only too painfully aware of how he was constantly under attack from the outside world up to his end. They would have seen in any open discussion of Toni Wolff's role a kind of delivery of just another weapon of attack into the hands of Jung's enemies. But Jung is dead and that time is long since over, and no full account of the man is possible without inclusion of Toni Wolff and a proper and decent assessment of her role. I would go further and say that I believe all that is true in Jung in so inspired a measure (and I deliberately use the historical present because I am certain the truth of the man is so great that it will stand) despite the withholding of his consent implied by burning of letters which must have been an agonising reminder of suffering, confusion and near defeat, would demand that it is done.

I think I have an inkling of why the letters were burnt, not for any unworthy motive but out of the most understandable of human reasons: he could not bear the thought of strange, impersonal eyes of future generations prying into what had been of such intimate, immediate, desperate and secret concern to him. I believe the key to understanding is in the word secret. All that happened took place in an area of the personality where the secret must be kept forever of the growth of the future self in the presence of the *numinous*, since no-one, except the *self* committed utterly to it, can know the reality of the experience without destroying it—a principle we have already seen so clearly orchestrated and obediently observed in Jung's own childhood and adolescence and initiation into manhood. He has kept it thus, I believe, so that we can understand it according to our several capacities not only with the kind of "not-understanding" he mentioned before.

but also understanding through our own need of a secret that is sacred and vital to the growth of our own self.

I believe this to be true all the more because of something he wrote on love to Mary Mellon who had been a patient of his and to whom he was especially devoted. The letter seems to me to gain in point because it was written during the dark night of the Western spirit we call World War II. "You should come up to the level of such understanding whose vehicle is love and not the mind. This love is not transference [a psychological state of projection frequent between patient and psychiatrist and which Jung always guarded against] and it is no ordinary friendship or sympathy. It is more primitive, more primeval and more spiritual than anything we can describe. . . . That upper floor is no longer you or I, it means many, including yourself and anybody whose heart you touch. There is no distance but immediate presence. It is an *eternal* secret—how shall I ever explain it?" And the key words are "eternal secret" and confession of his inability to explain. Yet though one cannot explain the "eternal secret" one can understand and explain the inability and indeed is forced to if one's evaluation of the man is not to be maimed.

And I assert the right of freedom to follow the meaning which the omission has for each of us with greater confidence because he told me he emerged from the long years of his encounter with the collective unconscious convinced that it had enriched him so that his life was no longer his own or his family's but belonged henceforth to the generality of man. All that battle and suffering and shaping of unknown forces ultimately had meaning for him because it was a specific of experience that was capable of transformation in a great universal.

As for Toni Wolff the woman, who was to be his companion, she was a great and rare spirit; one of the few most truly Patrician in Jung's immediate company of collaborators. She had a courage and vision of conduct perhaps alien to the *haute* Swiss and international bourgeoisie who surrounded Jung. She brought with her what was best in the spirit of a family with a proud aristocratic continuity that could be traced back into the early Middle Ages, so much so that she struck one more as a Bernese phenomenon than a native of Zürich. One uses this parallel because in this country of city states, as I have described Switzerland earlier on, Berne too was unique. Basle might have had more intellect and sense of history; Zürich more of the life of commerce and exchange with the material world; Lucerne more of the evolution of a Swissness from the foremost aboriginal Swiss stock; Geneva sees its role as the fortress of the conscience and

spirit of the uniquely French contribution to Switzerland; but in
Berne, where the Latin and Germanic in the Swiss character met
and were united as a double-edged one, there grew in time a truly
classical, aristocratic approach to life. The Bernese too thought themselves a cut above the rest, but a cut not of the qualities of which the
others boasted but of superior "breeding" which imposed responsibilities that made them almost the most serious of citizens in a naturally
serious country.

Toni Wolff had in full measure all that is best among these attributes,
oversimplified as they are here, perhaps all the more impressively
because they had to be maintained in the paradoxical context of an
increasingly naturalistic and *arriviste* city. She was an aristocrat of mind
and spirit and capable for a role in Jung's life outside the realm of the
eminently respectable. Anyone who has read her essay on the psychology of type in woman will instantly recognise how conceivable and
natural it was to her. In this essay she added to Jung's future definition
of the four functions a concept of woman born into four types: the
woman as mother and wife; as Hetaira—companion and friend of
man; as Amazon—the woman with a calling of her own, self-contained
and independent of man; and finally woman as Medium—at home on
the frontiers of the unconscious and conscious in the human spirit, as
unegotistical in her seeking as the Amazon tends to be egotistic, if not
egotistical.

She herself seems to me clearly to have been born an inspired
Hetaira, and one cannot read what she has written on this type without
experiencing it as reflection also of her inmost self. In this essay and
others, she was to make her own contribution to Jung's concepts of
the masculine in woman and the nature of feminine psychology which
were hidden even to such a man, precisely because out of an inherited
sense of a special right of breeding, she placed herself outside the
restriction of the conventional.

Even her clothes proclaimed the manner of the person she was. In
an unworldly society such as that which surrounded Jung, no-one paid
undue regard to style and indulgence in dress. Toni Wolff was always
a notable exception for she was always fastidiously dressed. She carried
herself with natural elegance, had a formidable intelligence, and a
general air of being something select and special. Even the bone
beneath the skin of a fine, distinctively modelled face seemed to be of
an unusual precision and delicacy. I myself remember above all her
wide dark eyes. I thought when I first met her that they were eyes
capable of seeing in the dark.

Great as Toni Wolff's services were in the conscious orchestration of Jung's psychological themes, I do not think they can compare with the service she rendered Jung in an inner way. I, for one, believe the world, on this account, owes her a gratitude which no-one yet has attempted to assess, let alone openly express. She was so singularly qualified for this purpose because she had come to Jung originally as a patient. Few know what was his diagnosis of her condition. All one is permitted to say is that it must have been affliction of stresses proportionate to the meaning that came out of it. That presupposes something considerable. As a result, at the moment when Jung decided to "let himself drop", she was the only person capable of understanding, out of her own experience and transfiguration, what Jung was taking upon himself. This world of the unconscious which he was entering as a man, she had already inhabited and endured as a woman. Thanks to Jung's guidance she had re-emerged, an enlarged and reintegrated personality.

Already for some years she had accompanied Jung and Emma as an honoured colleague to all sorts of psychological conferences, and was a co-delegate to the famous conference with Freud and his followers in 1911, the first of its kind ever to be held. In the official photograph taken of the occasion she is conspicuous among the other participants, staring wide-eyed with a wondering and totally un-preconceived glance at the camera.

As a person whose thinking and intuitive functions were her superior attributes, she appears the one person in the group to look almost overwhelmed by the importance of the breakthrough into a new level of human awareness to which the occasion testifies. Yet she was so innocent of the exacting role which was to be imposed on her later that one is strangely moved on her account. I say "exacting" but can hardly avoid adding adjectives like "harsh" and "cruel" because I believe that she suffered much. She was by nature too proud to complain. In any case she found reward enough in the meaning she had gained in being Jung's most intimate companion and guide during those long, protracted years of his critical, and at times, psychologically speaking, dangerous moments of his encounter with the "blind Salome forces" of his collective unconscious. But the dignity and willingness with which she accepted this role and the apparent ease with which she ignored the envy of a world jealous of her special relationship with Jung should not be allowed to disguise the staggering burdens it all imposed upon her.

I have known men and women who were hosts to Jung and Toni

Wolff when they travelled on psychological missions outside Switzerland. They spoke, sometimes, of their dismay when they surprised Toni Wolff, in the intimacy of their homes, repeatedly in the grip of great and demonstrable distress. I doubt whether any man is capable of a full comprehension of what she was called on to endure, let alone measure her achievement. I have a feeling that to do her justice in this regard it needs a woman aware of the burden of the projection of man's own blind and demanding feminine self which her sex has had to carry throughout the ages. Yet even a man can guess at the scale of both stress and achievement through the difficulties he himself encounters in being the subject of the projection of others. This ruthless mechanism of the projection of that which is rejected in a personality on to some other suitable and convenient human being demanded in the first instance (in a nature so profoundly introverted as that of Jung) an externalised form that would not give way under its weight. Indeed, it demanded a living personification in the world without sufficiently faithful and authoritative in its own right not to surrender to the forces that invested it; nor to disintegrate under doubt of the other being who could so use it.

Throughout these long years Toni Wolff stood fast, and in the process not only sustained the full weight of Jung's undiscovered feminine self, enabling him thereby to live it out through her into maturity. But inevitably she became, also, the vulnerable intermediary between himself and his embattled shadow. Both these burdens, of course, were proportionate to the man and the greatness of his seeking. When, years later, the time came when the projection could be withdrawn and received back with honour into Jung's awareness, and when the heavy problem of the shadow was firmly positioned between his own immeasurably broadened shoulders, it must have been a moment of almost miraculous resolution for them both.

Yet one wonders if at that moment of what appears to an outsider so great a victory for the human spirit, Toni Wolff did not find herself, as it were, to use one of the most sinister euphemisms of our day, suddenly redundant. She certainly would have been less than human had she not been tempted to feel so. But whatever problems she had, she accepted them as her own, and ready material with which she should look for work. Indeed, with the insight gained into her own nature and that of men through this close alliance in Jung's battle, she became self-employed with an effect greater than is already acknowledged, as will soon be evident when her last collected works and papers are published.

What she meant to Jung on that perilous journey can perhaps be summed up best by something he told me towards the end of his life. He was carving in stone, which had become his favourite visual medium, some sort of memorial of what Emma Jung and Toni Wolff had brought to his life. On the stone for his wife he was cutting a Chinese symbol meaning, "She was the foundation of my house". On the stone intended for Toni Wolff, who had died first, he wanted to inscribe another Chinese character to the effect that she "was the fragrance of the house". The imagery of meaning of this ancient Chinese ideogram is a direct visual expression and part of the symbolism of an element in the human spirit which informs it of what, though still far off and invisible, is inevitable and leads him towards it.

Finally and most conclusive of all, there is the testimony of Emma Jung herself. Just before she died she told a friend of mine close to both herself and her husband, "I shall always be grateful to Toni for doing for my husband what neither I nor anyone else could have done for him at a most critical time."

This gap, this silence then, is the guiding and the bridging that was Toni Wolff in Jung's hour of trial and peril. She was the significant outside aid that brought him to total emancipation from the negations personified by a "blind Salome". Now he was armed and prepared for his discovery in the most profound inner level of all of the rejections of the feminine of which even this man had been capable. This was specifically the rejection in the depth of woman's spirit of her own creative masculine element. This can be personified in the imagination as a "man". But it is as sexless in its intent as is this other feminine in man.

However honoured woman has been in history as mistress, wife and mother, Toni Wolff and Jung discovered together on this journey that there is no sustained period wherein woman had been acknowledged in this other, this "masculine" aspect of herself. This is a state beyond the recognition of her being and all the exacting biological and social duties to which she belongs. Beyond that, she exists at a deeper level, in order to create in her own right as man has always done. History remains unilluminated by any realisation that just as man has a feminine self through which he creates, woman has this masculine self (not to be confused with the man without), through whom she is equipped to make a contribution to life; not as wife or mother, but in her own unique right. What there is in history is ominous evidence of the failure of men to recognise and honour this aspect of woman's spirit. And a backlash of revenge over this ignorance produces woman's slanted and one-sided association with man.

There was the phenomenon of the Amazons in the myths and legends of Greece, and the fact that they were one of the forces with whom Jason had to come to terms before he could successfully accomplish his mission to retrieve the Golden Fleece; an image of life transformed and made whole. The Amazons were one of the earliest manifestations in the Western spirit of the phenomenon we know today as "Women's Liberation". And, of course, there was the Virgin Goddess, the huntress Diana, to provide a portentous image, serving notice on our imaginations of this urge in women to give birth also to a meaning peculiarly their own. But the hints were not taken up and the warning notices ignored.

All our yesterdays contrived to determine that when Jung set out on this journey, it was in a context of life where what woman personifies was twice rejected; first in the shape of the feminine in man; and then in her own masculine creative self. One of the most significant facts that Jung brought back from this journey was that man and woman are not merely a biological twosome joined through sex, to carry as best they can the burdens and mysteries of life. They are a foursome; the man and this feminine self personified by the Beatrices and Ariadnes of history and legend; the woman and a masculine self not yet accessible to understanding because, due to the heavy duties imposed on her by her own biological nature and her exploitation by man, she has not, up to now, been allowed, except vicariously, to articulate it for herself. Indeed, she became so much part of the machinery of her own rejection that she was largely unaware of it save in imageries that came unbidden to her spirit.

There is, for instance, such a hint in the pseudonym adopted by Olive Schreiner, in the writing of her first book about Africa. There the feminine in man has been most ruthlessly rejected, and this rejection is largely responsible for Africa's terrific miseries. Olive Schreiner called herself Ralph Iron, as if something in her knew that she was writing through a man in herself. It is a revelation of how only a spirit of iron could stand fast in this unproven masculine aspect of herself against the terrible and wholesale rejection of the feminine values in southern Africa, so movingly symbolised at the end of the book by the death of the boy who is its nearest approach to a hero. He died for no apparent reason in the light of a bright sun—that ultimate in human symbols for the masculine. Only the heart knows that what he represents had to die young in a world belonging so completely to all-powerful man as that of Olive Schreiner's. There is also the case of George Eliot, perhaps England's greatest woman novelist, who in the male-dominated world of Victorian England chose this masculine disguise for her pen. Her identification with her masculine self and her concern that it should have equal freedom of expression as men made her, as indeed it made Olive Schreiner, both a forerunner and an inspiration of the feminist movement in Britain.

The havoc caused by the long denial of this element in human relationships between men and their women, mothers and sons, fathers and daughters, as well as the disorder and disaster in societies and their cultures, has been immense. It cries out for historical recognition and definition if history is ever to achieve its full contemporary meaning.

Anticipating one set of the main conclusions Jung drew from this journey into the unconscious, one can say that for the first time it now became possible for man and woman to join together and stand, as it were, foursquare in the battle for new and greater being. The prospect of enrichment and enlargement of life was immeasurably increased. A greater relationship between man and woman, a complete renewal of their attitudes to one another, promises a richer partnership of the human spirit than any life has ever seen, despite the confusion and chaos of the present moment. Considering that on the long journey which lies behind us from that first theft of fire—man's earliest image of consciousness—on and beyond to his first act of disobedience in the Garden symbolic of another fearful step towards a conscious individual striving, the human spirit has been largely served by only two aspects in both man and woman, the achievement and the illumination still are immense and outweigh the burden of failure. So, once life can be served by all four aspects in man and woman, this should be the measure of the promise for our future on earth and among the stars to which we are now heading. I suspect that this partnership of four depends on man following his own feminine self, as Dante followed his poetically, and Jung his empirically. The balance between the two in man and the two in woman depends, in the first instance, on the differentiation of the twosome in man.

But none of this, of course, was to be foreseen at the start of Jung's journey wherein the only forms of guidance were discredited, in advance, as mentally deranged and sick. Even apart from the doubts induced thereby, he had troubles of another kind. From the day on which he said, "Well, Jung, here you go", and let himself drop, he had nothing in past experience to help him in his own evaluations. He did not know how to deal with the strange material gushing up out of this underworld like the lava of a volcanic eruption. All he could do was to take seriously the promptings of a long neglected instinctive self, however trivial, absurd or improbable. He had already had to learn, like a child of the spirit learning to walk, to take everything, no matter how formidable or chaotic, with the utmost seriousness and give each trifle the expression and form of which both he and it were capable. Now, in addition to his modelling, he found it necessary also to write down his dreams and put into words the erupting visionary material. Where words and his considerable powers of articulation failed him, he took to drawing and painting. He read deeper than ever into history and mythology, and whenever he found a parallel he followed it, in an endeavour to recover the continuity which he appeared for the moment to have lost.

His first record was kept in a black book, which in itself I find most meaningful. It is yet more evidence of how in this world of the unconscious there is nothing that does not matter and is not there for a purpose, however enigmatic and infinitesimal its manifestation. An imperative of underground logic seems to have demanded that Jung should begin with something black if he were to proceed on his journey accurately. The law of symbolism through which this great unknown of the human spirit speaks to us, presupposed a black book, because always with all acts of creation there is "darkness at the beginning". The light that the spirit is allowed in the first instance came from a dark night dreaming of transformation into the light of day. Just as meaningful, therefore, is the fact that some relief came to him from the pressures of his journey by their transformation into the words of his black book. The "Word", as we know, was synonymous with light at the beginning.

Jung steadily became more confident of the worth of the material so recorded, and this relief and confidence impelled him to transfer the record to a greater book, known today as the Red Book. There was the same progression of unconscious logic in that too. Red is the badge of life-giving intent. It is almost as if this Red Book was both pledge and armour for a questing spirit, and so a parallel of the imagery in the legend of the quest for the Grail of a Parsifal vulnerable in the simpleness of spirit and humility of mind so typical of the state which precedes the greatest of human ventures, and which threatened Jung's attitude in this initial phase of his journey of descent. It is significant that the armour which Parsifal's mother gave him for protection at the outset of his quest also was red. It is no accident therefore that round about this time, in this netherworld of his imagination, Jung should have a vision of a fountain of fiery blood rising up and spurting high and wide through the earth. This fountain of blood is an image of a re-quickening of the spirit and a drive upward of long buried meaning hastening to bring new light against the darkness which presses so urgently and so blue against the little glass of our day.

One longs for this Red Book to be published in facsimile. It is Jung's first and most immediate testament, and infinitely evocative. When I first saw it, my eyes were stung by its beauty. There was something numinous about it. A Merlinesque gift seemed to have determined the deep colour and grave proportions. My first reaction had been not to open it. Yet had not Jung himself discussed it openly with me and others, referred to it in several books and used visual material from it whenever necessary for illustrating his meaning? Also, I knew that nothing Jung ever did was private in any egotistical or collective sense. All that he did in this regard was on behalf of a gift which demanded that he should be one of the foremost servants of meaning in the life of his time.

All in the Red Book was ultimately intended to help the cause to which his life was dedicated, and was important to every human being with a problem. The instant impact of beauty was, I believe, a consequence of the movement from black to red and so an annunciation of transfiguration. Metamorphosis is even in the writing. The ancient illuminated script glows with the light as of a dream and shows something old and forgotten, yet remembered and made new. The parchment is of a thick, medieval texture, and the painting which illustrates the text is of royal authority.

All in the Black Book is dark, and such light as there is dwells in the words. But in the Red Book all is light and colour, the smouldering glow of new meaning caught and made visible. For perhaps the greatest of all forms of beauty of which our senses are capable is inspired by a meaning that has been denied life. It is the welcome to aspects of the spirit returning from a dark night of exile into the company of its peers. It is the Cinderella in man at last arriving at the ball. It is, if one were to use the language of theology now somewhat dishonoured and rejected, an expression of joy over evil redeemed, the sign of grace that what was base as lead has been transformed and transfigured in some alchemy of ourselves, into gold. It is chaos made free and accessible in form and proportion. For all these reasons and more, the imagination is compelled to salute arrival at a new stage of the spirit at some remote frontier hospice of meaning with an assertion of beauty in whatever is nearest at hand as Jung was doing. It is the final imperative of a demand of life which cannot be evaded without mortal injury to itself. It insists that all should be lived in the grace of all such beauty as any given circumstance is capable. It is obedience to a law of a life demanding to be lived with the harmony called beauty. Ethics, in so far as they are real, also have their own aesthetic of behaviour.

Jung, of course, had never thought of himself as a painter. Yet the painting of dreams and visions in the Red Book are not unworthy of comparison with William Blake. Blake's work, for all its authority and power, has a graveyard monumentalism about it. Jung's drawings, even where the hand is less experienced and certain than Blake's, is warm and rich. They are all the more moving because they are proof that, in every human spirit, there is provision for doing whatever is basically necessary for its increase, provided it has the humility to accept the unfamiliar forms in which the means reveal themselves.

The Red Book shows this most clearly. In the confrontation of Jung with the great unknown in himself and the life of his time, strange material yielded itself progressively in increasingly significant form. At times as abstract as any pattern inflicted on Euclid, the vision is none the less given definite shape, until suddenly the abstraction becomes capable of personification. The material is orchestrated in recognisable forms of life. It is as if the word at this strange beginning in this chaos of himself suddenly becomes flesh and blood, and the fear one has felt for Jung vanishes and one's pulse quickens as some of the paintings come to assume a Hieronymus Bosch character. But soon they are like those of Blake again, magnetic with prophetic shapes of man.

One of the first is of a world under a sun with a red crusader's cross inscribed on it, the cross that is the sign of all four seasons and four quarters in man, and so a compass of a life to be encircled and made complete. Last of all there is a painting of a castle, foursquare in a green-gold haze of space and time. It is of a design Jung was later to recognise from the Chinese material brought to him from the lonely Wilhelm as another imprint of the abiding theme of China's yellow castle. One glance shows that this is the end of a great beginning; a Prospero moment in Jung's life when, figuratively, the book and all its magic is about to be buried "deeper than any plummet's sound". In all its austerity, it is the most moving of all the paintings because it confirms Jung's safe arrival at an impregnable destination. It is the moment of which Kipling wrote: "Let down the drawbridge for the dreamer; the dreamer whose dream has come true."

The last page of the Red Book is finally turned. Jung, fortified, returns to the world of recorded history and time, to put his journey in the context of his own increasingly urgent day and produce facts and evaluations of his achievement in an idiom that contemporary man can understand. The confrontation had lasted long, and in what protracted detail it had been fought, recorded and all the psychological treasure specified and classified, emerges from the single statistical fact that the year wherein he painted the castle (which announced the last battle won) was the year 1928. The immediate practical message of all these years for Jung was clear. All the great imponderable, ineffable and yet objective demonic images, dreams and fantasies with which he had been concerned were not just to do with himself but with modern man as a whole. He had not only ceased to belong to himself in the process but had lost the right to do so. He had always held the belief that it was immoral to know just for knowing's sake and yet remain without a moral commitment to the knowledge: and without trying to live according to the ethics of total commitment in the cause of life. This commitment had now been, as it were, empirically established for him.

The long *queste* and *aventiure*, as he once called it to himself, might be over. But knowing himself in a way he had never done before, he accepted that he would have to take the treasure of new meaning for all to share in the world from which his deepest self had for so long been withdrawn. He must give to it, moreover, in the only way he knew it could understand, and that was in the hard, empirical and scientific way wherein he had been trained. He knew he could only do so by a re-dedication of his total self to his psyche, and the search of modern man for a soul which was as masculine as it was feminine.

He was as always confirmed in this step by the dreaming of a new dream—perhaps the most moving, evocative and beautiful of the many great dreams he dreamt in his long life. It was set in Liverpool. Why Liverpool? Because the "liver" in antiquity, in anatomical symbolism, was the source of life; "pool" the water which was the most evocative of images of unconscious creative elements. The city therefore was not the drab, dingy, sprawling harbour city of England but a place of singular meaning in the imagination. The harbour aspect of it was important of course, because it suggests an image of the area of his imagination where voyages began and ended, where outward- and inward-bound traffic met, and the cargo of his own spirit went out for vital exchange and gathering of meaning from beyond the seas of himself home in its place.

The streets of this place still were dark and the real inhabited part of the city on cliffs high above him, but he could not fail to notice that all was arranged radially as if presupposing a circular perimeter of the township with a square at the centre. Why circular and why square? Both were images of totality and wholeness as Jung was to amplify and demonstrate empirically with circumspection. In their city form they were images moreover of collective wholeness, and indeed the company of six other Swiss with him in the dream, suggesting human collectivity, not only failed to be interested in any of this but just complained endlessly, he told me, how awful the weather was, as it is indeed only too often in the Liverpools of the world. He in the dream hardly noticed them because he was utterly absorbed, senses, spirit and all, in another kind of vision. In the centre of the square, despite the fog, rain and smoke, was a round pool and in the centre of the pool blazing in sunlight, a small island. In the middle of the island stood a splendid magnolia exploding into flower with reddish flames which added a light of their own to that of the sun. His companions could not see the tree and spoke only of another Swiss who lived there. Only Jung, enchanted, saw it and knew why that strange other Swiss lived there in such a city, because that was his new and as yet strange self, coming home at last to his island totality.

It is because of this that I find the dream almost unbearably moving. It confirms all that we have suspected of meaning in the mythological groping of our confused, muddled and bloody yesterdays; we have all an island self with a tree of life in flower. The tree might be winter-bare on the first day of sailing. But if the endeavour is continued to its true end, it is in flower and in the sun on the day of return

Here Jung is about to complete the golden chain of the authentic spirit of man, however lost, over the horizon of history. He is at one with Odysseus and his return to Ithaca, as he is with us who are still seeking similar self-realisation; reunited too with the impoverished boy who walked down-at-heel in cheap and patched clothes along the Rhine to school, experiencing a foretaste of his island self manifested in this dream, through the creation in fantasy in midstream of the urgent mythological river—a fortified island kingdom of his own.

It is not for nothing that the tree is a magnolia and in full flower; there was meaning still to be extracted from it. The magnolia is a tree of the Far East brought to Europe about the beginning of the eighteenth century by a Frenchman, Pierre Magnol. Not the least of the dream's by-products therefore is that the tree in flower symbolised a truth the Romans had discovered in their conquest of Greece; the spirit of the vanquished could invade that of the conqueror and vanquish it in return. Pierre Magnol's flower, together with the first translation of the *Upanishads* which his great countryman Auquetil du Perron had brought back from India, showed how a profound process of re-orientation of the all-conquering European spirit had truly begun by infiltration of Indian, Chinese and Japanese values.

And now, for the first time in the history of man that I am aware of, East and West were in possession of a great dream wherein they could equally share without surrender or partial loss of their own higher meanings, and this profound historical process of inter-penetration made capable of conscious integration on uncommon common ground.

How this almost miraculous result came to be confirmed was not the least of the consequences of Jung's return to the world and his taking it on as if it were his asylum.

POINT OF TOTAL RETURN

*You yourself are even another little world and have within you
the sun and the moon and also the stars.*

ORIGEN, *Leviticum Homiliae*

The deepest of all the patterns in the human spirit is one of departure
and return, and the journey implicit in-between. The life of man is the
journey, a voyage such as that of Odysseus, a travel downward into
cataclysmic depths like that of Orpheus in search of his lost Euridice;
Dante's wandering through hell and the dark streets of the city of Diss,
and the journey of exile inflicted on the first man and his woman Eve
from the garden to which they have not yet returned.

There are also the stories of the wanderings of the Israelites from
bondage in Egypt in search of a promised land where they could live
after the fashion of their own unique monotheistic conception of the
divine and its commandments. There are those strange walkabouts of
aborigines in the never-never of Australia, and of my own Stone-age
countrymen in the vast wasteland of southern Africa. The same pattern
leads to the road which the Sanyassin takes in India; the Tao of China
which was both journey and purpose to Lao-Tzu; and the one and
only way of Confucius, conceived at the still centre of togetherness
in the storm of all our tumultuous being. There is Bunyan's *Pilgrim's
Progress* and others far too many to mention which all tend to illustrate
how in the beginning man at his best is outward bound only in order
to return from across the seven oceans the inward way from where he
started, and to see the place for the first time, as T. S. Eliot put it in
a precise poetic statement.

Perhaps one of the most concise and dynamic definitions of this
pattern of departure, journey and return and its meaning is to be found
in the New Testament parable of the Prodigal Son. Taken at a manifest
level the parable is a story of a great injustice. The son who takes his
inheritance in advance from a rich father, spends it and is reduced to
such a state of poverty that he lives with swine, is welcomed back by
the father as if he had done more than was expected of him and fulfilled his youthful promise to an extent not achieved by the brother
who had stayed at home and done all that duty to father, family and
society demanded of him. No wonder he feels himself unjustly treated,

but this injustice is condoned in religious convention by the fact that it enables the father to demonstrate his capacity for forgiveness. For this is the one lesson derived by theologians from the parable and preached from Christian pulpits all over the world to this day.

But there is another and I believe far more significant symbolic level to the parable, designed to sow quite a different seed of being and a new sort of truth in us, totally apart from the concept of our obligation to forgive one another—important as that so obviously is. This truth is that the parable dramatises legitimately the imperative of the need of man when young to separate himself from the father and live a life of his own. The money he receives from the father is an image of the talents he has been given by life, and the story tells him that far from hoarding these talents, which the New Testament has already warned no-one must bury, far from being thrifty about them as the brother left at home is, it is the duty of the young to spend them fully; in other words to use his talents until they consciously seem worn out and he is enabled to see at last how impoverished his collective self is, how inadequate and provisional the world and the social realisations demanded by it, so that he is driven to live with swine, and all the pig in himself symbolises of instinctive life closest to the earth and most dependent on its roots. Only when he has lived through all these aspects of himself as well, come to terms as it were also with the pig that there is in himself and all of us, is he ready for his prodigal return. And this return in a sense is all the more meaningful not just because of the reward the prodigal son receives, but because it enriches the father too, by bestowing on him the grace of spirit we call forgiveness with such inadequacy and patronage of sentiment.

And yet even so, considered in both these meaningful dimensions, the parable is still strangely incomplete. Why is there no mention of the prodigal's mother? Surely she must have rejoiced too at the return of a long-lost son out of the natural love of which the feminine in man is the keeper. Was she dead? The parable does not say, but if so it means that even in the New Testament and its profession of divine love, there was lacking the feminine element necessary to complete it. Or was she alive and not considered worth mentioning? If so, worse still, because though there for the asking, the feminine in life has been wilfully repressed. The parable for me would only have been totally fulfilled if both father and mother had been present to welcome in equal measure the prodigal in man home from the world. And this is why I think Jung's own return to the world after this great dream, which reveals him as it were homeward bound the inward way, means so much to me and constitutes I believe an Archimedean point for lever-ing our civilisation and time out of a perilous position with all its boulder-like weight poised on a catastrophic abyss of itself.

His too was a prodigal return, but to both the masculine and femi-nine in man strengthened by trial as few have been tried. To put it in its Classical Odyssean imagery, he had returned, despite the numerous shipwrecks, storms, encounters with one-eyed Titans, like the gigantic scientific establishment of his day whose traditional inadequacy of vision had already been summed up prophetically as "one-eyed" by Blake in his famous accusation hurled at Newton nearly two centuries before. One-eyed too, in its vision from the spires of the vast edifice of organised religion, had been the formidable enmity incurred from eminent divines and theologians. There had been too the temptations of siren song like that of the lady posing as anima who tried to lure Jung from science into art. He had suffered and survived abandon-ment, Odysseus-like, after his crew, his colleagues and friends forsook him when Freud excommunicated him for the heresy of denying a dogma and doctrine of psycho-sexuality. He had to endure more ship-wreck again in his voyage within until he must have felt in his final encounter with the collective unconscious, as Odysseus did in the storm to end all storms hurled by Zeus against him, that the gods were resolved never to let him see again the smoke of evening falling over the housetops of his island home. Yet in the face of all this and more, he had endured to come at last to the true feminine in himself. He had walked out of the deep sea on to firm land in the here and now as Odysseus had done, to be welcomed by his own inner version of Nausicaa, and now could be made ready for total return to the island harbour of himself already foreseen in a dream as some Liverpool.

What was even more astounding is that, in the midst of so much, he had made time to fashion the one instrument essential for communi-cating his discovery to the world without danger of being misunder-stood by anyone willing to hear and examine the evidence. Of course he knew that one never has armour adequate for turning back the assaults of those who just would not want to hear and look objectively. They of course would be the vast multitude. But what he could do was to make certain that he should not be misunderstood by men and women of good will and good faith. He told me how often he thought in this regard of the example of Christ whom he saw as the Western world's total revelation of the eternal pattern of the anthropos, the self, in the spirit of man.

He would remind himself again and again how Christ appeared to have addressed himself only once to the masses of his time, and that was in the Sermon on the Mount. Thereafter Christ had behaved as if he too cherished at heart the truth of the ancient Chinese saying, "The Master speaks but once". Henceforth he had confined himself to those who sought and asked for him in their hearts, and concentrated for the rest on his twelve disciples as if to imply that if he could transform only those twelve he would have accomplished what he had been born to do.

When I said once, in the course of a discussion of the growing peril of numbers to the integrity of man, that I had been tempted to think of Christ's remark that wherever two or three were gathered in his name as almost his definition of a maximum and not a minimum, Jung did not smile as I had perhaps hoped he, who was so quick to warm to irony, might have done, but added gravely that he often did not even have the comfort of two or three in his far less exalted role on the journey behind him but had to find his solace from the saying of the James referred to in the Apocryphal New Testament, "And where there is one alone, I say I am with him."

So he had concentrated what there was of him to spare on making certain that there was a new psychological form of understanding, a common key for deciphering all the many human codes of communication present in life, to make for a disastrous confusion of form with content of their meaning. Those who searched and asked the sort of questions he was asking, he knew could only be prevented in this way from getting at cross-purposes with him or themselves and have a chance of understanding as they wished themselves to be understood.

This new psychological language was set out in a long book published in 1921 when the campaign, though far from over, was beginning to release a feeling of ultimate victory through the atmosphere within. It was called *The Psychology of Type* or—and the *or* is of utmost significance since it proves that already Jung had a clear intimation of the ultimate of his seeking—*A Theory of Individuation*.

In this book he had typically also turned his mind to the task which seemed nearest at the time. He had realised instantly that the unconscious in man could be observed only through what was conscious. Therefore, unless this phenomenon, so subjective and diversified in its quality and extent in every human being, was not itself most carefully investigated and its working understood, no common evaluation of its role and consequences would be possible. The book was therefore also the first serious empirical examination in our history of the phenomenon of consciousness.

Its immediate motivation was rooted in Freud's traumatic quarrel with him. After the first shock Jung rediscovered that profound inner calm of his. He discovered that far more interesting and important than the personal pain inflicted on him was the motive of Freud's break with him. They were both persons of good faith, dedicated to the service of truth. Jung never doubted Freud in this regard. And yet they had fallen out with each other. Why? He knew all the rationalisations of their differences, all the plausible excuses and justification both for Freud's decision to break with him and Jung's to go his own way, but none satisfied the sense of truth in him. He was convinced that there was more to it than that and wanted at first to probe into the deeper causes he suspected of the quarrel in Freud as in himself. But he felt incapable of doing so impartially at that time. He was too closely and painfully involved in personal history and consequences with Freud that were to pursue him to the end of his day. So instead he turned to ground where he could explore similar material more objectively. Freud and another of his earlier adherents, Adler, had also quarrelled. It was out of an examination of the underground of this epoch-making dispute that the larger work commenced.

I remember one cold winter afternoon walking with him by the black Maggiore water, the snow pink in the evening sun. He was unusually depressed, had upon him one of those moments of self-denigration which came to him from time to time. He complained with heart-rending conviction that he had done nothing, absolutely nothing of his essential task in life and with each "nothing", he would hit a rut of snow beside him with that stout English country walking stick of his. I protested vigorously and said, "If you had done nothing else but given us your book on psychological types, and made us capable of speaking at last a common psychological language, you would have done more than enough."

I said that because I believe this difficult and much neglected book of Jung's is a turning point in the art of human communications about which we hear so much and do so little these days. It is a discovery, as it were, of a foolproof technology of mind for making communication intelligible between all men, no matter what their differences. It is deliverance, at last, from the confusion of tongues which made the building of the Tower of Babel impossible, that ancient story which all of us can take to our twentieth-century hearts with profit. In the middle of his life-and-death confrontation with the forces of the unconscious, Jung had had the space of mind and time to devote himself to finding why it was that persons so absolutely dedicated and honourable as Freud, Adler and himself should disagree. I tried to tell him

how great and heroic an achievement I felt that to have been, and
added that I could never forget the excitement racing through me
when I came to his conclusion that it was in the first instance a problem
of inborn type. It was a breakthrough of such importance, I felt, that
if he had accomplished nothing else, it alone would more than have
justified his life.

It was not the easiest of his books to read, it is true, because the material
was utterly new and he had no precedents of form or example of mind
to guide him, and something of his own difficulties affect his presenta-
tion. Yet the central message emerges as clear as it is startling and leaves
one's imagination as if unchained for the first time in an essential
function of itself.

All human beings, he demonstrates in this book, are born either
extraverted or introverted. Freud was an extravert, Adler was an
introvert. They represented two extremes of psychology that cut
right through life and made a great divide in the history of the human
spirit. Here was the origin of the Classical and Romantic urges in art;
the Apollonian and Dionysian in the mind; the Greek and Trojan in
legend and history, and so on up to the mechanics and vitalists in the
sciences of our day. The extravert tended to be as at home in the world
without as he was embarrassed by the world within; the introvert
uneasy in the external world and naturally confident only in this other
"objection within of life."

Historically the extravert had tried to achieve meaning by outer
form, shaped to contain; the introvert by inner realisation and change.
One sought his meaning as it were by breathing in; the other by
breathing out. But what life demanded was a state of being where the
spirit breathed both in and out.

Jung's book supported this with detailed evidence from the progression of philosophy, religion, art and science and then went further.
He found that within these two great divisions there were also other
differences. Each human being had four "functions"; two rational and
two irrational or, as I prefer to call them, non-rational, since "irrational" in its common usage tends to be synonymous with "unreason".
The two rational functions he called "thinking" and "feeling"—
equating the "feeling" not with emotion but the process of evaluation
in awareness. Thinking needs no such defining, seeing how much it is
the speciality of our own time. The other two functions were "intuition"—the sense in man of all the unrealised potential in life and time,
his awareness of what though invisible is yet to come and the source of
his greatest creativity—and "sensation" (not to be confused with the

nucleus of sensationalism), which is awareness through the senses of the immediate world, the here and the now.

These definitions are of course simplifications of an extremely complex concept. But what it is important to realise is that Jung's empiric evidence proves that man is born with *one* function (either rational or non-rational) being consciously in command, and another (its opposite in rationality or non-rationality) working in close support of it. The third and fourth are relatively repressed in the unconscious. One of man's supreme tasks in achieving wholeness, therefore, was two-fold; to resolve the imbalance in the spirit of man not only between the superior and suppressed functions, but also across the great divide of the extravert and introvert. The human spirit, seen in this way, is deprived of any justification for the state of civil war in which it has existed.

As a writer I was only too aware of the feuds caused by unawareness of these differences in literature alone, and it seemed to me that no critic, philosopher or statesman—in fact no-one at all—can afford ignorance of this invaluable code Jung has provided for translating all the languages of the spirit into a common idiom. I think always in this regard of Anatole France's saying, which had travelled the battlefields of Europe, Africa and the Far East with me: "Human beings are forever killing one another over words, whereas if they had only understood what the words were trying to say, they would have embraced one another."

After Jung's *Psychological Types* we no longer have any valid excuse for not realising that we are all ultimately trying to say the same things and express the same longings in terms of our own unique natures. We have no excuse for destroying others just because their psychology demands a different idiom of utterance.

The consequences of providing mankind with a common code for the first time in history are formidable. The achievement is a preliminary towards attaining the brotherhood of man which I shall try to show is already waiting prepared and fully armed in Jung's hypothesis of the collective unconscious. I told him so plainly during those walks at Ascona. But he was not in a mood to be comforted, and remained uncomforted for a long time. Soon after my return to England I had a letter from him in which he concluded: "I am an increasingly lonely old man writing for other lonely men."

In all this he did not fail to call himself to account and measure himself with the utmost exaction in terms of his theory of type. What matters, therefore, despite the deprecation by himself that day at

Maggiore of a book written nearly forty years before, was that it proved that no-one could succeed ever in freeing himself of profound bias, acquire a free ranging taste and evaluation of life, science and art unless he had some idea of the kind of type he himself represented. Unaware of our "inferior" functions, we certainly cannot set to work towards a full realisation of greater selves. In this regard, one clear example from history is perhaps helpful. Goethe, for instance, plainly was not only an extravert but an "intuitive-feeling" type, with thinking and sensation in the shadow. *Faust* is only partially understood if it is not seen also as an orchestration of Goethe's inferior aspects; thinking and sensation. That is why Goethe was of so great importance to the German spirit. He was a compensation to the Faustian will and the predominant thinking and sensation functions of Germanic culture. *Faust* achieves universality because, through it, Goethe brings into light what is dark, dangerous, archaic and angry both in himself and the spirit of his time. I choose Goethe because of his relevance in this regard to Jung, and in particular for his orchestration of what Jung was to call the "shadow" in the human spirit. Jung took the task of Goethe in this regard symbolically upon himself and tried to correct through his own example, what he thought inadequate in *Faust*. Faust's murder of Philemon and Baucis, the masculine and feminine who had been worldly hosts to the god, Jung regarded as a sin. For in his pact with the devil, Faust committed the classical hubris of swinging over from one opposite into the other and thereby setting up another form of tyrannic partiality as a whole. This eliminated man from his instinctive experience of the mighty other activity that Jung called God.

One of Jung's main tasks therefore was to enable modern man to allow these two elements of Philemon and Baucis to be reborn, as he worked incessantly on their rebirth in himself. He laboured in vain as far as Germany was concerned, but he need not have laboured in vain as far as we and our future are involved in the same dilemma. It is for this reason that his Number Two personality was called Philemon. Some two years after publishing his difficult book on types, Jung installed him in the tower retreat he built at Bollingen, calling part of the tower, "Shrine of Philemon: Repentance of Faust". As token of the antiquity and validity of this process of atonement and redemption to which he had subjected himself, he carved the phrase in Latin firmly in yellow stone.

How deeply he had taken this problem to heart and how much he had worked on it to the immense benefit of his own awareness, is illustrated for example by the difference in attitude displayed to the first and second World Wars. The first, judging by his correspondence and conversation, did not strike nearly so deeply as the second. There was little outside mention of the first, partly, perhaps, because his own desperate battle had started within, and the war seemed to him then mainly a great portent of confirmation of the war raging in a similar pattern within himself. But the march of Europe and the world towards the war of 1939 was a totally different matter.

There was a brief moment, at the beginning, when this stirring of unconscious forces that he saw in Germany seemed to him to be capable of a positive potential. This may seem surprising in someone who from so early an age had been aware of the perilous and rapidly widening dichotomy in the German spirit. First there had been Goethe's *Faust*: then the example of Nietzsche's tragic genius soaring with a demonic zeal towards an ideal of a super-man: then Burckhardt and his grim foreboding of the consequences of this uncorrected slant in modern German history. Finally there was Jung's own experience in trying to deal with this dichotomy in himself and others. As early as 1918 he addressed a sombre warning against the possibility of a breaking out of a "blonde beast from an underworld prison" of the German spirit with disastrous consequences. Yet his mistake as to the positive potential of the Nazi upsurge in Germany is only too understandable if one remembers that he himself was still under the spell of how much his own encounter with the collective unconscious had enriched him. He was therefore inclined to assess any activation of it in others positively rather than negatively. But within two years he had changed his mind. His warnings against events in Germany became more frequent, urgent and unqualified, ending in such outright condemnation that when the war broke out his own books were banned in Germany and he himself placed on the Nazi black list for liquidation at the first opportunity.

No-one who knew the man and has studied the facts and read his work can honestly doubt that, if he had foreseen in the first instance the catastrophic potential of evil in the first Nazi stirring in Germany, he would have given it in his own mind even the slight short-lived chance that he did.

Had this been his only human error—he was after all no politician— the matter may have been overlooked. But unfortunately he did two other things which were to become more debatable. At a moment when the Nazis were beginning to accuse the Jews of defects of spirit and cultural attributes which deprived them of all right to common human consideration, and were using this patently spurious and amply discredited approach to justify their persecution of the Jews in Germany, Jung spoke publicly of the differences between the culture, psychology and character of the Jews and others. Not only were his remarks misunderstood and taken out of context to be used by the Germans as additional justification for stepping up their inhuman campaign against German and Austrian Jews, but they also gave great offence to the Jews and opponents of Hitler everywhere in Europe. Jung was totally taken aback by the storm he had gathered about himself. His remarks were truly innocent of any derogatory or malicious political intent. Utterly bewildered, he asked why it was in order for him to discuss differences in French and English psychology, or Western and Chinese psychology, without reprisal, but he could not do so about the Jews? He ignored, of course, the timing of the affair, not all too surprisingly if one considers how profoundly he was engaged in a totally different dimension of reality. He was even more dumbfounded when the Jews resented his reference to the Chinese and his comparison of the Jews with the "Mongolian hordes". But at that moment Jung was working hard on the *I-Ching* of Richard Wilhelm and the *Secret of the Golden Flower*. Deeply impressed as he was by it all, he meant the comparison as a compliment! His letters to his Jewish colleagues at the time, like those to James Kirsch, himself a most distinguished German scholar, show how baffled he was by the accusations of anti-Semitism hurled at him.

Indeed, however much one deplores the timing of Jung's remarks on the Jewish cultural character, one has only to read the letters he wrote in defence of Neumann who had escaped from Germany and settled in Tel-Aviv, to find reassurance. In these letters he shows such a profound understanding of the plight of the Jew in history, such compassion for all they have suffered from Christian projection of the Christian shadow on them, such appreciation of their unique and indispensable contribution to the spirit of man, that they would shed the last traces of suspecting him as being anti-Semitic. But best of all, perhaps, is Aniela Jaffé's analysis of the whole affair as set out in her masterly essay *Der Nationalsocialismus*. As a Jewess herself, a refugee from Nazi Germany, a pupil and collaborator of Jung, she has said all that there is to be said about the matter with final authority. She deals admirably with the second reason for Jung's pro-Nazi, anti-Semitic labelling; his acceptance of the Chairmanship of the International Society for Psycho-Therapy in those dubious Nazi years, which meant that for a while he had to work with the head of the German branch, a Göring who was a cousin of the notorious Hermann.

Aniela Jaffé states that one of Jung's main considerations was to protect
his Jewish colleagues in Germany and to provide them with some
international status if expelled from Germany. None the less his participation in this form was abused by Göring and others sufficiently to
provide his accusers with more ammunition to use against him. Yet
Jung did so much for his Jewish colleagues and, even after his resignation, continued to help them with immense courage, ingenuity and
generosity as to prove the persistence of the anti-Semitic, pro-Nazi
charge to be invalid. It is possible, too, that there is a mythological
origin to all this. The traumatic break with Freud has an importance
in this not generally perceived. Never in the history of the world had
two such great personalities, in so charged a dimension, been so con-
spicuously placed in the centre of the stage where a new drama of
time was being enacted. Immediately both, in their various ways,
personified the projections and aspirations in the unconscious of an
entire age. Unfortunately, in the way of all collective projections, the
personifications were over-simplified. So finally Freud represented the
great benevolent, wise, generous Jewish father, the patriarchal dominant of so much of Hebraic seeking. Jung became the "adopted" non-
Jewish son, the Gentile, who betrayed the great father, so reducing the
relationship to which we owe so much to an unworthy Jewish–non–
Jewish conflict. It is true that Freud himself did think of his psychology
as sufficiently a Jewish phenomenon to greet Jung's support of him as a
welcome correction and enrichment of his cause. But Jung never
thought of it in any similar terms. His psychological approach was on
so profound and universal a level that racial implications were not
involved. None the less a vulgar mythological use of the personal
story of Freud and Jung continues, and it is the mythological aspect of
the story of their relationship which contains the real explanation of
this continuation of the campaign against Jung for having been pro-
Nazi and anti-Semitic. Consequently there remains a certain number
of the public who to this day believe that the real cause of Jung's
differences with Freud are based merely on the fact that Freud was a
Jew and Jung a Christian.

One of the final ironies of this false situation is the contribution
made to it indirectly by Freud himself. Until the 'thirties Freud had
been the only distinguished Jew whom Jung had known intimately.
What he knew of Jewish psychology and culture was in large measure
picked up from Freud himself. But Freud, unhappily, was shockingly
ill-informed about his own people and their post-Old Testament
evolution, as so many German and Austrian Jews were to such a large

extent. Even what Freud knew about the Jews was restricted to the narrow confines of his own scientific approach which dismissed as "occultism" the Jews' greatest contribution to the history of man, their national genius for religious experience and revelation. Freud knew little, for instance, about Jewish mysticism. He was not aware of the eventful evolution of Jewish religious awareness through the mystique of the Kabbalah and Chassidic phenomenon in central Europe. It was not until the Nazi horror brought Jung into wider contact with Jews that this side of Jewish culture became available to him. Then his response to it was almost immediate and creative. Evidence of his admiration for the inspired concern of the Jews for all things of the spirit is to be found in the fact that, of the three literary trustees appointed by him, two are Jews. As conclusive is the fact that the gallant Leo Baeck, when he heard Jung's side of the story at a meeting that they had in Zürich immediately after the war, became completely reconciled to him and announced the fact publicly.

One further anecdote to illustrate where Jung, the man, stood in these desperate years of the 'thirties. He told me that at one of the last conferences of the International Society in Germany he heard the goose-stepping Nazi hordes from the hall where he was speaking.

He paused to say to someone on the platform beside him "There goes the march of an age into the night."

The same day he was summoned to see I think it was Goebbels himself. Reluctantly, but with studied correctitude, he went. The city was reverberating, night and day, with the tramp of vast armies of fanatical men marching with what Jung had already described, as Caesar had once done, *Furor Teutonicus*.

"I am told you have something of importance you wish to say to me", Goebbels demanded in his most aggressive manner.

"On the contrary, I was told you had something to say to me. I have nothing to say to you", Jung declared.

For a while reiteration and counter-reiteration between the two men continued until Goebbels, enraged, banged his desk with his fists.

Whereupon Jung stood up, totally uncompromising, and walked out; as he had already walked out in early 1933 of any idea of giving the Nazi phenomenon any further chance.*

When war finally broke out, he was deeply committed in spirit to its meaning and consequences. He made no secret on which side he had

---

* This encounter with Goebbels produced so profound a revulsion in Jung that when he returned to his host's home, he was violently sick.

committed himself. "Three cheers for Old England", he wrote to "Peter" Baynes with his youthful turn of English phrase.

"The devastation of London", he wrote to Mary Mellon, "hurt me as if it were my own country."

He called the war by many names but always with the Germanic adjective of possession as in terms of "the German evil", "the German disease", "the German poison", and so on. After the war he had no patience with Germans who were prepared to behave as if nothing had happened to them in the process and that they themselves had not been responsible.

It is true, Jung thought it important that we should realise how the whole trend of spirit of our time had contributed to the catastrophe of the war. We too were not without blame in a spiritual sense. But he made it absolutely clear that the immediate responsibility was a German one. He wrote in this regard a scathing letter of rebuke to a German notability who seemed to feel that business as usual of interchange of spirit with the rest of the world could be carried on without admission of responsibility and plea for forgiveness.

"It was most remarkable", he told me once, "how as the war became more desperate and widespread, I found myself dreaming more and more of Churchill. It was almost as if there was a kind of dream telepathy and state of dream participation between us. I would wake up in the morning having dreamt of him and read, for instance, that he had just been on another long and dangerous journey by 'plane. That happened not once but lots of times."

So I mention these two differences of attitude because without this book on the psychology of type and the movement it initiated towards individuation, with its underlying assumption of a collective unconscious in man, he could not have moved so far from a personal self-awareness to its universal counterpart.

These two signposts of war must stand as milestones of the immense distances he himself covered between 1913 and 1939. But long before 1939 he had left his work on psychological type far behind him. It was never meant to be an absolute but a relative aid to navigation of oneself, and an exhortation to all men to realise how important it was to work towards raising what was dark and inferior in oneself to the same honourable estate as what was light and superior without any sacrifice of the illuminated values.

His first immediate concern, thereafter, was to establish the validity of the objectivity of the "collective unconscious" and all the material uncovered in his encounter with it. This material went far beyond the personal. Indeed, Jung even during his earliest psychiatric years had discovered in his most profoundly disturbed patients, elements of meaning, patterns of fantasy and symbols which seemed to him of a disturbing relevance to the great objective universals of the history of civilisation. He had, he was certain, established that there were similar objective forces of indescribable power active in himself. Empirical as his approach even to himself had been, he knew that the hypothesis which the facts were massing to impose on him, and which he was ultimately compelled to accept (since he hated theorising), would not be acceptable to others unless supported by outside evidence.

He embarked therefore on an immense historical enterprise in search of evidence beyond doubt in the consciously recorded story of all that we call civilisation. That the instinctive objectivity of this new world was an established fact he could prove from his clinical work and analytical sessions with his patients. Its validity was proved by the fact that, when uncovered, taken seriously, and restored to a role in the life of his patients, they were healed. The problem, of course, the apparent causes of the neurosis and its symptoms, did not disappear. But the energy necessary for dealing with them would re-emerge in the stricken personality and the neurosis itself vanish. "Why", he was driven to exclaim again and again, "cannot men who call themselves psychiatrists and doctors see that acceptance of the reality of this discovery and its activities works, and heals people whose sickness orthodox medicine could not help?"

And yet there is no need to examine in detail the way he accomplished the historical aspect of his task. It is best followed in his own words and the several books devoted to it. They, unlike the book on psychological types, are easy to read; clearly and forcefully set forth with elaborate and convincing detail in a manner no educated reader interested can fail to understand. *Roots of the Conscious, Archetypes and the Collective Unconscious, Psychology and Religion, Modern Man in Search of a Soul*, though only a selection of some of his major works and exclude any reckoning of the great stream of relevant seminars that poured out of him all the while, convey through their titles the range and ordered progression of this self-imposed historical endeavour.

Jung made his point of departure from what is primordial and primeval in life. His work established also that there was a primitive self in civilised European man which had increasingly been denied a legitimate participation in his life. Because of this denial and the rejection of natural feeling values which inevitably followed, civilised man had become less and less civilised in the classical sense and more and more of an "intellectual barbarian" or "technological savage", as Jung often called him. And here perhaps I should reaffirm that Jung was never in any way ranged against genuine intellect but felt free only to fire great broadsides at it because, of all our psychological functions, it was least in danger of being ignored. His voyage to Africa in 1925–6 provided the final proof of what is first and primitive in even the most modern of spirits. Similarly, as far as the history of antiquity was concerned, he discovered an embarrassing wealth of illustration and proof in the story of civilisations as remote as those of Babylon, Assyria, Persia, Egypt and, somewhat nearer to us, those of Greece and Rome. But between them, the emergence of the medieval church, and himself, there were wide and disturbing gaps, an apparent dissociation and lack of continuity which could not have been there if his hypothesis of the collective unconscious possessed the universal objectivity that now he knew it did. There were hints that the theme had not altogether vanished as, for instance, in astrology. Astrology for Jung had little to do with the stars as such, and their direct involvement in the fate of man. It was a projected form of psychology, an attempt of antiquity, by way of the instinctive attitude, of seeking for a new truth in its reflection in the mirror of the world about us. But this aspect of it can perhaps be best reconsidered in his ultimate investigation into the role of time in the life of man.

There was another intimation of the continuity he sought in the history of the Christian Gnostics so ruthlessly repressed and persecuted by the early church. He recognised a kinship in Gnosticism with his own experiences. But its representation in history, almost entirely by Church fathers ranged against it, was too partial and uncertain for him to take up the thread with confidence, until much later when the discovery of the Dead Sea Scrolls and new Coptic papyrus scripts from Egypt gave additional scope to this line of his investigation. He was to find the ultimate realisation of continuity in the hitherto obscure and much despised story of alchemy. He would not, perhaps, have been able to do this even had not the external world at the appropriate moment provided him with the right key to a door so firmly shut.

The dream of the magnolia tree, the flower of East and West, aflame in blossom, was proved to be prophetic, because soon after this he received from Richard Wilhelm the translation of an old Chinese alchemical text called, with uncanny pre-recognition, *The Secret of the Golden Flower*. Through this alchemical text (the year in which he received it was 1928), added later to Wilhelm's translation of the even older *I-Ching*, he found the door to European alchemy wide open.

The validity was established beyond doubt of the universality of his hypothesis of the collective unconscious in man, and its revelations of distinct, diversified patterns of energy active in incalculable numbers in the spirit of man.

He was no Chinese scholar and had made no special study of Chinese history or culture. He had read with great profit the *Upanishads* of Sanskrit India which was geographically near China but in reality as remote from its spirit as its European kinsmen. There was obviously no connection or possibility of influence from China in the conclusions he had reached. But now, through Wilhelm, he was introduced to a progression of culture older than our own wherein all he had learned from psychology in Europe was made manifest and worked on as established facts. He needed to go no further than to give the Chinese material its exact European parallel in the dreams and fantasies of his patients as well as in the purpose of all Christian seeking—above all in its living revelation of a transcendental self, the Anthropos, the "golden flower" or "diamond body", as his great spiritual forebears, the ancient Chinese sages and alchemists, had called it. They had endeavoured, with an integrity and passion not seen in Europe for centuries, to arrive at the lasting translation of their ephemeral selves into a continuous and endlessly continuing truth beyond the here and the now, beyond our prescribed cycle of birth, life and death.

The Pauline "Not I but Christ in me" had always been for Jung an arrival at a self-realisation far beyond any egotistical aspiration of man; an achievement of an everlasting state of truth where at last man, in living bondage to a value greater than himself, was freer than he had ever been. And this conviction now was confirmed as a clear parallel by the over-riding Chinese alchemical seeking of the creation through a union of two great opposites of spirit symbolised in dark and light, the yin and yang in themselves, ringed with fire as in their visual image of Tao itself. A golden flower of light in the "diamond body" which was the same incorruptible greater self Paul discovered through the pattern of Christ within himself.

"On the one hand Christ the sorrow-laden hero", Jung wrote. "On the other, the Golden Flower that blooms in the purple hall of the city of Jade: what a contrast, what an unfathomable difference, what an abyss of history." Yet he was to show that, although they started poles apart in the transcendental symbol of their final seeking, they were one, as the spirit of East and West could be at one.

From that moment, Jung felt no further need for proof of the hypothesis of the collective unconscious. His contact with Indians in America and, above all, the Elgonyi in Africa had demonstrated how it held good for the primitive as well as the "civilised". His contact with Wilhelm proved in a much more complex and evolved manner how another great civilisation like China, without any tangible connection with his own, had come to the same conclusion. The *Upanishads* had already established the same pattern in the sophisticated culture of Hindu India, and a brief visit by him to the sub-continent itself was to demonstrate how the Lord Buddha too, after high Himalayan fashion, was another realisation of the pattern of the greater self in man. Jung found himself immeasurably enriched thereby but in an honourable and dignified way, as of the spirit, as of a pupil learning humbly from the masters in this field. And characteristically as a result, he addressed an urgent warning to his own culture, more urgent and relevant today than it was when he was alive. The warning had its roots in his basic conviction that science is the finest instrument of the Western mind. That did not mean that he saw it as the end in itself it is far too often presumed to be. But that on no account should it be abandoned in the approach of the Western mind to all this wealth of empirical material from the East. More doors could be opened with science than with bare European hands. Picking the pockets of wisdom of his Chinese pioneers was not valid as a serious task. Ancient China, for instance, could help Europe to wider and more profound as well as higher understanding of life. But it was of no use to us if indulged in as "Eastern Wisdom" and we were consequently pushed into the obscurities of archaic faith and superstition. For Jung this Oriental material, far from consisting of exaggerated mystical intuitions, was wisdom based on practical knowledge, hard spiritual empiricism and a totally original exercise of intelligence of the finest kind. He could not bear to see it abused as magical formulas or spiritual amulets for correcting our own European disorientation. Above all, he warned against blind imitation of Indian and Chinese practices, as he had warned, and been warned by himself, against adapting primitivity in the African way. Western imitation of China and India was doubly tragic in that it arose from a psychological understanding as sterile as "current escapades in New Mexico, the blissful South Sea Islands and central Africa, where primitivity is staged in all seriousness in order that Western man may conveniently slip out of his menacing duties".

It is not for us to imitate what is organically foreign, Jung urged, or worse still to send out missionaries to foreign peoples. It is our task to build up our Western culture, which sickens of a thousand ills. This had to be done on our own doorstep. "Into the work must be drawn the European as he is in his Western commonplaces, with his marriage problems, his neuroses, his social and political illusions and his whole philosophical disorientation."

In fact Jung had nothing but pity for the spiritual impoverished European who went, as it were, to beg for spirit in the East. He would say in their regard that one did not do one's best by beggars when giving them all they ask for as alms. One helps most by freeing them for the re-learning of the value of work. So we could justify what we gained from the East by translating the meaning of Chinese wisdom into our own humdrum European lives. In this way we could live out the meaning together in the same devout measure of integrity and honesty as those others who had lived their lives in their own context and at their own peril in order that they could acquire so great a wealth of wisdom. But how close Chinese and European parallels are was evident even in a common negation; in both there was the same formidable denial of the feminine. Both were essential manifestations of the masculine domination of the evolution of the spirit.

This is a brief and simple summary of the redirection of spirit Jung gained from China through Wilhelm. The immediate link between the two, apart from the dream mentioned before, was appropriately a symbol. One does not diminish thereby the pre-eminence of the dream. Indeed, the older Jung became the more he dreamed, and hence the greater the use and meaning dreams assumed in his work. Not the least of his services to his time was his demonstration of how the dreaming process in man, far from being archaic and redundant, was more relevant than ever. If honoured and given the same attention that we give the other objective externals of our lives, the process could be evolved and raised to the status of real partnership with conscious man in the most contemporary way.

However, one symbol, moving between his dream and daylight self, was crucial at this moment. For years Jung had observed a circular movement of awareness, dreams, visions and new inner material round an, as yet, undefined centre like planets and moons around a sun. It was a strange rediscovery of what had once been called the "magic circle". Christian use of this symbolism of the circle was common in the medieval age, usually in paintings of Christ at their centre and the four Apostles arranged at the cardinal points of the compass around him. But no-one had ever seen the symbolism implied in the pattern. Some of Jung's women patients, who could not describe it in words or paintings, would even dance the magic circle for him. And, as I was able to tell him, so does the Stone-Age man of Africa to this day. I recalled instances, too, of outbursts of apparent madness in the bush in Central Africa where I had seen whole communities, grey-headed, middle-aged, youth and young children, dance from sunset to dawn in a circle round and round a deranged person, exhorting in song and chanting the soul, whose loss they believed had deranged the spirit, to return to the body. I had been amazed how invariably the dance succeeded in its purpose. Jung's gratification when I told him this was due to the fact that, imperilled as he was under this bombardment of his conscious self with unconscious material, he had found this circular pattern such a compulsive one constant in himself and others, that he had started to paint it and derived such comfort and meaning from it that for years he hardly drew anything else. He called the process and the movement of spirit the "mandala", taking an old Eastern word for a circle, because by this time he had seen drawings of this pattern by his patients that were almost exact copies of paintings used for religious instruction in a Tibet they had never known. When I told him that mandala was the Arabic (as used in Africa) for spectacles, signifying an enlargement and two-way traffic of spirit, he was deeply interested.

He told me how important a piece of evidence the discovery of the famous "sun-wheel" in Rhodesia had been to him since it was perhaps the oldest visual representation of this pattern. Indeed, his own confrontation with these aspects in the unconscious had ended with some superb paintings of mandalas. One called *Window on Eternity*, though painted long before his meeting with Wilhelm, is included in the illustrations of *The Secret of the Golden Flower*, of which the dream magnolia was obviously an example. It shows a flower, diamond with light in the centre, the stars in their courses about it and surrounded by walls with eight gates. The whole is conceived as a transparent window, constituting as complete a visualisation as imagination is capable of rendering of the whole of life and its meaning.

It was followed later, however, by another, the last of all his work in the Red Book, the painting of the yellow castle. He always thought of it as oddly Chinese. Hence the name yellow, not only because it is the colour associated with the Chinese, but also because it is the colour of resolution of the gold of *being* which both Chinese and European alchemists sought. So without sacrifice of special meaning in terms of his own life and time, he returned to alchemy more zealously than ever before.

Yet this return, despite the Chinese precept, was as difficult a task as any he had attempted. He bought all the modern books on the subject available and, when these failed him, went about the market places to buy the work of long-forgotten alchemists in their original Latin. He came to possess what I believe was the largest library of original alchemical books in Europe. But they all seemed at first obscure and meaningless, until he decided to write down carefully all the more constantly recurring patterns of phraseology, and so finally, like an intelligence officer engaged in breaking the cipher of enemy messages in a great war, he broke the remote code. Just as the Chinese, the alchemists were his true, authentic remote forebears. When the medieval church began to fail the questing spirit of Europe (as it increasingly did from the first Christian millennium onwards), and when such thread as it had with the living historical past appeared irrevocably cut, the alchemists had increasingly taken over the original quest. Their persecutors who accused them of being vulgar materialists in search of the wealth that was gold could not have been more wrong. Much of what they had done was inevitably achieved in secrecy and expressed with great obscurity for reasons of security as well as the originality and intractability of the material which confronted them. But Jung, the code broken, soon saw that the gold they were after was no common gold. The philosopher's stone they sought was no ordinary stone. With their al-chemistry they were trying to achieve through the external world what he sought through his psychology. As always, the authentic process of arriving at new meaning began by seeing its reflection and symbolism mirrored in the world without. They were seeking to create a new sort of man, a greater awareness of reality and increase of meaning.

It was obvious to Jung now that their work was full of living symbolism of the most transformative kind. There was not one of any distinction among them, from Hermes Trismegistus to Paracelsus, who did not lay down as the first and most important law of his science purity of heart, honesty of mind, love of God and the patience of that love which endured and bore all things to the true end. And so at last from as far back as an unremembered African hand which inscribed a rock in Africa with its version of what the Tibetans call the "wheel of life", and on through the story of Babylon, Egypt, Russia, Palestine, Greece, Rome and up to the present day, the continuity of the essential theme of life was empirically established as having remained unbroken and intact.

The detail of all this is there irrefutably in Jung's *Psychology and Alchemy* and so there is no need to follow it further. With all its essential and elaborate footnotes, the book appears forbidding enough and fit only for the most dedicated of scholars. Yet far from difficult, it is a great Homeric epic of the Western spirit and a resounding poetic statement which leaves one humble, grateful and infinitely reassured. For there were in the past so many forgotten men working with the zeal of Old Testament prophets at material abhorred, and even ridiculed, and serving such improbable and fantastic initiations of reality with patience and forbearance, seeking nothing for themselves but light of the truth. The astonishing illustrations in this book show them in their curious, precarious places of work serving their improbable vision at odd hermetic vessels, little charcoal fires, glass burners and other baroque chemical retorts, and make one realise what a debt we owe them and what a great river in man is his passion for truth. One starry utterance after another comes out of the alchemical dark. "I sleep and my soul awakens"; ... "Imagination is the star in man": ... "Thus there is in man a firmament as in Heaven but not of one piece; there are two. For the hand that divided light from darkness and the hand that made Heaven and earth has done likewise in the microcosm below, having taken from above and enclosed within man everything that Heaven contains." ... "As the great Heaven stands, so it is implanted at birth." ... D. H. Lawrence wrote that "in the dust where we have buried the silent races and their abominations we have buried so much of the delicate magic of life". Through his re-interpretation of Chinese and European alchemy, Jung uncovers much of this "delicate magic of life" and shows that it is not dead but relevant and alive in the symbolism of our imagination and continues to be of great concern to our well-being in the present.

Perhaps one example may help to underline how relevant even the most trivial of these forgotten issues can be to the individual today. In all these researches, Jung had done what the Chinese had always prescribed as a pre-essential for living one's own life with meaning in the present; he had honoured in full the spirits of the ancestors in the field. All sorts of men who had laboured for the truth in obscurity against cynicism and persecution were brought out and resurrected each one in his own individual right and restored in honour to their place in the procession of the spirit of man. For instance, in Dante's *Divine Comedy* there appears in this crepuscular world a being who is hailed joyfully as "Michael Scott". So British a name among the scores of Greek, Roman and Italian ones, is so unexpected to the ordinary reader as to be comic. But in Jung, "Scott" is resurrected as an alchemist of distinction, and one can see immediately why he would have been important to Dante in an age when alchemy was of such essential interest to any free-ranging spirit.

With all this and more done to Jung's empirical satisfaction he was free to evaluate and interpret in detail all he had brought back with him from his journey. And, above all, to set forth in depth, and fill in with substance, his hypothesis of the collective unconscious. Until this moment it would not be an unfair generalisation to say that in so far as the existence of an unconscious in man was accepted it was in a negative way. This, in a sense, was not surprising. Both Jung and Freud had come to it initially in their search for the causes of neurosis and derangement in human personality. Both had traced the source of neurosis and derangement to an unconscious area in the mind of man. There was a moment even when this unconscious appeared as a comparatively shallow area, existing not so much in its own right as created out of a conscious and wilful suppression of instincts and experience too painful for the comfort of man. In so far as it was thought of as existing in its own right, it seemed to be in active opposition to what was conscious in man. Both Jung and Freud themselves had established significant patterns of conflict between the conscious and unconscious. But in Jung's view it was a vastly different matter. The negative aspect of the collective unconscious dwindled into insignificance beside his revelation of its positive objective nature, and its vital involvement in the enlargement of consciousness in man.

The conflict between conscious and unconscious forces which filled mental asylums and crowded out the consulting rooms of Freud, Jung and their collaborators was nothing compared to the problem of enrichment and increase in the conscious life of man that Jung found concealed in it. This was no dark, disordered world, basically antipathetic and committed to war on consciousness. Where it was dark, it had its own form of starlight and moonlight by which the probing spirit could steer. Its laws of order and determination were as precise as those that kept the stars in their courses in the universe without. The negations came only when man's conscious self ignored his dependence on this world of the collective unconscious and tried to establish some kind of independent tyranny over what ultimately only sought to nourish and increase what should be a partnership. The disturbance started in human personality when consciousness behaved as if it were the whole of man. There was nothing the unconscious world abhorred more than onesidedness. When one extreme of spirit attempted a monopoly for itself, sooner or later another extreme in the unconscious rose titanic to overthrow it. That is why the history of man is so often a swing from one opposite of spirit into another, as Heraclitus had observed. This new and revolutionary view of an unconscious was set out by Jung with an immense wealth of empirical detail, drawn not only from his work in the mental asylums and in his practice, but from history, art, literature and the mythologies and religions of the world. The labour and scale of imagination and concentration that he put into this work makes nonsense of the charge that he was some gifted but vague mystic let loose on the scientific scene. He established in a way that no scientist can deny that this collective unconscious within man was objective; that the visions and dreams and imagery in which it communicated with man's conscious self were utterly objective facts, however subjectively they were experienced. Jung showed clearly how conscious man ignored such facts at his peril. Moreover he taught himself and men how to read the language of dreams as if they were the forgotten language of the gods themselves.

He revealed that in the collective unconscious of individual man were infinite resources of energy, organised in definite recognisable patterns. Each of these patterns had at its disposal its own form of energy located, as it were, at the centre, between the unconscious and conscious. There was a master-pattern to which all other patterns subscribed, and all their energies could be joined in one transcendental orbit. He called these patterns, first of all, "primordial images" (a phrase borrowed from Burckhardt) but later changing it to "archetypes", rediscovered from St Augustine and before him even used by Hermes Trismegistus, who exclaims in the *Poimandres*, "You have seen in your mind the archetypal image."

In this one detail one sees the selfless unfailingly exacting worker, Jung, determined not to set himself apart or above history, but wherever possible to contain all he did in the context of his own culture. It became a fixed article of work and faith that he should never throw away his own cultural inheritance but accept it, however imperfect, as the basic material of his work, and as the only aboriginal stock on which his own contemporary spirit could flower. This was the more remarkable because he was always open to all cultures, and religions. The temptation to copy them at times must have been considerable. But his capacity for deriving new meaning from all civilisations was unbounded. He drew on the experience of such different extremes as the Chinese and Red Indian, Sanskrit India, and primitive Africa, not as substitutions for but as enrichments of his own cultural inheritance.

Meanwhile, he found that these archetypes (a word that is so much in use these days that it is in danger of losing its value) were so highly organised and vivid in the unconscious, impinging so sharply on conscious imagination, that they could be personified or at the very least given abstract expression, as in that final drawing in his own Red Book of a yellow castle. An example of how vivid and complex this world of archetypes was, of course, to be found in the instinctive and intuitive representations in Greek mythology. This system of spirit is perhaps the most highly differentiated, accurate and detailed model of the forces of the collective unconscious we still possess. It is precisely because of this exceptional instinctive awareness of the collective unconscious, demonstrated in their myths and legends and all that flowed from them, that the Greeks were able to make so formidable a contribution to the evolution of the human spirit.

Jung himself in his Red Book, in the mural paintings he did so magnetically on the walls of his tower at Bollingen, and in his carvings on stone, gave visual expression to his own personifications and abstractions of some of these great archetypal images and powers. He himself indeed had been familiar with one in personified form when still a boy. He had visualised and had had a dialogue almost as far back as he could remember, as we have seen, with one of the greatest of all archetypes, that of the wise old man, the inner master or guru of India, or the *sensei* of Japan. He had discovered with great benefit to himself how this pattern was formed of all the experience of life since the beginning and its intimations of where and how it wants to take itself further, implanting in it the imagination of every human being, so that did we but know it we are not born utterly naked, ignorant and unarmed in the jungle of the world but also have great guidance and protection within.

As one looks back from this high, assured new vantage point Jung had achieved within himself in a life lengthening so fast behind him but closing in on him so swiftly from ahead, there is nothing more poignant than this vision of him as a young boy, when a father he had loved had failed him, and putting a trusting hand instead in that of this wise figure who came to him unsolicited in the stillness of his own imagination and letting it lead him on safely to his meeting with the destiny to which he was committed at birth. We have seen how in all his moments of greatest abandonment, when he had no male company of any kind, this archetype stayed firmly with him. Embattled as he was, Jung was moved to go on painting and repainting his portrait at Bollingen in a manner which is so decisive that no imagination can look at the painting and doubt the validity of the pattern he represents. One could hardly sleep in one's bed there at night, so alive and urgent was his presence in the murals around the room.

And perhaps strangest and most significant of all, the relevant coincidence, in high Chinese fashion, had come to confirm the authenticity of the vision the first time he tried to paint it. The vision came to him in kingfisher-blue wings. Jung painted it with an electric blue immediacy that to this day is quite startling. Some time afterwards, walking in his garden by the lake, he found a dead kingfisher lying there. The bird in any case was rare and he had never seen one there before, nor was he to see one again. Since the bird, always and everywhere from Stone-Age man to Stravinsky, has been the image of the inspiration, the unthinkable thought which enters our selves like a bird unsolicited out of the blue, it was for Jung, as a Zen priest once put it to me, one of the signs of confirmation from nature that sustain the spirit in its search for enlightenment and emancipation from the floating world of appearances.

Unfortunately, the archetypal patterns of Jung's evolution are far too many to be enumerated specifically, and there are probably more even than either the massive assembly recorded in Greek mythology or those Jung delineated. But two deserve special mention because of their unique importance to our own time. These are the feminine in man and the masculine in woman—the great twosome. Jung called the latter "animus" and the first, as mentioned in his encounter with Salome, "anima", thereby using again a term borrowed from the forgotten language of Christian religion when it was still aflame with its new message of love in the power-obsessed world of Rome. It was precisely because of this denial of the archetypal aspect and its supreme value of love that Jung saw the history of the world as such a cataclysmic wasteland. It was this denial that made modern man increasingly sick in mind and spirit, so great was the loss of sense of direction which resulted from this rejection. It was the equivalent of what my African countrymen (as Jung had appreciated when he lived among them) call the "loss of soul". This they fear and abhor as the greatest disaster that can befall any human-being. And this loss of soul, joined to what he had experienced as a psychiatrist, convinced Jung that it was the main cause of man's private and collective derangements.

The soul of man, after all, as one of the earliest fathers of religion had said, was naturally religious. Now it had been proved to be so scientifically. Clearly it gave man a hunger greater than any physical hunger. And if this hunger were not nourished, men and their societies either withered or perished in some disaster unconsciously brought down on themselves. Wherever Jung looked he saw a world increasingly sick because of a loss of soul deprived of its meaning. "Meaninglessness" was the greatest disease of his day, as it is of ours. We all, to a greater or lesser degree, whether we know it or not, are Pirandello characters in search of our author.

From that moment on, Jung's work became more and more a religious concern, however scientific and empiric were the instruments chosen for the service. The unconscious was no longer a source of conflict and derangement but a world in which health and sanity and salvation had to be sought. Important as it had been to discover and explore the unconscious in the interests of the abnormal, it was now recognised as an affair of life and death for so-called normal man.

Derangement and neurosis were regarded by Jung as a measure of man's estrangement from his full unconscious self; an affliction sent to redirect him and set him on his true course. Consequently, in every neurosis there were the seeds of something positive, of new growth and new meaning. The moment he could direct his patients to see a meaning in their own suffering, the suffering became endurable, even if it did not vanish. More and more he found in the suffering of the individual a mirror of what was culpably inadequate in terms of the collective unconscious in the life of a whole time. No recovery of a sense of meaning seemed possible without a recovery of personal "religious" experience through the collective unconscious.

The churches for many had ceased to be places of living religious experience. The psychiatrist had to heal where once the priest had been effective. Never before had he realised so clearly how the future of man depended on a rediscovery of his capacity for religious experience accessible in a twentieth-century idiom, rather than in the dogmatic doctrinal in which it had been imposed on him for centuries. It is remarkable how always those who in the end could gain most from Jung's work misunderstood and attacked what he was trying to do; namely the churches and institutions of science. Yet he knew, and protested over and over again, that only living religion could replace literal religion. He had not abandoned his own Christian inheritance because he acknowledged the validity of the religious experience of other races and cultures. He was concerned only in making religion real again for modern man. He recognised that exhortation, dogmatic utterance and conventional religious ritual and symbolism still worked for a number of people. He acknowledged that there had been a moment when the creed and dogma of the Christian church had achieved as complete and accurate a definition as possible of the aspirations of the Western spirit. That was why not only the spiritual aspirations of man but all that he possessed of art, science, music and grace had been put to its service as well. But that moment had long passed. If Christian exhortation had been the whole answer, surely two thousand years were more than sufficient for it to have proved its efficiency?

But clearly, as our disastrous yesterdays showed, it was not enough. Indeed, it looked as if in the church's insistence on dogmatic utterances of a bygone age, its effort to arrest the evolution of the human spirit in one moment of divine revelation of the Son of God nailed to a cross, the churches had failed both themselves, civilisation and the religious urge they proposed to serve. His task was to make religion once more credible to unbelieving modern men and women for whom exhortations to belief were useless. He had to do it in an empirical and scientific way in the first instance, and then through the objective eventfulness of their dreams, fantasy and imagination bring them to an area of the spirit where the mystery, the "awful" mystery, he stressed, of the Divine was more likely than not to present itself again.

The mystery of what happened there was not mystification. It was the mystery of re-growth. Dr C. A. Meier, Jung's collaborator, explained something of the event in his book on ancient Greek healing. He said it was like bringing together, as it were, the two ends of a broken bone. There was no doubt that, as a rule, the bones would join and grow as one again, but how they did it was a mystery. No scientist could, as yet, know exactly what this growth was. It was a great mystery, yet it was real and it worked.

The role of the dreaming process was crucial. Writing to a friend later, Jung was to say something to the effect: "You tell me you have had many dreams lately but have been too busy with your writing to pay attention to them. You have got it the wrong way round. Your writing can wait but your dreams cannot because they come unsolicited from within and point urgently to the way you must go."

As always he himself put it clearly and, as always when in the presence of his own greater truth, with the humility and poetry which he possessed in no mean a measure. He writes of the dream: "The dream is a little hidden door in the innermost and most secret recesses of the psyche, opening into that cosmic night which was psyche long before there was any ego consciousness, and which will remain the psyche no matter how far our ego consciousness may extend . . . All consciousness separates. But in dreams we put on the likeness of that more universal, truer, more eternal man dwelling in the darkness of primordial night. There is still the whole, and the whole is in him, indistinguishable from nature and bare of all egohood. Out of these all-uniting depths arises the dream, be it never so infantile, never so grotesque, never so immoral."*

* *Civilisation in Transition*, Collected Works, Vol. 10.

Of the psyche, the soul which invokes the means of all the love of the feminine in man and which is at one with the source of the dream and as such must be defined with it, he wrote even more evocatively: "If the human soul is anything, it must be of unimaginable complexity and diversity, so that it cannot possibly be approached through a mere psychology of instinct. I can only gaze with wonder and awe at the depths and heights of our psychic nature. Its non-spatial universe conceals an untold abundance of images which have accumulated over millions of years of living development and become fixed in the organism. My consciousness is like the psychic non-ego that fills them with non-spatial images. And these images are not pale shadows, but tremendously powerful psychic factors . . . Besides this picture I would like to place the spectacle of the starry heavens at night, for the only equivalent of the universe within is the universe without; and just as I reach this world through the medium of the body, so I reach that world through the medium of the psyche."*

Yet even in dogma, pre-eminently a theological field, he did what he could to preserve its symbolic validity. His correspondence with numbers of clergymen, priests and philosophers testifies unquestionably to his undying efforts despite their scepticism and prejudice. He wrote profound essays on the meaning of the trinity, the Mass, transubstantiation, the Immaculate Conception and other basic aspects and articles of Christian faith, making them contemporary and accessible to ordinary educated men and women in a way their rational preconditioning could not deny. But the churches did not seem to want to be helped. Then, most important of all, he established that no matter what the race or creed or colour or culture, the need for a living religious experience was equal and vital, and that in this collective unconscious the same patterns never varied, but were all of one and the same measure. It was a great, impartial, undiscriminating area of spirit where all men were one in what they could receive. The scale and detail of the work on the life of his own time and in the history of man, art and religion, are so vast and impressive that no-one who will give the facts a hearing can remain unconvinced that in this collective unconscious the brotherhood of man already exists and is ready and equipped to be lived consciously. That is why the compulsion to find it haunts the human spirit, as the ghost of his father did Hamlet, and will not leave it alone until we give conscious expression to what is already a great, dynamic unconscious reality.

In the collective unconscious, already all men and all races and

* *Freud and Psychoanalysis*, Collected Works, Vol. 4, p. 331.

colours are kin and enjoy one and the same parentage. It is the great religious ocean into which all the religious streams of the world flow. For the first time in the history of man, religious imperialisms are outmoded; are, in fact, irreligious. Religious colonisation is at an end. Even sectarianism or the equivalents of caste and class systems in religion are out of date, and man can unite in the service of a common religious search derived from the same experience in one uniquely contemporary idiom. We are only at the beginning of the consequences for man of this aspect of the discovery of the collective unconscious. The societies of man and his political systems alone can ultimately never be the same because of it.

Ignorance in English law is no excuse for breaches of the law. In the collective unconscious, ignorance, unawareness, are not only inexcusable but the greatest offence which carry the most dire consequences. That is why in Greek myth, legend and art, the villain is always the ignorance where it serves as representative of inner unawareness. It is always the "not knowing", the non-recognition of man's own inner eventfulness, which is the real crime. Always it is man's unawareness that evokes the vengeance of fate. It is man's lack of knowledge of himself and his motives that calls up disaster. How much greater, therefore, the culpability of a consciousness like our own that knows and will not face up to the responsibility of what it knows: for no-one since Freud and Jung can any longer plead ignorance of where our failure starts.

Theologians always firmly held that all men were equal in dignity before God. This pattern in the collective unconscious is precisely of so great a potentiality for the human spirit because all men are equal in dignity before it, in the sense that in that area they are all raised and equipped with equal impartiality.

Jung put all this forward not as argument but as experience. Experience is before and beyond argument. One of the gravest indictments of the intellectualism of his and our age is a strange determination to deny human-beings the validity and dignity of their own experience and to subject it to some external, preconceptualised devaluation. Jung held on to the experience of all these patterns in the collective unconscious as vital points of departure. When asked in public if he believed in God he said, "I do not believe . . ." and then paused.

I who heard him at the time remember the sense of darkness that came in at the windows at the pause, and how it dissolved swiftly into light when he added, after what seemed an age, "I know."

He knew because he had experienced what was once called the living

God. He had that experience, I believe, in a measure no other man of his day had done through confrontation with the collective unconscious. He apprehended God as the ultimate and greatest meaning of which life is capable and in whose direction all our searching is turned. God revealed himself immediately through this master pattern in the collective unconscious in a manner that no man could have endured had he not possessed an intermediary, an intercessor, between himself and this fearful reality. This intercessor, of course, is this only partially apprehended, and as yet inadequately explored, pattern of the feminine.

"I cannot define for you what God is", Jung wrote to me just before he died. "I can only say that my work has proved empirically that the pattern of God exists in every man, and that this pattern has at its disposal the greatest of all energies for transformation and transfiguration of his natural being. Not only the meaning of his life but his renewal and that of his institutions depend on his conscious relationship with this pattern in his collective unconscious."

So in the final analysis Jung's life was that of a profoundly religious person, lived to a truly religious end, however scientifically committed his work. His last years were spent almost entirely in exploring this relationship between individual man and the pattern of God in the human spirit. He was convinced that our spent selves and worn-out societies could not renew themselves without renewing their concepts of God and so their whole relationship with them.

Jung, in this journey into his own unconscious self, had discovered another "archetypal pattern" of the utmost significance in this regard which he called the "shadow"—a pattern that had at its disposal all the energies that man had consciously despised, rejected or ignored in himself. One sees immediately how aptly the term was chosen, because it is an image of what happens when the human-being stands between himself and his own light. Whether this shadow should be properly regarded as archetypal in itself, or whether it is another shadow of archetypes themselves, is almost academic. The dark, rejected forces massing in the shadow of the unconscious, as it were, knife in hand, demanding revenge for all that man and his cultures have consciously sacrificed of them in the specialised conscious tasks he has set himself, are real and active enough to keep us too busy for scholasticisms. They show how all our history is a progression on two levels—conscious and unconscious, a manifest and a latent level. The manifest level provides all the plausible rational justifications and excuses for the wars, revolutions and disasters inflicted on men in their collective and private lives. But in reality it is in this other latent level where, unrecognised, the real instigators and conspirators against too narrow and rigid a conscious rule are to be found. There, proud, angry and undefeated, they move men and women on the visible level as puppets in pre-determined patterns of their own revengeful seeking, like a magnet conditioning from underneath a field of iron filings on a table above.

This is why all men tend to become what they oppose. The New Testament exhorted us not to resist evil because what follows, logic-ally, is that the dark, dishonoured self triumphs and emerges to form another tyranny, thus producing the swing of the opposites of which Heraclitus spoke. The answer, as Jung saw it, was to abolish tyranny, to enthrone the two opposites side by side in the service of the master pattern, not opposing or resisting evil but transforming and redeem-ing it. These two opposites in the negations of our time are turned into tragic enemies. But truly seen, psychologically, and perhaps best defined in the non-emotive terms of physics, they are like the negative and positive inductions of energy observed in the dynamics of elec-tricity. They are the two parallel and opposite streams without which the flash of lightning, always the symbol of awareness made impera-tive, was impossible.

Containing those two opposites, putting the light of the superior functions at the service of the dark, bearing all the tensions induced thereby, the individual could grow into a resolution of the two on to a greater realisation of himself. One says greater because the self realised thereby is more than the sum of the opposites, because in the process of their resolution the individual is enabled to join in the universal and continuing act of creation and add something to life which was not there before.

So this role of the shadow in the life of the individual, the life of civilisation and the reality of religion, not surprisingly, was one of Jung's closest concerns. He demonstrated in a way that cannot be denied how this mechanism of the shadow was at the back of the phenomenon of the persecution of the Jews in history, how Christians for centuries blamed their own rejection of the real meaning of Christ on the Jews who had crucified him, ignoring how they were recrucify-ing him daily in their own lives. It is an elemental part of the mytho-logical dominants of history, as I called them to myself in the begin-ning. The mechanism of the shadow, for instance, was the explanation of Hitler and his own persecution of the Jews, and also of all racial, colour and personal prejudice—all were consequences of forms of a profound process of self-rejection.

Jung revealed in great detail how the individual imposed his quarrel

with his own shadow on to his neighbour, in the process outlining
scientifically why men inevitably saw only the mote in the eye of their
neighbour. It was not just out of ignorance of the beam in their own
eye but unconsciously to avoid recognising it as their reflection
because of the self-responsibility that would entail. He defined for the
first time in a contemporary idiom a primordial mechanism in the
spirit of man which he called "projection", a mechanism which compels us to blame on our neighbour what we unconsciously dislike most
in ourselves.

All at once it was clear that man could only be well and sane when
this quarrel between him and his shadow, between the primitive and
the civilised, was dissolved. Only when the two were reconciled could
they enter together into the presence of the master-pattern, as Jung's
experience had already done. Only then did man become whole.
Wholeness was the ultimate of man's conscious and unconscious seeking. Consciousness was important because it was the chosen instrument
of the unconscious seeking the abolition of partialities in a harmony of
differences that is wholeness. This wholeness was only possible through
a life lived religiously. To heal, or make whole, once more was demonstrated to be a Pentecostal task of the utmost holiness.

The message to the churches and temples of the day was clear. They
were emptying fast because they had defaulted on their mission of
enabling men to become whole. They would empty altogether unless
they returned to healing in a contemporary way leading to an achievement of wholeness in a twentieth-century context. And none of this
healing was possible except by facing honestly and with the utmost
courage the problem of the shadow cast not only by man in himself
but by God on life.

This last, at least, should not be too difficult to grasp because its
impact on the human imagination has been so great and is of such
long standing that it is amply personified in religions, mythologies,
art and literature of the world. One is speaking of something that goes
by many names. Generically the shadow is the evil spirit, the devil.
More particularly in the European tradition it is known as Mephistopheles, Lucifer or the proud Apollyon of Milton, who preferred ruling
in Hell to serving in Heaven. It was typical of Jung that he did not
make any attempt to establish the shadow as a great universal, before
he had sorted it all out scientifically within his own nature and in the
individual problems of his own patients. He had faced up to the problem of his own shadow so squarely that one of the most significant
paintings in the Red Book is a portrait of his shadow personified.

There, in what looks like a room in some basement, covered with black and white tiles, the colours of the two opposites, Jung portrays his shadow as a cloak-and-dagger figure cowering against the far corner of the walls. It is done with such confidence as if the outcome of the encounter were already decided and Jung could afford an enigmatic, affectionate smile in his approach to it. "Cornered at last", one could add, and cornered in the right place below street level.

I myself have often been taken to task for not speaking more about Jung's shadow. But I cannot speak of what I myself did not experience. I knew him only in the closing years of his life, when he was much more resolved and the shadow less evident than when young. Of course, great a person as Jung was, he must also have had a great shadow. No-one could be real and not throw a shadow. I had learned this as a boy from my own black friends in Africa, who, if they wanted to pay one their highest compliment, would say, "But you do throw a shadow!" They would look at their own shadows, la Mancha long and lean at sunset, and say of them, "You see that man down there? When I die he goes up into the sky to join the sun, but I go down into the earth where he now lies."

The important thing is not what Jung's shadow was but the fact that he never ceased to work on it. Coming to terms with the shadow, the problem of reconciling the opposites in a whole greater than their parts was an ultimate of his seeking. And for him, if we were not to destroy ourselves, it was also the most urgent practical necessity of our time. Working at this aspect of himself brought him into conflict not only with himself but with the churches. He never wavered in his acceptance of Christ as the West's greatest symbol of the self. But he could not accept that the coming of Christ, or any blind imitation of his being, had abolished the reality of the shadow, whether in man or God.

As far as the shadow of the All-Highest was concerned, it had bothered Jung all his conscious life. The significance of it both for God and man was expressed in one of its earliest and most dramatic forms in the Book of Job. For years Jung had talked about it to his friends, as many others before him, but in a new way. It was talk of his in this regard which had much to do with the writing of H. G. Wells's *The Undying Fire*. Froude, too, an unjustly neglected Victorian historian and essayist, had been obsessed with the problem of Job. He answered his doubts ultimately by interpreting Job's meaning as an inspired allegory designed to show that worldly wealth and success were no proof of God's blessing as the Victorians were over-inclined to assume. But, on the contrary, those whom God loved most could be made to suffer most. That satisfied Froude for, of course, it is a vital point, but only a point. He leaves the "why" of the suffering out of it.

Jung in all honesty, however, could not do so and finally wrote one of his most subjective of all books—and one all the greater for it—as a dialogue with God on the drama of Job. Only a simple version of the main conclusion is possible here. Job proved that man found his greatest meaning in God's need of man's conscious awareness, which inferred a freedom of choice between good and evil in order to deal with a cosmic shadow. Though God himself might be compelled to let the shadow, Satan, also have his say in reality, and so be forced, as it were, for the moment to lend Satan a certain tactical support in the long-term strategy of the campaign for meaning in the universe, God counted on man not to submit to his Satanic shadow. So in order to let man win both battle and campaign, God delegates his most valuable of all powers, the power of his love, to do battle with man and Job against Satan and himself. Job in this sense is a prefiguration of Christ and, implicit in this divine alliance with love, there is an intimation of the future greater role of the feminine, the anima in its most evolved form from Eve to Helen and Helen into Mary and so finally into that personified in Sophia, as the wisdom of love. Most important of all, there is a significant and disturbing hint, which one must not overstress and yet cannot ignore, that man, made whole through endurance in love of the shadow, is made so much more honourable and meaningful in his estate that he could ultimately surpass his Creator—a hint that makes the imperative of man's ethical obligations to what he knew and discovered increasingly of new sources of power over nature more urgent and awesome than ever before in history.

It is not surprising, therefore, that nothing made Jung more impatient and at times angrier than the conventional and stubborn religious insistence that evil was only the absence of good, a fault in man alone, and a result of indulgence in the seven deadly sins. His language, which could be just as earthy as it was poetic, when he was roused in this profound regard was worthy of an inspired peasant, and words like "shitbags" and "pisspots" would roll from his lips in sentences of crushing correction.

"Who the devil do they think put the serpent in the Garden of Eden?" he once exclaimed to me, talking about the fearful archetype of the shadow, and then suddenly laughed out loud at himself. "Did you notice how my unconscious intruded to point a finger at where the answer could be? Certainly not Adam. Maybe the devil, but certainly not man."

Perhaps he put his objections best of all in the most carefully considered, measured, and considerate fashion in a letter to Father Victor White, because he was fond of the man. Victor White had come to him for psychological understanding of his own religious beliefs. As so many others before him, he ultimately went away in the main with what suited his own preconceived beliefs and provided the latest modern ammunition for promoting them while rejecting the rest of Jung, on which the very illumination he took away depended. Jung, who longed to work with a serious, intelligent theologian qualified in depth, had turned to him with unusual warmth, not surprising in one at the same time so lonely and so concerned for restoring modern people's capacity for religious experience.

Victor White was to turn on Jung later with, it seems to me, unnecessary violence and disregard for what he owed him both as teacher and friend. At the time this particular letter was written he had already had a stab at Jung's broad back which Jung magnanimously overlooked, as he did other attacks and certain studied indignities inflicted on him by Victor White. Jung's *Answer to Job* at a first reading, if Victor White's immediate letter of appreciation can be taken at its face value, had both excited and uplifted him. But very soon he had second thoughts, began to decry the book in public, and became increasingly critical of Jung, not hesitating to call him naive and ill informed on matters of theology—terms that were as undeserved as they were inaccurate. For if anyone were in a position to know the extent of Jung's theological knowledge, research and interest in religion, and his grasp of its implications for life past, present and future, it was Victor White. Yet despite this, Jung, up to the end, respected what had brought him and White together and understood White's situation, committed as he was to a priority of prescribed faith, as much as the latter failed to understand his ultimate meaning.

Considerate as Jung was, however, his meaning and the quality of the temper of truth at work in the writing of the letter itself is clear.

Accordingly he wrote: "This *Privatio Boni* business [the Catholic doctrine that evil is a privation of good] is odious to me on account of its dangerous consequences; it causes a negative inflation [overvaluation] of man, who can't help imagining himself, if not as a source of the good, at least as a great destroyer, capable of devastating God's beautiful creation. This doctrine produces Luciferian vanity and it is also responsible for the fatal *underrating of the soul* as being the original abode of Evil. It gives a monstrous importance to the soul and not a word about on whose account the presence of the Serpent in Paradise belongs!

"The question of Good and Evil as far as I am concerned with it, has nothing to do with metaphysics; it is only a concern of psychology . . .

"As long as Evil is not a living entity *nobody will take his own shadow seriously*. Hitler and Stalin will go on representing a mere 'accidental lack of perfection'. *The future of mankind very much depends upon the recognition of the shadow* . . . Evil is—psychologically speaking—*terribly real*. It is a fatal mistake to diminish its power and reality, even merely metaphysically. I am sorry, this goes to the very roots of Christianity. Evil verily does not decrease by being hushed up as a non-reality or as mere negligence of man. It was there before him, when he could not possibly have had a hand in it. God is the mystery of all mysteries, a real Tremendum."

And there the final enigmatic, paradoxical truth was out. God was a reality man had to fear as much as to love, Old and New Testaments of the spirit did not abolish but complemented one another. Yet before one follows this final storm-bound perception further, it is important to stress that this evaluation of the shadow in Jung's psychology is followed at its simplest and most immediate best in his letters to Victor White and many others. It is significant how Victor White was to go on from there to reject the post-war reassertion of the feminine in Catholic doctrine. For the feminine soul in man is the go-between and guide to reconciliation of man and his shadow. That is why Jung attached such an enormous symbolical importance to the Vatican's proclamation of the new doctrine of the bodily assumption of the Virgin Mary into Heaven. For him at last in the highest dimension of reality and its greatest symbol, the masculine and some of the feminine were at one, the conscious will of the masculine in creation was increasingly being joined to serve the love of the feminine and a creation, no longer static but procreatively on the move again. It was for him a welcome sign that the Christian myth which mattered so much to him was still alive and breathing; that its content was not one of mere "historicity" but of an historical conception of a profound need in man still capable of growing in meaning.

White was among the foremost of Catholic intellectualists who pronounced the doctrine as a religious scandal, reading it literally of course and not symbolically as Jung did. The objection is all the more glaring when one considers that, even symbolically, only part of the feminine had ascended to Heaven. The woman so translated was the image of the feminine in man, the mother of the son of man, Dante's virgin mother, daughter of her son. Woman and her masculine self, as far as Christian dogma was concerned, were still left stranded on the earth.

It was only after coming to terms with the role of the shadow in himself that Jung took upon himself the dangerous task of approaching its universal aspect. It was typical of the man that he did this first as a living experience, exposing his imagination and all of his conscious self as a kind of Job on an ash-heap of himself before all that was terrible, ruthless and aweful in the human spirit's experience of God. Out of these experiences he emerged with an enriched awareness of the paradoxical nature of all reality, even that of the ultimate.

In this paradoxical pattern the image of God was both terrible and lovable. There the fear of God always was the beginning of all wisdom; the love of God the only protection of the spirit that ventured in his presence. Fear and love were mysteriously joined to enable both man and God to achieve greater meaning. From that moment on, Jung saw the relationship between man and God in a way it had never been perceived, however mystically and intuitively it may have been pre-experienced.

He saw man and God, as it were, in partnership; the traffic between them no longer one-sided but two-way; man no longer alone at an almost intolerable receiving end but also at a giving end. Man now too could contribute to the conscious reality of God, as God contributed to his power to do so. He found man and his unconscious self, man in all four aspects of himself, the man and his feminine self, the woman and her masculine self, joined with God in a task of transcendental meaning.

Man was the chosen instrument for enabling life to answer the problem for which it had been invented. Life was a process of living an answer to a problem implicit in its creation. The suffering of man was meaningful because it reflected the suffering of its creator. In this role, man might look as exposed as Job to what appeared at times to be an almost capricious exercise of divine power. But even in his most miserable state, man was not alone. Jung had clearly demonstrated that where man and God were encountered face to face, a vital, indescribable element of the greatest transforming energies at the disposal of this master-pattern was delegated to intercede for man. This was the long rejected and despised feminine and its highest value of love. The history of man's experience of God had been a miserable, one-sided affair, the catastrophic, disaster-pitted dimension of history it has been,

precisely because this love of God and its averted feminine face allotted
to man for his protection had been spurned.

No-one has worked harder to bring more light to the darkness that
still surrounds our little day. No-one has worked harder to push back
as it were the frontiers of the mystery which encloses us. Yet no-one
has shown so great a respect and reverence for the mystery. Indeed,
Jung could not have worked so well to reduce the mystery of life had
he not done so utterly in a spirit of reverence and love. As a result,
one finds that at the end of his days, when he is ready to close his own
account of what he had laboured to do in life, he leaves the last word
not with these great new concepts of his but with a mystery which he
confesses he is incapable of articulating; the mystery of love. And that
love in the last analysis is a feminine mystery.

Indeed, one of the occasions on which I saw Jung most moved was
in the course of an account of a dream which illustrated this. It was
the dream of an old lady whose last years had been full of pain and
sickness. Before she died, at a very great age, she had a dream experienced as near to death as any dream on record. Like so many dreams
of greatest meaning it was almost epigrammatic in its imagery. In the
dream, all her pain and sickness were gathered together into a bed of
roses and she knew that roses would always grow. And the rose, one
felt instantly, was chosen by her unconscious because it is the image of
everlasting love, the Eros in life as only a woman can know it and
which enables her to lead the masculine to achieve its greatest meaning. One thought of Dante's reunion with Beatrice and their ascent at
last to Heaven in the rose as well as that poetic statement of total finality
in one of the last of T. S. Eliot's poems on how the end of all our
seeking was a state of being where fire and rose are one.

The essence of Jung's message then is that, as far as the future is
foreseeable, the highest task of man once more is the old religious task
of the redemption of Evil that he called the shadow. As shadow, Evil
was not absolute and final, but redeemable and through its challenge
to be redeemed an instrument of enlargement of human awareness. In
this transfiguration, the last word is with love. In *Modern Man in Search
of a Soul* there is a sign of what his feelings, as opposed to his thinking,
were about it. At the end of the search he describes there, he writes:
"Who are forgiven their many sins? Those who have loved much.
But as to those who love little, their few sins are held against them."

Jung was possessed by a capacity for love so great that it included
a love of all that life until now had rejected, reviled and persecuted.
In all this he was more than a psychological or scientific phenomenon

—he was to my mind one of the most momentous religious phenomena the world has ever experienced. Until this central fact of his work and character is grasped and admitted, the full meaning and implication of Jung for the future of life is missed. But once this fact is grasped and experienced, the life of the individual who has experienced it can never be the same again. However dark, disordered and desperate this moment in which we live, the individual who finds himself in this way will, I believe, change the course of life in the direction of a greater wholeness of being, lived in greater awareness of the mystery of love. And this love is so pre-eminently in the keeping of the feminine in life, and presides so archangelic and constant over the passion of truth in Jung. Perhaps this is why such numbers of truly remarkable women rallied round Jung.

I remember as a young man going into northern Zululand because of a report that a great new prophet had arisen among the Zulus. When I found him at last I was amazed that there was hardly a single man in his following, but vast numbers of women. My guide, a remarkable Zulu himself, as well educated in the tribal as the European ways, was not at all surprised. "You can tell the greatest of new prophets among us from the numbers of women who flock to him long before the men have the courage to do so", he told me. And in time I saw the uncommon good sense of what he had said. More intuitive than men, women to this day are quicker at spotting a revelation of new truth. The man who is the keeper of the rational conscious self in man—the Logos principle as Jung called it, or the Word as St John called it—needs a clear progression towards conviction by way of ideas and logic. The woman, in her role as chatelaine of the Eros in life, needs no such guidance and gets there first as if on wings of the heart. This to me is one explanation why the numbers of women working around and with Jung were so great. But even more important was the fact that Jung was working ceaselessly to bring back into equal partnership with the men all that was feminine in life. How right therefore that modern woman rather than the modern man often should have been the first to recognise what he was essentially doing.

Late as I came to know Jung, it was still soon enough for me to meet some of the most remarkable of this impressive circle of women colleagues and friends. His own wife Emma was still alive and taking an active part in the work of the Institute founded for the study of his psychology after the last World War. I went regularly to her lectures on the myth and legend of the Holy Grail. She was an immensely sensitive, shy, solicitous, circumspect and introverted spirit, and must have found public exposition of a task of such intimate concern extremely difficult if not painful. Yet she was dauntless as she was enduring, and delivered her meaning with great precision, erudition and understanding. At the same time, she was working as a lay analyst herself.

And then of course there was Toni Wolff of whom I have said almost all that is relevant here. She died suddenly and without ostensible physical warning. Jung saw her only two days before she died. Although he had no conscious idea that her end was so near—he himself was far from well at the time—a dream of Hades some months before had made him uneasy in her regard. And there had been other recurring dreams even before then, started by one of a great black elephant uprooting a tree. This too, he realised, could be an image of death approaching to take away another to add to the many dead who had mattered specially to him.

But there remained many others. Linda Fierz-David whose work on Francesco Colonna's *Hypnerotomachia Poliphili*, *The Dream of Poliphilo*, shed new light on the inner motivation of spirit of the Renaissance and the pattern of its preliminary convolutions in the imagination of that singular Venetian monk who was its author. This dream, as she said herself, was "the symbol of the living process of growth which had been set going, obscurely and incomprehensibly in the men of his time, and made the Renaissance the beginning of a new era".

There was Barbara Hannah, who had come for a visit straight from an English cathedral close, and remained to make her home in Zürich where she lives to this day working as analyst and writer. If her essays on Stevenson, "R.L.S.", the analysis of his evolution as a writer, and in particular how his story of Dr Jekyll and Mr Hyde, inspired by a dream, is high drama of the conflict of man and his shadow played out in the hidden heart of each one of us, were her only contributions, it would have been enough. But of course there was more work still to come.

There is Aniela Jaffé, who had come to see Jung before the last war after a skiing accident that seemed too portentous to ignore. She went to see Jung for months and sat silent in his presence, not knowing what to say or ask, so remote was the world of psychology to her. Jung would just go on patiently and calmly talking to her while sheer intuition that one day she would know what he meant kept her in her chair. And then one day she did know, and knew to such an extent that she could set out on her own, explore what was nearest to her imagination, the area of psychic phenomena, write revealingly about it, and from there move on to her remarkable book *The Myth of Meaning* and her essays on other aspects of Jung's work. In addition, she found the energy and capacity, perhaps unexpectedly in someone ostensibly so delicate and vulnerable physically, to become Jung's secretary, co-author of his *Memories, Dreams, Reflections*, co-editor of his letters, and to perform many other tasks.

There was Dr Marie-Louise von Franz, then the youngest of recruits to those formidable ranks, yet one of its greatest acquisitions. She was to collaborate closest in a psychological sense with Jung and his wife in their last years. It was she who finished Emma Jung's work on the Holy Grail and did much of Jung's special research for him. A natural scholar by instinct as well as by training, she has been able to carry on Jung's work now to an historical and archetypal depth unsurpassed by any co-worker of her sex.

There was also Jolande Jacobi, one of the members of the founding committee of the C. G. Jung Institute. In a world of profoundly intro-verted feminine personalities, she was the unashamed extravert. As such she was of immense value to them. Also by temperament she belonged neither to the German complex of European culture nor to the English-speaking version. She was actually Hungarian, although she had worked in Vienna. She was Jewish and converted to Catholicism. Through her own differences of temperament and approach she diversified and en-riched the feminine contribution to Jung's work. Unafraid of the world and completely at peace with a fate which had so violently uprooted her from a culture she loved, she performed an invaluable service in establishing Jung's psychology in terms an extraverted world could un-derstand. She spoke her astringent mind without fear or favour, perhaps at times too much, as Jung was once moved to warn her gently.

There was too, and happily still is, Cornelia Brunner, wife of one of Switzerland's most distinguished surgeons and for many years the respected head of the Psychological Club at Zürich. Her mastery of English enabled her to follow her instinct on the trail of the anima at work in the books of Rider Haggard, and so provide a clear mirror wherein reflections of this profound, hidden process in men can be clearly and precisely seen. Her work and research into the life of Rider Haggard exceeds anything yet produced on him in the English-speaking world, and demonstrates how negligent Rider Haggard's own country-men have been in their assessment of his real achievement.

First under Toni Wolff's chairmanship and then under her own, the Psychological Club became a positive communal expression of colleagues, friends, pupils and analysands. But it was no dead and perfunctory body sealed in academic and professional solemnity. Jung saw to it that its beginnings were as alive as he felt himself to be. Those meetings at the club could be as Dionysian as they were Apollonian, and the last word of the profound lectures often lost in the sound of music and laughter that followed.

There was Alice Lewisohn Crowly, co-founder and director of the Neighbourhood Playhouse in New York, who also came on a visit and, like many other American women, remained to the end of her days. She took no active literary part in the work of the others but she was always a rare psychological presence in being, an indefinable but abiding influence more than a substance, who through the atmosphere she evoked became a rare and essential element in the feminine establishment of those days. Above all she kept open house to the young who came to Zürich to study, and gave them a personal human centre of their own on which to turn and return.

Finally there was one other remarkable woman, not in Zürich but nevertheless in Switzerland and out on a wing of her own at the Casa Gabriella in Ascona on Lake Maggiore. She was the Dutch lady, Olga Fröbe-Kapteyn, a profoundly introverted personality, sensitive, shy and, with reason enough, not without fear of the external world. Yet she made of her shadow, her averted self, so positive a force that she created the Platonic institution of Eranos around her. She made her home a place where great scholars came annually from all over the world to talk to a select public on a common theme of abiding human concern. It was she who had gone to visit Jung in Zürich in the 'thirties and persuaded him to come to lecture at Ascona. As a result of his first experience there, those meetings at Ascona, the *Tagungen* as they were called, became an ideal platform for delivering what was new, active and immediate at any given phase of the swift progression of his work.

When the last war broke out and it looked as if Eranos might have to close down because the world could no longer come to it, Jung insisted with Olga Fröbe-Kapteyn, so she told me, that the meetings had to continue. Jung saw the mountains around Switzerland, he told her, as a kind of magic circle, a mandala, a protective movement of the earth itself, to provide a still centre where the search for meaning could be carried on in the midst of the storm of the madness of war around it. So Eranos went on and continues to this day.

There are of course many more, but this must be enough to illustrate the quality of Jung's feminine following in Zürich at the time. Their unceasing work and care for the implications of analytical psychology, added to the efforts of other women elsewhere, constitute a unique feminine phenomenon. Both in sheer numbers as well as in texture and measure of what was achieved, they led a breakthrough of the feminine into a field almost exclusively reserved until then for men, with rare exceptions that only went to prove the historical masculine rule of law.

The outside world, far from appreciating its significance, made light of the fact that Jung had so much feminine support. I remember how everywhere negative men prophesied that when Jung died, Zürich would see such a dire harvest of feminine suicides as no city had ever experienced. Yet on the terrible blank morning after the afternoon of storm wherein he had died, not one of those ladies cancelled an appointment but every one reported for duty as usual to their patients and students. They had not fallen out of the march when many a man had done, and it is a convincing proof of both their quality and the stature of Jung that not one faltered in step on the sombre march to his grave and on afterwards to a future where he was no longer present physically to guide them.

The world of women around Jung even to this day has no clear intimation, I believe, of how rare and great a little universe it constituted. Its members could not, out of a natural modesty and respect for the reality of their own shadows, see the unique wood they planted because of the trees of themselves. But I never think of them without raising my hat to them. They loomed all the larger because the men around Jung, when I first met them, were so few. Dr Ludwig Binswanger, the Existential psychoanalyst, who had been a steadfast friend to Jung all those long years, was about to withdraw from active participation, so the main role of representing Jung in the world fell on Dr C. A. Meier. He was the head of the Institute and had been a close colleague of Jung's since long before the war. He was soon to leave the Institute and take up Jung's professorship at the federal Polytechnic Institute but had already, in addition to dealing with all the practical daily applied issues of Jung's psychology, performed a great historical service for it. A profound scholar of Greek and Roman antiquity, he had firmly traced the continuity of a Jungian theme back into the heart of the Greek world in its great mysteries of healing exercised at Epidaurus and Eleusis; hence his book *Ancient Incubation and Modern Psychotherapy*. He never wavered in his attachment to Jung's work but carried it on in scientific fields for which only he had the technical equipment. As well as the Professorship held so ably that it has now been converted into a permanent chair instead of the temporary one it had hitherto been at the Polytechnic Institute, he established the Clinic and Research

Centre for Jungian Psychology in Zürich for further scientific Jungian research and treatment. He consolidated and expanded Jung's earlier scientific work in the association experiments, and has published in German two revealing books on dreams and the role of the unconscious in man. Since dreams and their interpretation have always been elements especially dear to him and for which he has a special gift, these books are indispensable for the understanding of the inner foundation of Jung's work and Jungian seeking. Yet at the time, Dr Meier tended to be an isolated masculine phenomenon.

The one other person of real stature who could also have supported him had long since returned to his native England. That was Dr Helton Godwin Baynes—"Peter", as he was known to his friends. He had been for years the man closest to Jung and uniquely equipped to establish a Jungian school in England, as his *Mythology of the Soul* was to prove. In England, many of Baynes's immediate supporters too were women of great calibre, and the Zürich pattern remained relevant to a remarkable if not total extent. But in America the importance of women in the crucial formative years of Jung's work was even more pronounced than either in Zürich or England. This was all the more remarkable because it was the interest of American scientists in Jung's earliest work that had brought him and Freud to America in 1909. But this interest declined after Jung's break with Freud.

Women like Frances Wickes, who tragically was deprived of her son in a fateful yachting accident and came to write with such profound insight about the psychology of the young, took over where the men left off for the moment. Her influence spread far beyond the frontiers of psychology into American art, even the dance and ballet of the New World. She was a most impressive old lady when I met her, totally unembittered by the loss of her son and blindness, and went on working until her eighties.

Then there was Dr Esther M. Harding, who died only recently in 1971 but made one of the greatest American contributions of all in volume of work and depth of character, although she was English. Her books on various aspects of psychology, literature and history, seen from a feminine point of view, have far-reaching consequences for the nature and wholeness of human awareness. Close beside her was Dr Eleanor Bertine—I speak only of those I knew personally— and many others like Elined Kotschnig and the gallant Martha Jaeger, both Quakers who laboured to carry Jung into the Society of Friends and make those indomitable "children and servants of the light" realise that the clearer the light the more precise the shadow.

To this day, American women help pre-eminently to maintain Jungian institutes and societies from East Coast to West, and from Montreal to Houston in Texas. Although the numbers of notable men have happily increased thanks greatly to the example of distinguished émigré initiates like James Kirsch and Max Zeller, the women still seem to set the general tone and maintain the growth.

One final example from the unlikely world of Japan that cannot be ignored. A Japanese woman who trained in Zürich too has inspired there one of the fastest-growing Jungian schools of all, near the ancient capital of Kyoto and its thousand and one temples of Buddha and Zen. To put it in terms of Jung's great dream of transition, the magnolia tree brought back from Europe is in flower again in the Far East, and this interpenetration of spirit and traffic between East and West is becoming an affair of increasing depth. Without this mobilisation in the world of the feminine, one could easily despair of any resolution to the clash of the opposites and the problem of the shadow which is basic to Jung's approach and the greatest challenge confronting our world.

I knew Jung only in the last sixteen years of his life. When I first met him, this problem of the universal shadow was his greatest concern and was soon to lead to his *Answer to Job* which I have mentioned. I remember him saying clearly that the individual who withdraws his shadow from his neighbour and finds it in himself and is reconciled to it as to an estranged brother, is doing a task of great universal importance. He added that the future of mankind depended on the speed and extent to which individual men learnt to withdraw their shadows from others and re-integrate them honourably within themselves.

One of the paradoxes of the unconscious is that ultimately it abhors collective expressions of itself. However important collective expression in the world without may be as a defensive measure on behalf of a new-born and vulnerable value in the unconscious, ultimately what is sought is an individual realisation of that value. One sees an example of such a defensive collective expression in the movement known as "Women's Lib". This movement is clearly intended to serve a new awareness of the importance of the masculine in woman. But it is only an archaic, defensive preliminary to a specific individual realisation of the feminine which the collective unconscious seeks.

Jung in his darkest hour after his break with Freud already had a clear, intuitive intimation of the importance of this irresistible drive in the collective unconscious. To describe it, long before the close of his own confrontation with his own unconscious, he had coined the phrase "individuation". If one wanted slogans for what Jung stood for himself, and sought for his patients, they could be found in the two words, "differentiation" and "individuation". But in this role of making the collective specific the importance of the individual was given another dimension, when Jung saw the individual raised in worth and dignity as a working partner in the pattern of God. The great theological scandal of our time is not the fragmentation of the Christian churches but their failure to take up the inner findings of Jung and the instruments he laboured so long to create on their behalf. He has placed in their unwitting hands the means of their renewal and their recreations as organs of living religious experience.

Yet the churches continue to exhort man without any knowledge of what is the soul of modern man and how starved and empty it has become. They have done nothing to inform themselves in a contemporary idiom of "The Dark Night of the Soul" to which St John of the Cross pointed so poetic and saintly a way. They behave as if a repetition of the message of the Cross and a reiteration of the miracles and parables of Christ is enough. Yet, if they took Christ's message seriously, they would not ignore the empiric material and testimony of the nature of the soul and its experience of God that Jung has presented to the world. He did his utmost to make us understand the reality of man's psyche and its relationship to God. But they ignore the call. Even William Temple, one of the most charismatic of archbishops since Becket, turned a deaf ear to Jung's plea for a hearing.

" 'Please send me an intelligent young theologian' ", Jung begged him. " 'I will lead him into the night of the soul so that one of them at last may know what he is actually dealing with.' But nobody came.

"Naturally they knew it already, and much better", Jung commented wryly. "That is why the light in the churches has gone out."*

As a result, in a world mainly obsessed with political patterns and socialistic values, the churches have failed to realise how all systems and institutions are psychological groupings before they become movements and forces in the world without. Marxism, for instance, is spoken of as if it were purely a science of politics and history and not, in the first instance, the expression of a partial psychology. Life teams with psychological Marxists who, though they may not ascribe to political Marxism, aid and abet its causes through their own state of mind. Christianity itself is more and more being taken over by a form of spiritual Marxism, a totalitarianism which sees religion's highest value as a political and sociological one. Instead of making politics religious

* Letter to Max Frischknecht, 17 July 1945.

the tendency is to make religion political, and slanted. A so-called love of the oppressed and poor in the material sense makes religion fight with the sinned against the sinner, poor and deprived in spirit as he is, ignoring that love demands as great a compassion, if not greater, for the sinner than the person sinned against.

This love in its partial and slanted state is doomed to decline and die, and already the hallmark of condemnation is present in a condition of the modern spirit, where love is not only not recognised when held out to it but cannot be experienced. Yet the truly religious approach demands that the whole of life and the whole of man is involved. Nothing that is inadequate, rejected or delinquent is excluded. Its purpose was never to bring about some welfare state of the mind. Rather it was a reaching out in the dark areas of his spirit and the soul, to succour and heal all impartially from the wounds and suffering they have incurred, no matter on which sided aspect of life they are ranged. But through Jung, the priest is once more enabled to take upon himself the task of healing in its full, ancient sense.

The priests who take to following their calling the Jungian way, no matter whether Buddhist, Hindu, Protestant or Catholic, joined as one in enabling man to recover a soul that is full of his contemporary meaning. Although this would be, as it has always been in the past, a task performed for its own sake out of the need of a new kind of man on earth and not a political one, the social and political fall-out would be incalculable, and the result a greater evolutionary revolution of life than man has yet seen.

It was in regard to this overwhelming importance of the individual's coming to terms with his shadow through the intercession of his highest feminine self and its medium of love, that Jung saw the true meaning of the coming of Christ. Struck as he was by the absence of love and the presence only of the power and fear of God in our Old Testament beginnings, Christ to Jung was the love of God made specific in man, and constituted a transcendental tradition to which both God and man were subject. Christ was an expression of cosmic love made specific, delegated to stand up with man to the terror of God as with Job on his heap of ashes.

One sees how far the relationship of man and his highest meaning had travelled since the first hint of partnership between God and man in the dream of Jacob's ladder and its traffic of angels. In the coming of Christ, the angels and their role of messengers are superseded by a divine plenipotentiary born of woman and made flesh and blood in the person of the Son of Man.

Jung never denied the historical reality of Christ, and indeed stressed and restressed that only a real and specific person born in response to the greatest need of his time could have done what Christ had done. He thought Christ's life was of greatest immediate meaning as one fulfilled in obedience to an overwhelming symbol active in all men to this day. He therefore traced an inborn and constantly recurring and therefore also a contemporary pattern of Christ in the spirit of every man so that one could, in a psychological sense, declare with Paul that the redeemer still lived. One of the most important statements Jung ever made, therefore, was his definition of what was meant in a twentieth-century way by the imitation of Christ.

He said quite plainly that the meaning of Christ's example was not that the individual should imitate blindly the life of Christ and make himself a pale, insipid copy of what that crucified person had been. The true meaning of Christ for him was that every individual should live out fully his own natural and specific self as truly as Christ had lived his unto the end to which he had been born. But this was only possible if man was re-integrated with the shadow in all the despised and rejected aspects of himself and his time through intercession of the universal feminine in himself.

It was through the intercession of the feminine that Goethe had struggled to achieve the redemption of the shadow of Faust. Jung knew that it could only be done by uniting it with the eternal feminine in man which in its highest form he had called Sophia, as Goethe had done in *Faust*, and which was beatified in the person of the saintly Christian lady of a name that in its Greek derivation means "wisdom". Jung personified the evolution of the feminine in four self-evident ascending feminine models: Eve, Helen of Troy, Mary and Sophia. Equally he saw four masculine patterns to support his own achievement in this rising scale in priorities; Lao-Tzu, Mani, Buddha and Christ. All were illustrations of how all streams of inner eventfulness can meet. Yet the churches remained indifferent instead of submitting themselves to the hard, bitter task of "individuation", and the unmasking of all worldly and theological presumptions that it demands.

"It is a gigantic task", Jung once exclaimed, "to create a new approach to an old truth. The old way of interpreting itself has to be interpreted now with the help of science. I do not combat Christian truth. I am only arguing with the modern mind."

As he spoke there came to me again the line from Dante's *Paradiso*, "Virgin mother, daughter of your son". Instantly it took on a completely new meaning. Biologically, this great poetic statement makes no sense. Symbolically, it could not be more meaningful. It is a symbol of Euclidian accuracy. The Christ that was crucified was a creation and symbol of the feminine love (anima) which came from the master-pattern in the collective unconscious in order to help man in his awesome task of serving the unconscious consciously. Man has a biological birth through woman of flesh and blood. He can have a spiritual or psychological rebirth within through his feminine self. Man's biological birth provides him with the base material for creating something unique and individual of himself. The act of individual creation and recreation within is achieved through the feminine, but fathered within by man's male spirit. That is why in a moment of his greatest agony Francis Thompson wrote: "Yea, in the night, my Soul, my daughter, cry—clinging Heaven by the hems . . ." This, surely, is the contemporary meaning of the Immaculate Conception which so much troubled the literal spirit of post-Renaissance man. He insisted on regarding it practically instead of symbolically. But here is one example of what appears to be dead, dogmatic doctrine brought back alive and meaningful into the life of our time when reassessed in the light of the symbols that rise from the collective unconscious.

Jung never defined precisely where he stood in terms of religion perhaps because the transcendental is ultimately beyond definition. But he did stress how all-important his Christian heritage was to him. He worked scientifically to keep the door open in the imagination of his time for admission of the full meaning of Christ. But the cosmic shadow that fell over Christ's life was that he was also the Son of Man.

Even at work on the apparently remote, esoteric story of alchemy, he had a vision of Christ one night that stayed with him all his days. In a bright light at the foot of his bed he saw Christ on the cross, and his body was made of greenish-gold—the combination of values in metal which was for the alchemists the expression of the life spirit that motivated the whole of the universe. That for Jung was proof enough of the universal importance of what Christ represented in the spirit of all men whether known by that or any other and even no name at all.

But this was by no means the end of the road for Jung in his search for the totality of the self. I could easily show how the dialogue continued until the end between his own awareness of the self and what the self reflected. But it is best followed in the correspondence he had with countless theologians, artists, philosophers and others. The efforts to involve him in the semantics of definitions of the indefinable were as remorseless as they were vain. Yet none of this endless process of cross-examination, to which he was subjected from without, was nearly as exacting as that which he asked ceaselessly of himself. This ruthless demand from within is best left unsummarised because of its complexity and subtlety, and because ultimately it can be followed only in his own words. All that is important here is to grasp the central fact. He established beyond doubt that the glory, as well as the agony, of the Promethean gift of consciousness in man meant that he was free to choose between good and evil. This mysterious gift of consciousness inflicted responsibilities on the human spirit which had previously been only in the province of the gods. Moreover, responsibilities of which men are still insufficiently aware contain implications for the future as disturbing as they are full of promise. They are disturbing because consciousness presupposes a form of bondage far more rigorous than any predetermined form of existence ever could have been. This paradoxical freedom is a life sentence in the new prison of a necessity. Night and day man must decide what is good and evil, and then choose between them. However provisional the human assessments of good and evil may be, they are an abiding feature of the inscape of man. Indeed, the enlargement of man's awareness and the possibilities of achieving a position of meaning in life and time depend on how he discharges this responsibility of being both the beggar and the chooser. In spirit he is compelled to be in accord with his own growth of consciousness. This ultimately is what Jung's harsh path of differentiation and individuation is all about.

This painful process of unrelenting evaluation imposed on the individual human spirit does not deprive man of significance. On the contrary it raises him infinitely in meaning because the evaluations are directed at renewing his relationship with God. In this re-delegation of responsibilities between himself and God (which increase of consciousness implies) man's own individuation becomes meaningful because it aids differentiation and individuation in God Himself. So, in this regard, the question has to be honestly faced. Was Christ, whom Jung regarded as Western man's greatest realisation of the symbol of the Self, the final totality? Or was even He, son of man and of God as He was, but another stage on the way towards making this traffic between man and his Creator ever more meaningful? Christ himself proclaimed that only the truth could make men free. How could Jung therefore not conclude that his own meaning had continually to be tested and re-tested in the progressive evolution of man's grasp of living truth? Christ's answer, though implied, seems clearly to suggest that He too was but a stage on the everlasting way. Hence the symbolic meaning of all the Apostolic references to His second coming.

This could only be relevant in so far as it implied that Christ would be coming in a form not yet revealed. That is why at His going, He left man the disconcerting legacy of a Pentecostal spirit, to lead him on to the unimagined day of His return.

Seeing how far short modern man still falls from this crucified example of the self, it might seem arrogant to talk of an increased "totality of the self", were there not clear evidence that we have failed the example of Christ so ignominiously precisely because we have ignored the provisional nature of Christ's self-realisation. We have ignored also the problem of the shadow which the light of His coming cast over our lives. By the inertia of our own spirit we hide behind the sacrifice of Christ, instead of using the meaning He achieved as a new point of departure.

The task of differentiation and individuation of our meaning, so dependent on transforming evil through love without sacrifice of the good, is as unending. Thus the imposition of what might appear so monstrous a shedding of cosmic responsibility on mere flesh and blood, would be unpardonable were it not for the fact that, at the core of this symbol of the Self of which Christ was a living symbol, creation has placed at the disposal of the spirit of man the greatest of all weapons; the power of a love that is beyond good or evil, light or darkness. Here for the first time in all the religions and mythologies of the world, God and man have a centre of increasing awareness of each other and in an area where they are the instruments of one another. And Jung's contribution is simply this; he established, scientifically, that God is no longer a wishful, remote, super-reality somewhere out in the blue of the universe and His great intermediary, the Son of Man, was not just a single, never to be repeated historical event. On the contrary both are immense recurrent and daily transforming activities in the soul of each one of us. We have only to acknowledge their presence and dedicate all that we have of consciousness to the partnership they offer us, to free life on earth from the last of the impediments which have hitherto excluded us from full participation in the act and deed of creation. For this exclusive service we ourselves were designed, and its unfolding has barely begun. Jung lived and worked out his religion in a way that made definition unnecessary if not redundant. For him, it was never an arrested but always a continuous and continuing process. There was no finality to it. Creation for him was only the first commitment in a continuing act of creation wherein all life participates every second of night and day. The exposition and formulations in which it came, temporarily, to rest were only wayside inns of the spirit. And its atmosphere was around him in even the lowliest of tasks, as, for instance, that of cooking food.

But just as he never rejected his cultural or domestic inheritance, nor did he evade his own religious aspects. I remember how we talked about this and the evolution of Christianity. Jung mentioned how the Book of Revelation, which Calvin had rejected as "a dark and dangerous book", but which showed how the Christian dream did not end with the coming of Christ but that the search, of which His coming was a consummation, had still to be carried on into the Apocalyptic future of which John of Patmos had had such disturbing visions. For him the Christian vision, however final its relation to an abiding master-pattern of the objective soul, had hardly begun to unfold.

It was when we came to this stage that Jung turned to me with a great laugh and said, "Of course, as you will have noticed, at heart I'm only a determined old Protestant of the left".

And of course this was true. He was a Protestant in the sense that he could not run spiritually to the shelter of some great mother church, however much he admired it and wished it well, as he did, for instance, the Church of Rome. He was a Protestant in the sense that he had to put his own individual conscience, the commandment of his own unique contract with life, above that of any doctrine or church. For those who needed a church he thought the Roman Catholic church, with its roots in the pagan as well as Christian world, its ancient ritual, dogma and symbolism, was the best available collective home. He thought it an immense pity that the leaders of the Reformation had dismissed the appeal of Pope Paul III to come to Trent in the sixteenth century under promise of safe conduct, to try and reconcile their differences. He thought it scandalous that the Christian churches were so fragmented and almost at war with each other in the face of the growing peril threatening the Western spirit. But his concept of the Protestant was that of a person operating as an individual and, however much prepared to honour the need of institutional religion, committed ultimately to following only the Pentecostal flame sent to guide the fearing disciples after the Ascension of Christ.

Religious revelation had not ended for Jung with Crucifixion, Resurrection, Ascension, but had barely begun. He took the Book of Revelation, with which the Christian message is supposed to end, as only the beginning of a disconcerting call to resumption of religious searching. But this, in actuality, was only part of the truth, because he worked really beyond the frontiers of even the boldest speculation and certainly outside the fortifications of any church. He was a born frontiersman, and there were times when he would say to me, "I am only an old African for whom God is the dream."

He said this of course because one of the things that had impressed him about Africa was the fact that he found Africans drawing the same distinction in dreams as he did. They talked of "little" and "great" dreams; whereas he talked of dreams from the personal unconscious and from the collective unconscious.

His voice was sad when he told me how an old African witch-doctor had once told him that he no longer dreamt any "great" dreams because the English District Commissioner in his *boma* now dreamt them for him.

I told him how the great African seer and prophet I had been to see as a young man implied something similar when he said to me, "People no longer talk of the First Spirit. His praise names are forgotten."

Jung nodded and smiled before saying that, of course, it must be far worse in Russia, because it looked as if people were not allowed to dream any dreams at night because the State was doing it for them.

Saying that, he became unusually sombre and silent, and after a while stood still and pointed with his stick at a cloud in the sky that was swollen with snow as the sail of a great ship with wind, and said: "It is pitiful how ignorant we are of such things. Man everywhere is dangerously unaware of himself. We really know nothing about the nature of man, and unless we hurry to get to know ourselves we are in dangerous trouble. I should have been a mathematician and a physicist and God knows what else beside, perhaps even a musicologist, to do my task properly. I am appalled by the inadequacy of what I have done."

I took all this as another sign of his greatness, because only someone truly great could see the vast, unexplored prospect in front of him and experience the shrinking of his own measure of achievement in the full scale of his vision. I saw him as I have always seen truly creative pioneering spirits, as a Moses who can lead millions to a new land of promise, which is our inherited image of greater being, but are forbidden to enter it themselves. That reference to music in particular had an association for me with that kind of burden of isolation Jung carried around with him all his life. It was only the second, and last, time he ever referred to music in conversation with me. I thought of Socrates' own sense of separation from the life which had condemned him, falling like a shadow over his regret, uttered not long before he took his hemlock, that he had not learned to play the lute.

I found this black mood of self-deprecation unexpected and almost unbearable, and protested all I could, but in vain that day. It was one of those occasions when one's own sense of his unfairness to himself was irrelevant because through it he achieved his warmest, greatest human stature. He was too aware of his own inadequacies to exceed his humanity. As a result he gave out a feeling of being known and belonging, and a sense of involvement in the unfolding of an expanding universe, that I have only experienced among the despised first people of my native country.

As we stood there beside the dark, troubled Maggiore water, he pointed with his stick at another great cloud full of thunder and lightning which made one feel small and insignificant, saying in a voice low with awe: "It makes me shiver to think that such a cloud is unfolding and forming also in us, and we both partake with that cloud of what is being formed and unformed in this moment in time."

I told him how on a hot day in the southern desert of Africa I had wanted to go and speak to one of my favourite Stone-Age hunters. He was sitting in the middle of a thorn bush around which the sunlight crackled like electricity. He was huddled in an attitude of the most intense concentration on the sand in the scrub. His friends would not let me get near him, saying; "But don't you know, he is doing work of the utmost importance. He is making clouds."

Jung laughed as only that desert maker of cloud had laughed in my experience, and we went on to talk at great length about time, and how a great many of our modern errors arose from our misunderstanding of the nature of time. He had already written a book outlining some principles towards a non-causal explanation of life and time. He said he was compelled to do this by unexplained empiric evidence obtained in his work of a principle in life beyond cause and effect. For instance, in certain dreams the future already seemed to exist and was sometimes presented in precise detail. Events occurred, too, long before any known cause could explain them. Coincidences in his own life, and that of others, the Chinese experience of an inherent time sympathy in men, things and events, the *mono-aware* of the Japanese, all challenged him to propose another exposition of its nature. His own intuitive attitude in this regard had been reinforced through Richard Wilhelm, and his introduction to the Book of Changes. The Chinese, he felt, possessed one science that was uniquely their own and had been for thousands of years. This science was based on a total a-causal principle of approach. It was a profound observation and exploration of the pattern of meaning unfolding through time in the universe which was utterly beyond and before our own conceptions of cause and its effect. The *I-Ching* was for Jung the greatest textbook for this classic Chinese science which had constructed its own method for divining the meaningful context of any given moment of time, seemingly manifested through what we call chance or coincidence. Through his own experiments with this Chinese 'time machine" he was convinced of its efficiency as a measure of meaning in time, and confirmed him in his concept of time as a continuous stream of dynamic energy of a character and drive peculiarly its own. But there was more to it than that. It was precisely one of those areas he felt he had been unable to explore sufficiently and of which the thought depressed him so. He longed for physicists, mathematicians and astronomers to take over and go further than he had done.

Even so, the book Jung wrote as a result of this and more is not so difficult as men make it out to be, but its importance on this particular day was the fact that, as far as I myself was concerned, its message still is that time is not merely the measure of our days. It is a reality in its own right as much as a dimension. It is an element vitally involved in the evolution of the human spirit. It has a character of its own which it communicates to life. Everything in life not only has its own but also a time-character which it shares with all other things existing at that unique moment. There is not an idea even that is free of it, and growth itself is possible only in so far as it corresponds to time and conforms to the overall character of a great togetherness.

All living things, consciously or unconsciously, partake of that character in any moment of time (an axiom almost so over-axiomatic that Jung, not long before he died, called it tautological and spoke more and more of time in physicists' terms as a stream of infinite energy). They share it no matter where they are. It is another great partner of man, and in so far as it yields a scythe, it is only to cut what is provisional from what is permanent; the false from the true. It carries a portion of the responsibility of living the answer for which life was created that would be unbearable if left to man alone.

The liberation of spirit implicit in such a concept is immense. It means that life is not a process of mere predictable cause and effect. Both cause and effect are aspects of something greater than either, and there is no real necessity for man to be merely an instrument, a prisoner in a chain-gang of action and reaction. What men call a "cause" is the raw material over which man, out of his full, rounded awareness, exercises a freedom of choice. He can choose, in harmony with time, to add something to the cause which was not there and making it more meaningful than it was before. Between cause and its so-called effect, there falls a cosmic shadow. Out of this shadow man can accomplish a transfiguration of his own, participating, however minutely, in an act of universal creation, and something emerges that no cause all alone and purely out of itself could have produced. Above all, not only life and men on earth but meaning has its seasons. Time and meaning in their interdependence are themselves profoundly seasonal. Only in loving bondage to the elemental seasons man was free. Here Jung stressed the importance of astrology. It was not only an ancient effort at developing a psychology of its own by projection on to the stars and their courses. It was also an effort to relate and read the meaning and character of man in terms of the quality of time. Astrology, for Jung, as any study of the real zodiac would show, had nothing to do with real astronomy. The stars and planets were used only as mirrors to reflect inner psychological patterns. He could not follow it alas, very far, because of the absence of empirical evidence to support its observations, but he emphatically thought, as he would put it to me with his love of slang, that it was "on to something".

He took seriously too the intuition of the seasonal character of time born in Greece about two centuries before Christ. This was the concept of a Platonic year of about 26,000 years, a complete round of all time seasons, divided into months each of about two thousand years. Christianity was also in part the product of both such a season and response of the spirit to its own inner sense of season. Jung felt this season of the Christ and anti-Christ was approaching its end. A new season was about to begin wherein the great opposites of light and shadow faced each other openly, and the task of transcending them could be completed without sacrifice of the Christian values which preceded it.

It is not surprising that, having come to terms with the reality of the shadow not only in himself, his own time, but in the pattern of God, Jung felt more free not to *do* so much as just to *be* within himself all that he had discovered and wanted life to become. An overvaluation of *doing* and a tendency to measure the importance of men exclusively by the importance of the functions they performed in the external world had long since struck him as part of the slanted character of his day. More and more he was concerned with men as they were in the quality and texture of their own being and less with the kind of things they did in the world, however impressive or powerful their role. Indeed, he knew already only too well the damage which that kind of obsessive doing inflicted on men and their societies unless it was an issue of the necessities of their own inner selves. All round him he saw the fatal consequences of the power to do and act conferred on men whose being did not match the responsibilities of the functions entrusted to them. He was to reiterate again and again, as the Chinese of the *I-Ching* and *The Secret of the Golden Flower* had done, that the right cause entrusted to the wrong man was disastrous. And as always what he preached was only uttered after he had practised it himself. Accordingly his intuition, that faculty for seeing below the horizon of time and round the corners of life, had already prompted him to build by the lake at Bollingen, according to his own design, a house wherein he could just *be*; or perhaps "design" is a shade too blunt and self-conscious for what came about as the result of inner thrust and organic growth in phases over more than a decade.

It is an interesting example of how intuition was really his own superior function—using superior and inferior in the technical sense used in his theory of type. He himself always declared that he was a thinking, intuitive, introverted person and that his sensation function, the sense of the here and now, and his feeling function, tended to be pushed down into a position in his unconscious.

One does not doubt at all the introversion. Only introversion of the deepest kind can explain why outwardly his life was so uneventful and inwardly so packed and overflowing with an historic eventfulness. Nor does one question Jung's judgement on the relative inferiority of his feeling function. He was singularly aware of it and worked hard to compensate for its deficiencies. Indeed at times he would appear hypersensitive in that regard, and I was amazed how relatively often after visiting him I would receive a letter excusing himself for some inadequacy—in the course of a discussion—of a feeling response, which I had not even noticed.

By the time I met Jung, of course, he had worked so long and with such effect at his own individuation that it was not easy to say what "type" he was. He had always stressed that no man was wholly extraverted or totally introverted, nor were the inferior functions ever completely unconscious. These were all relative states. But what he did stress was that all men and women, particularly in the second half of their lives, if they were to avoid this swing from one opposite to the other in themselves, had to labour at differentiation, raising their inferior functions and making them equal partners of the superior. That was an elementary goal of individuation and of immense importance in redeeming one's shadow. Jung at that moment was, in those terms, too highly differentiated for anyone to define his basic type, as it were, just from appearances.

Yet I do question the position he gives to his powers of thinking, considerable though they were. The history of his life, to my mind, shows beyond doubt that he got himself somewhat wrong and that intuition was his superior faculty. Only a man of the most highly fortified and precise intuitions could have gone against the trend of a whole age, correct it on his own spirit, and maintain this course against the most formidable opposition, as Jung had done. This intuition prescribed relatively early on in his life that one day he would need a house and trees in isolation, and silence also by water which all his life had meant so much to him. At the home at Küsnacht he had made a fortress in the world from which he went out daily to function and work. It was in this home where he lived with his wife and children. But the house of stone which he built at Bollingen was where he could just *be*. This being, in the fullest measure, was his own preparation for the end to come and what might be beyond. Thus he could make his life in the final season a living testament of the measure of wholeness that he had been able to achieve. Significantly enough he built the house with the utmost simplicity so that, as he was fond of saying, a man of the sixteenth century would have felt at home in it. He chose as a site a promontory of land some twenty miles outside Zürich on one of the least populated parts of the lake. It was a place where he had often camped and picnicked with his family. I have seen many photographs taken on these and similar occasions. They tell one thing about Jung that the writings—both his own and that of others—do not. Most writings and recollections about Jung are obsessed with his work and thought. This is understandable because of the significance of the work and the great and immediate originality of the thinking. Judging by those, he is almost without exception pictured in terms of a somewhat Olympian image as an unrelenting servant of science, and in the culmination of life, as a man of immense wisdom, of great Chinese *sensei* or classical sage-like proportions. But I have copies of photographs where he stands with an air of almost boy-scout triumph, complete with alpenstock, on the peak of some mountain that he had just climbed. I have others which show him dressed with abandon in aggressive knickerbocker or plus-four fashions, jauntily wearing caps with loud check patterns, that seem more appropriate to a bookmaker shouting the odds at some race-course than the solemn, contemplative, far-seeing great man that his official photographs make him out to be. I have other photographs of him dressed like a stone-mason, happily extracting the appropriate symbol locked up in yellow lakeside stone at Bollingen. Or some of him just sitting content in the sun slicing kindling wood, or busy chopping logs for the fire in the great open hearth of his medieval lakeside kitchen. But perhaps my favourites are those showing him at ease at the rudder of his boat, one or more of his young daughters sprawling nonchalantly on cushions in the boat in front of him.

He had often sailed to this anchorage at Bollingen, as if some wind of the spirit naturally brought him there. It was still a relatively bare place, and he had to plant most of the trees which now surround the building, dense and high, and on nights of storm serenade the house and it occupants with harp-like music. But here the house was built with stone. His first dialogue with something outside his lonely, introverted self, as we have seen, had been with the stone on which he happened to be sitting at the end of his father's garden in the vicarage at Laufen, where night and day silence was the sound of the Rhine. Here the sound was to be in different dimensions, first of all in the natural form of the lake water lapping almost against the foundations; then the wind and a certain star-crackle in the frozen silences of some unclouded night in the deep of winter. but finally, uncannily even for him, as if through the barrier of silence before and after his day, a distant sea murmur of voices of multitudes of being gone before and uncountable numbers still to come, was filtering through to swell the last chorale of this final orchestration of his being.

Appropriately, right at the beginning at Bollingen he delivered himself through the means of stone of another proof of his commandment to himself that, no matter how unfamiliar the form, all things had a character and meaning of their own not to be denied. When the foundations of the house of stone were being laid, Jung arrived there one day to find that the builders had rejected a cornerstone as too large for their purpose. They were about to send it back to the quarry, angry because with Swiss thoroughness their prescribed measurements for the stone had been meticulously laid down in the list of their requirements. But Jung would have none of it. There was a deep meaning for him in its appearance at such a moment. Not only the stone but the great "togetherness" seemed to demand of him some creative recognition of the event. He took the stone by sheer intuition and gave it an honoured position on a pedestal in the garden by the lake. To this day, though the colour has darkened and the surface stained as with the patina of time itself, the impact of Jung's own work on it is still as immediate as it is authoritative. Indeed the imagery and inscriptions carved into the stone seem to issue direct out of the nature and texture of the stone as much as a product of Jung's imagination, and the result, therefore, of an unusual integrity of execution. However, he contemplated the stone for a long time, he told me, before he worked on it and only then when an image came to him, as it were, out of the stone itself.

On one side he carved an inscription in Latin taken from a medieval alchemist, showing how for him this stone was more than just a stone. On the face directed towards the terrace of the tower, he chiselled a kind of eye, a vision which the stone seemed to insist on focussing on him. Within the pupil of this eye, the tiny reflection one sees of oneself within the eye of another, like the Telesphoros of Aesculapius—the mythical pointer of the way in antiquity and the child in man who fulfilled dreams and prayers. Below that he carved an inscription in Greek composed of lines from Heraclitus, Homer and the Mithraic Liturgy, beginning significantly enough with the words: "Time is a child—playing like a child—playing a board game—the kingdom of the child." Imagery and lettering in both Greek and Latin are chiselled with precision and a devout hand.

On the face towards the lake he let the stone speak for itself in quotations from alchemy also inscribed in Latin. He followed this up by carving the names of his father's ancestors on stone tablets which he placed in the courtyard of the tower, and painted the ceilings with the main features from his own and his wife's coat of arms, as well as those of his son-in-law. So, out of his own instinct, he had given the illustrious dead not entombment so much as an enthronement in the deed of grace that we call gratitude, and rendered them lasting recognition.

It was his private and personal affirmation of the human-being's continuity of responsibility for taking on the past and living it as an immediate present, and with increasing relevance to the future. It was his own version of the ritual of reverence for the spirit of our ancestors. The proof of its necessity and validity was that once the ritual was over, he was at one with life as he had never been. Night and day the tower seemed peopled by a greater family from far down the well spring of the first century of man, and he could see life in the round forever coming into being; renewing itself and then not coming to an end so much as passing on, to make way for another version of itself not possible before.

Jung always held that one reason why modern man was so significantly poor in spirit was because he no longer lived a symbolic life. This stone, saved from rejection, which started this process I have described, once made into a memorial of the meaning and the magic lost in man's rejection of the symbols that would inform him of a deeper self, not surprisingly led him to make Bollingen a place built of other stones where, even more than enacting the symbolism of himself, he could also let the symbols be.

Only a very partial rendering of the extent to which he exercised his own symbolic self at Bollingen emerges from his writing, but he went to immense trouble to live it out in great detail. For instance, when in the course of the building, a skeleton of a man was uncovered, Jung took pains to discover whose skeleton it was. When it was found to be the skeleton of a French soldier killed there in the course of the Napoleonic wars, he insisted on re-burying it with full military ceremonial, appropriate to the day of the death of the person who had once invested the vanished flesh and blood.

When a friend died, he carved a memorial for him like a small shrine in the walls of the house, covered with curtains so that it should not be exposed to irrelevant eyes. When his wife died, he designed a memorial stone for her too, carved his own epitaph in it and set it up where both sun and its reflection in the water of the lake could warm and illuminate it. All round the building and in the walls are more stone carvings of images of the unconscious which had a special meaning for him, or quotations from the Greeks, Romans, and the obscure alchemists whom he had honoured as pioneers in his own field. There are also heraldic patterns in vivid colours. The walls of the bedrooms are all painted over with immense, brooding, winged personifications of the prototypes tried out first in the Red Book, but given final authority here.

He built the house itself in three stages, and in the last stage, when already the trees that he had planted were tall and reverberating with the winds that came, long-maned, down from the Alps, he built, high up, a place for his own unique retreat and contemplation, He had often remarked how even in the poorest house in India there was some corner set apart whereby a man could go through the ritual of respect for the symbolism investing his life. This retreat became Jung's inner sanctuary; a holy of holies within the natural tabernacle which Bollingen was for him. There he could communicate in himself with life and time and whatever lay beyond. The old Zen Buddhists spoke of the importance of achieving action through non-action. At Bollingen, Jung sought it and achieved it, moreover, in a state of contemplation so great that one would not have been surprised if he could have heard the sound of one hand clapping—which is the Zen image of the ultimate in power of comprehension.

Modern men have forgotten the art of growing old. They have devalued it into an inferior state that they see as the decline and fall of the human spirit. They see life merely as an orchard full of bright, thrusting young trees and forget that they have still to bear fruit which has to be harvested. Jung's old age was old in the classical sense, where the fruit of his experience was gathered, stored and evaluated. It was no decline or fading away but a state of growth into death and beyond. As he grew older, the further away from other men and the lonelier he became in a human sense. But correspondingly he discovered a kinship with natural things at Bollingen that made loneliness his home. In that loneliness already he had made his peace with his own impending death. Life for him was greater than birth or death. During the second WorldWar he had nearly died, or rather died to the extent that he no longer wished to live. He had seen the world, and himself, as far out in space, the earth like an ancient geographical globe beneath him, its map contours distinctly outlined. The vision was distinct and haunted him and many years later compelled him to write to a fellow scientist, describing the view and asking how high that would have put him out in space. The answer came back: "About a thousand miles." His own return from that height was a deeper kind of dying which made his own personal death relatively unimportant to him. As a result he could comfort with authority those of his friends about to die; and they were many.

"Death", he wrote to Kristine Mann, one of the distinguished founder members in America, facing with indomitable courage her own death sentence from cancer, "is the hardest thing from the outside and as long as we are outside of it. But once inside you taste of such completeness and peace and fulfilment that you don't want to return. As a matter of fact, during the first month after my first vision, I suffered from black depressions because I felt that I was recovering. It was like dying. I did not want to live and to return into this fragmentary, restricted, narrow, almost mechanical life ... Throughout my illness something has carried me. My feet were not standing on air and I had the proof that I have reached a safe ground. Whatever you do, if you do it sincerely, will eventually become the bridge to your wholeness, a good ship that carries you through the darkness of your second birth, which seems to be death to the outside. I will not last too long any more. I am marked. But life has fortunately become provisional. It has become a transitory prejudice, a working hypothesis for the time being, but not existence itself.

"Be patient and regard it as another difficult task, this time the last one."*

* Letter to Kristine Mann, 1 February 1945.

By provisional, of course, he did not mean that one had to live life provisionally, He scorned such an approach. What he meant thereby was that one's life had to be lived as an absolute commitment, not just for now but forever. If one did that, one could arrive at the moment of the great order of release and see it as provisional. And there, at Bollingen, what was provisional in his life receded from what was lasting. He felt strongly at one again with nature, the clouds, seasons and those thoughts of God that the trees had always been for him. I have been back recently both to the house at Küsnacht and to Bollingen. Although I visited him repeatedly at Küsnacht and only rarely at Bollingen, and although Küsnacht is full of things to remind me of him and the library in which we so often sat and talked is lovingly preserved, he has gone for me from Küsnacht in a way he has not left Bollingen. There, in a house where I saw comparatively little of him, his presence still seems to me so near that one feels one only has to stretch out one's hand to touch it.

And these feelings are not just about some great marble solemnities but someone almost more human than anyone I have known. That was his greatness, being so human with all the human capacity for error and distraction, yet he did so much with his fallible spirit that is everlasting—more than any man for centuries. All these feelings of his greatness are accompanied by far too many intimate glimpses of the man to record in detail here, like the day he went out to buy some fresh lamb chops, wrapped them in decorative paper and special ribbon, to give to a little dog whose birthday it was. Since the dog had been given to him by an American, he spoke English—because he thought that would appease a certain nostalgia for its place of origin he sensed in the small animal—wishing it many happy returns and conversing with it. Or again, on one of his own birthdays, when like an old Chinese sage, he noted how loudly the wild duck called and how at evening a cold wind came down from the mountains. And then, of course, there was always that laugh of his and the look of incorrigible mischief in his eyes that often accompanied it.

But perhaps the most moving illustration of how he never exceeded his own humanity is a remark from a letter to a pupil barely two years before his death. He wrote, "In my case *Pilgrim's Progress* consisted in my having to climb down a thousand ladders until I could reach out my hand to the little clod of earth that I am."

All that I experienced and feel about Jung to this day seems to me to be focussed and most comprehensive in our last meeting. I remember,

I believe accurately, the significant details of our last encounter. I had just come from Zermatt where I had gone to climb the Matterhorn in the middle of the winter. Mountains have always meant much to me. I had been inflicted with a great longing to climb this mountain which, to me, because of it shape and name was some sort of myth. I climbed it a long way but I found the summit, in that bitter season, beyond my powers. I had to come down and go on to Zürich, feeling oddly deprived as a result.

I arrived at Jung's home just as someone was leaving. Jung, once the door was shut and I was safely inside, said to me, with a light of mischief in his eye and a smile that was a kind of reproof to himself: "I'm afraid I had to tell her that I really could no longer interest myself in which Jack went to bed with which Jill!"

When we were alone he asked me as always about myself before I could ask him about himself. I had to tell him, among other things, about my disappointment on the Matterhorn, which, to borrow an adjective of his, looked like an archetypal mountain to me. We talked about Whymper, his tragic fall to death after his conquest of the, as yet, unclimbed peak, and how not only he, but the Italian priest and his party climbing unbeknown to Whymper on the other side of the mountain, had also seen the cross appear in the sky over the abyss into which Whymper's guides and companions had just plunged to their death. After this, we talked about mountains at great length, from the Parnassus of the Greeks to the hills of the psalmist. He told me again how as an inarticulate boy hardly capable of walking, in the garden at Laufen at sunset he had had his first view of the distant Alps. He spoke movingly of a sense of destination evoked in him by the view. It was, he said, the vital point of departure in his own spirit, amazing and singular. Then he read an account of how the poet Petrarch who, like Dante, had in Laura a feminine spirit to lead him, became the first man in European history to climb a mountain in the Alps. If ever asked to fix a definite moment at which the long reawakening of the Renaissance began, he would place it in that precise moment. It was a sign for him that after long, Middle-Age introspection the European spirit was coming out of itself and moving into another opposite of extraversion. But paradoxically for him, in his own profoundly introverted spirit, that view of the mountain peaks had seemed to be a glimpse of a world within. And I wanted to tell him how, for many of us, that day he climbed the Rigi looked in retrospect like a great turning point in time; not, as always before, one into just another swing towards an opposite but an age new in history wherein life would no longer be divided against itself but rounded and full. I shall always regret that I did not do so.

We went on instead to talk about Dante, about the meaning of the smile on the face of the *Mona Lisa*, why Leonardo gave John the Baptist the face of Bacchus, and also about a ritual murder in Kenya. Jung thought the smile on the *Mona Lisa* was a "Sophia" smile, the smile of the eternal feminine transfigured into love as wisdom. Sophia knew the secret of the everlasting creation and recreation, and was aware that, as men and events come and go, so they will return again and again to new and more meaningful forms. Da Vinci had caught her with a look on her face of medieval confidence, and the certainty of knowing and belonging which distinguished Gothic humanity at its best. The artist showed her as if actually watching the great outburst of Renaissance activity; fleets of ships sailing out of ancient ports to discover new worlds; men at work in laboratories observing the sun and stars afresh and reappraising the arts, religion and societies all knowing the provisional necessities and, at the same time, certain it would not and could not last. Mona Lisa was there, great mistress and mother, watching her children at play, glad and sad that they would have to grow up and learn to make way, in their turn, for another succession of the living spirit of life and its love. As for Bacchus's face on the head of John the Baptist, symbolically for Jung nothing could have been more right. The revelation which St John came to announce so austerely came from a Dionysian, Bacchic element of that day. It needed the discipline of St John's austerity to contain the wild upsurge hinted at from within. It came from a profound change of focus in the underworld of the spirit of John the Baptist's Roman colonial day. We saw the same sort of thing going on as, for instance, when the young, and even grown men like Huxley, turned to drugs for their enlightenment. If one read the account of the coming of Bacchus in the legends of antiquity it was like a newspaper report of the drug traffic in our time. The drug then being wine which in the first instance of its invention was regarded as a means of spiritual revelation and transformation. It is a true parallel, Jung maintained, even to the extent that the authority in command, the King of Thebes, not only made no effort to understand the new phenomenon and its rapid spread but just cried for the application of more "law and order" against the recruits of the swelling followers of Bacchus. He ignored, as we do, that great inner eventfulness could only be dealt with from within and not merely by external sensation practices, and least of all blind suppression. As a result, the King utterly failed in his task and was torn limb from limb by his own wife and daughters; his own instinctive and feeling self with which he had obviously lost touch. So in this sense Bacchus was the classical forerunner of a regrouping of irresistible unconscious forces. The wine was an image of new vision and transfiguration, but not in regard to its negations as a representative of sheer licence and indulgence. Seen in this way da Vinci's association with Bacchus and John the Baptist was prophetic. We were all in danger of repeating the King of Thebes' mistake in failing to understand how great a shift there had been in the collective unconscious all over the world, how the season of time itself was changing. Unless soon we understood, those who opposed the new Dionysian upsurge manifest in our time, as well as those who were its instruments and victims would perish. These last, above all, seemed to be imperilled because they had forgotten the vital importance and validity of the ego in life. Egotism, like all "isms", was wrong. But the ego itself had to stand fast in its own validity at the core of the conscious individual if consciousness were not to fail. It could no more be ignored or by-passed than the psyche within. The archetype of the persona, or mask, which supported man in his relationship to the external realities, could not be rejected. It might be accused, psychologically, of representing man, in his maturity, as being everything that he and the world had thought him to be, but which, in his deeper individual searching, he was not. Yet the ego had to be firm and its living validity acknow-ledged if man were to grasp the importance of his own feminine psyche which regulated and observed his relationship with his own great objective collective unconscious. Somehow the two opposites had to be maintained and contained. Our greatest immediate problem was to prevent one disastrous opposite from swinging over into the other to the eclipse of its predecessor. If man stood fast and worked to bring his shadow (his neglected areas) into the light of consciousness, Jung empirically had proved that man and his ego were transformed into something greater than both. The ego, without loss of value and with immense enrichment of meaning, was enabled to surrender itself to the greatest individual archetype of all, the self. That self was the end of the harsh road of individuation and the purpose of all one's seeking, for in that self one experienced the presence of the author of the mighty activity that Jung called God. There one found clear reflection of the great mystery of the image of God. Only then could one set out with the right instrument for taking on the turmoil, confusion and sickness of our time. But to think one could gain self-knowledge and enlighten-ment from drugs like mescalin was almost the final depravity in the decline of the great passion of the spirit into mere flirtation with intellect, reason and sensation. Drugs, of course, had their role in medicine and healing, but as a source of enlightenment Jung viewed them with total distrust. In the first place they disregarded the natural ethical accompaniment of their use. The view, as of Everest, which one gained after taking the requisite drug was in terms of meaning totally different from the view of the man who had climbed the mountain the hard and dangerous way. Not only was the view of the one an hallucination but it was in terms of life "not earned" as the climber had earned his and as indeed all meaningful reality had to be earned. Nor did it involve the drug-inflicted visionary with any moral commitment or exercise of conscious choice between the error and accuracy of his vision. Besides, Jung added, he himself, much as he knew of vision and the vista of the collective unconscious, did not know whether he had earned the right to know more of it. He would be most uncomfortable to know more, until he was certain he had done his duty by what he already knew. That was one of the great troubles of our day. We had in our possession perhaps more knowledge and power resulting from our knowledge than ever before in the history of man. But less and less were we morally committed to our knowledge and its power. Life demanded that all knowledge should be evaluated and lived according to the most accurate evaluation of which we were capable, if it were not to destroy us. What were atomic power and Hiroshima if not warnings addressed to us from life about how power without appropriate evaluation and obedience to our evaluation and greatest awareness could annihilate life on earth?

This had been summed up a few years before by what Jung wrote about Huxley's *Doors of Perception*: "If I once could say that I have done everything I know I had to do, then perhaps I should realise a legitimate need to take mescal. But if I should take it now, I would not be sure at all that I had not taken it out of idle curiosity. I should hate the thought that I had touched on the sphere, where the paint is made that colours the world, where the light is created, that makes shine the splendour of the dawn, the lines and shapes of all form, the sound that fills the orbit, the thought that illuminates the darkness of the void. There are some poor impoverished creatures perhaps, for which mescal would be a heaven sent gift without a counterpoison, but I am profoundly mistrustful of the 'pure gifts of the Gods'. You pay very dearly for them. *'Quidquid id est, timeo Danaos et dona ferentes'*."

In his published works Jung contained himself within the discipline of a reverent empiricism. He never abandoned the resolution taken as a student that, in talking to the world at large, he would do so no longer just out of intuition but only out of intuition supported by facts. On occasions such as this meeting, however, his mind ranged far and wide and he speculated about the possibilities of life and meaning not referred to or even hinted at in his work and seminars. On this occasion, too, we talked a great deal about the meaning of immortality and what faced life beyond death. We had discussed it many times before. He always said how impressed he was that even in the oldest of his patients, even in men and women he knew for certain were about to die, there was no sense of death in their objective psyche or in the heart of their collective unconscious. He was convinced that the objective psyche of man in an essential part of itself, behaved as if there were no death; as if it existed outside space and time and was therefore not subject to the majesty of death. He was impressed how old people lived as if there were no death. He urged one and all therefore to live on even to the last of his days as if the "now" were the great "forever".

To me he said specifically that although one must not think the unthinkable, although one must never use the mind for a purpose for which it was not intended (one of the outstanding hubrises of our time), we should always recognise that it was one's imagination that gave one the greatest guide: one had to follow it always with the greatest awareness. If, in the prospect of death, the meaning was derived from a feeling that death was not the end, one had to follow that and live that in terms of that feeling.

In this connection I had been much shaken once by an answer to a letter I wrote to him when his beloved wife Emma died. One knew that, in more senses than one, more than a wife and mother had died with her because of her recognition of the demands of the masculine in herself in her work on the quest of the Holy Grail. In his reply, in terms so moving and personal that I do not care to repeat them, he spoke of how he was faced now by a silence to which there was no answer.

My spirit went black because it seemed that he was denying his own precept of following his own greatest meaning and that clear conclusion of his that the psyche existed outside space and time and beyond death. Some months later I was relieved when he wrote to me that the silence had been broken by a dream. He dreamt that he entered a vast and darkened theatre. He walked down the aisle between the empty rows, leading to a brilliantly lit stage. He came to the orchestra pit which stretched like an abyss before him and which he could not cross. There in the centre of the stage, more beautiful and free of care than he had ever seen her, was his wife. He refers to this dream in his *Memories* as if through it he had received a portrait of his wife from "the other side" specially commissioned for him. His wife's dress in this dream was made for her by the young seamstress, the psychic medium whose claim to speak with spirits had helped to make Jung aware of the end to which he had been born.

There is also another and wider significance to the return, at this late hour in his dreams, of the psychic young seamstress who had impelled him on his natural course in his student years at Basle. It demonstrates how Jung's own interest in the question of life after death never diminished. Only a rigorous and scientific self-discipline prevented him from formulating a definite hypothesis about it. It was one thing to be convinced of a world of individual spirits, but quite another to produce objective proof either that they did exist, or were perhaps mere personifications of unconscious; the unlived elements of human personality that he had so often found them to be with his patients. How acutely the problem had exercised his probing mind is clearly illustrated for me by the manner of his recollection, in old age, of that fateful first visit of his and Freud to America for the Clark Conference of 1909.

The content of the papers delivered, and all the discussions they provoked of such critical concern as they were to the two embattled men, had sunk almost without trace into the sea of Jung's memory. No detailed recollection of the celebrated academics he met remained, with one or two exceptions. Of course his memory in this, as in all else he did, had a way of its own in measuring what was worth retaining. For instance, although not a fact or feeling of his meeting much later with Mountain Lake, an obscure chief of a despised and almost extinct Indian race, was ever erased, celebrity after celebrity of the high established American intellectual, social, and scientific scene of those years was made to walk the plank in the course of his passage through the years. But on this first occasion in America, the most notable exception was William James, and among those Jung remembered in old age, he seemed to stand out above all those many others with the precision and clarity of a silhouette against a sunset horizon.

Apart from more formal meetings, Jung spent what he called two delightful evenings alone with William James, and warmed to the originality and immediacy of the man. From what Jung told me, as well as from what I have read, James shared considerably the family legacy of the gift of the artist which made his brother Henry so articulate and remarkable a writer. In both his writing and conversation William James had a capacity for expressing psychological findings and speculation with the grace, lucidity and ease called art, and I myself if ever in need of a reminder of all this have only to think of the way he termed one of his basic concepts, "subliminal", which to this day is valid for me and expresses a nuance absent in both "subconscious" and "unconscious". James's clarity of mind and the total absence of prejudice accordingly impressed Jung greatly, all the more because James was so profoundly interested in the psychic, extrasensory and particularly spiritualistic phenomena encountered in his work. Indeed at that very moment, James's work on the reality of the spirits with the celebrated medium Leonora Piper was making him increasingly suspect to contemporaries, even to their staunch host G. Stanley Hall, despite James's reservation: "I remain uncertain and await more facts, facts which may not point clearly to a conclusion for fifty or a hundred years."

So deep was the impression James made on Jung that he never lost contact with James's close friend James Hervey Hyslop, also a psychologist in his own right. The two of them once had a session together to survey the investigation of psychic phenomena. Hyslop himself was convinced of the identity of the spirits in a life after death. Jung remained to the end in his scientific self closer to James's reservations than the absolutism of Hyslop's belief, but told me he had to concede to Hyslop that there was occasional evidence of a continuation of individual reality after death that could be better explained by some hypothesis of spirits than by the qualities and peculiarities of the unconscious. On the basis of his own experience, Jung still felt compelled to be sceptical in individual cases he encountered, since they were so often mere personifications of unconscious tendencies, but there were occasions when the spirit hypothesis seemed to yield better results in practice than any other.

The fact that in this concession to Hyslop's belief he appeared to go further than James himself had done is to be explained not only by the enigmatic variations on the basic theme encountered in his own research into the collective unconscious but by nature of Hyslop's own testimony.

This aspect of the matter is summed up best for me by something Jung told me, not long before he died, about Hyslop and James. I do not know if it is recorded elsewhere but I do not hesitate to do so here since it is little known and is such a striking illustration of how a psychological approach, particularly in this over externalised hour, is valid only as an interest in life continuous and whole, presupposing as great a concern for a destination beyond death as it does for an origin before birth.

Hyslop and James, Jung told me, promised each other that whoever of the two died first, the other would, if there were individual life after death, do all that he could to give the survivor proof of it. Men like Rhine in his book *Reaches of the Mind* have since produced a host of examples of this kind. But early in this century the pact between the two friends was as rare as it was a moving demonstration of a call of duty to truth to be carried on even after the dismissal we call death from the laboratory of life. It was evidence of how the lives of all three men, in passing, pointed to the importance of Michelangelo's observation that "whereas death killed all men, the thought of it had made many".

James died first and Hyslop waited, convinced that somewhere William James lived on. But proof did not come. Hyslop waited for years and had almost despaired when one day he received a letter from Ireland, a country he had never visited. The letter was from a husband and wife who apologised profusely for intruding unnecessarily on his time. They were, the letter explained, regular users of the planchette as a means of communicating with spirits, and for some months their experiments had been dominated by one who purported to be "a certain William James" and who insisted that they contact a Professor Hyslop of whom they had never heard. He made such a "nuisance of himself" on the planchette that they were finally compelled to make inquiries about Hyslop's identity and address and deliver this single message in the form of a question: "Does he remember the red pyjamas?"

Jung said Hyslop's first reaction was one of utter consternation. He neither remembered any red pyjamas nor thought that James had honoured their solemn pact by so banal and trivial a communication. But in the days that followed, he was more and more impressed by the fact that no channel of communication could have been more objective and protected against subjective elements than the one chosen. Then he remembered in one lightning flash the "red pyjamas". As young men he and James had been sent on a grand tour of Europe. They had arrived in Paris late one evening some days ahead of their luggage, and were compelled to hasten out shopping for immediate necessities like pyjamas. The only ones Hyslop could find were some "really fancy red pyjamas". James teased Hyslop greatly about his "dubious taste" in night wear for some days. But soon the episode was forgotten until resurrected by this intrusion on a planchette-scribbled message.

"Now, what in Heaven do you make of things like that?" Jung remarked, and before I could speak, added that he had never been worried himself, as so many were, by the apparent triviality of messages "from the other side". If there were a life beyond death, it would be in an idiom which we could not possibly possess in the here and now, and as such was utterly incapable of transmission in terms we could understand. What was surprising therefore was not the insignificant nature of these intrusions but that they should take place at all and imply, as Hyslop's experience did, that even in that extraordinary, transcendental state which a life after death had to be if it existed at all, nothing, however trivial, had not played its part or been overlooked.

Besides many of these so-called trivialities, if looked at in this light, were often not so slight and banal after all. If considered in terms of the imagery issuing out of the symbolic heart of reality and looked at as dream material imposed on men who were themselves stuff that dreams were made on, they made rare sense of a transcendental kind. Take the case of the red pyjamas. They were connected with an incident on a journey in James's and Hyslop's case to a world they had not been to before. They had arrived at a new stage of this journey, called Paris, ahead of their luggage which is the image of the sheer impedimenta and inertia imposed on the movement and change of life in the here and now. What could reflect more truly the state of spirit of two men, particularly that of James, pushing on well in advance of the spirit of their day than such a journey and such an arrival?

As for the planchette reference to the incident, was there not a recurrence of the same image for the purpose of demonstrating how James had arrived at another stage even farther in advance than before and, as popular image would have it, not died so much as passed on ahead? Surely the answer to this was in the fact that in the message the garments were pyjamas and moreover red. Pyjamas were a man's personal sleeping material, an image of the individual approach to the night, above all to sleep which always at all times and places symbolised death; red always was the colour of life. It is as if in this recurrence of the imagery of red pyjamas bought in advance of the baggage of physical existence in the present, James was saying to Hyslop that in this sleep called death he had only to look in his imagination they had called "fancy" and he would see that James lived on. No, far from dismissing manifestations such as these as trivial, there was cause for

humility of mind and spirit before such banalities and inspiration to
look deeper into their origin of meaning. Certainly for Hyslop the
message of the red pyjamas was conclusive and his belief and interest
never again wavered.

All this went on while there was no sign that Jung's own death
was near. He always had an enormous zest for life and it seemed to be
then as great as ever. We ate delicious meals. He and his other guests
also drank good and appropriate measures of wine and smoked with
great enjoyment. Even at the age of eighty-seven one had a glimpse of
the Jung who, in the midst of the first World War and all its agonies,
insisted that at the meetings of the Analytical Psychological Club its
members should not neglect their Dionysian needs. This love of fun
and alert, thrusting mind, active as ever, seemed undiminished.

On the last day when I said goodbye to him, I found him sitting
under a copy of the Holbein portrait of Desiderius Erasmus. The man,
the attitude, the book in his hand, and the background provided the
most complete visual and most precious rendering of Jung and what
he represented among the many I recollect. He was wearing a little
black skull cap and, with the light like splinters of glass around him,
looking as if he might have been posed there by Rembrandt himself
for his conclusive study of the perennial philosopher at work.

The contribution Erasmus made to Jung's own spirit deserves and
still awaits detailed evaluation, for it was immense. Jung was as aware
as anyone of what Europe owed him for standing fast at a moment of
great disintegration in the European spirit. He belonged to the natural
order of spirit of which Jung too was a companion of honour, and to
the end Jung loved and re-read him.

Just then Jung was looking through something Erasmus had written,
of course in Latin. Jung as an almost penniless student at the age of
nineteen had bought the book in Basle. He was turning the pages as
fast as someone reading a thriller. He excused himself for going on with
his reading because one of his guests wanted to know where he had
got the Latin inscription carved in stone over his front door: "Called
or not called, God shall be there".

He said, "Of course I know it comes originally from the Greeks but
I first came across it in Erasmus in Latin and I would like the exact
reference to give him."

And that is the focus of my last vision of him in Küsnacht: a vision
that seems to confirm the religious essentials of all his seeking and such
message as he lived for life. Called or not called, God was always there.
Known or not known, sought or rejected, this master-pattern

theologians call God, night and day is there in the collective unconscious of man, calling him to live and be his whole self.

It was a vision too of the confirmation of the importance he attached
to continuity and the sense of history which the world has lost for the
moment. It was a glimpse as though through a corner of a curtain
lifted into the deeps of his mind, showing how the future depended,
not on the abolition of ancient values, the ancient truths of the spirit,
but in their rediscovery and expression in a truly twentieth-century
way. In making the past contemporary, the now forever, man found
his greatest meaning and accomplished the wholeness that is true sanity
and health in all dimensions of body and mind.

Jung had never done anything which had not been a duty imposed
from within. The life of a man, he was fond of saying, is an event
which is completed in the here and now only through death. Psychologically, death was for him just as important as birth, and like birth an
integral part of life. So the event of the life of the man could not be
described until after death. That is why among other reasons, he refused to write a detailed autobiography. It did not mean, as I have
intimated, that death was the end for him and the last of the image
of a self fulfilled. There is clear implication in his writing and clearer
affirmation in his conversation that the self achieved lived on at least
as image and uncorruptible core of new being. Death freed it only
from what was false and provisional and sent it on, indestructible in
time, to serve in another season of itself. The walls between birth and
death, the known and the unknown, had always been no opaque
barrier for his spirit but transparent as the windows of a house of many
mansions amber with light at night. However solidly and empirically
drawn his own frontiers were for us, one was always conscious of how
for him they remained transparent with new meanings pressing out of
the dark against them. In particular one is conscious of how transparent with numinous light the answers he found for the two great
questions he had set himself at the beginning: "What is the secret of
the human personality? And what is my own personal myth and the
myth of my time?"

The secret of the personality was enclosed in the self, in the area
where in the silence of one's own truth achieved and fortified by oneself, the "I" and the "thou" of life could converse with each other. The
myth, of course, was that of the ancient quest of the Holy Grail, rediscovered and made modern and armed with scientific armour so that
service of the feminine that is love was provided with the protection
of the masculine that is the power of the word. How real and active

this myth had become for him was as always revealed in dreams and for me most conclusively in one which had come to him years before in India. In the midst of celebrations organised there in his honour, and bombarded as he was by the imagery of another culture of a sort which always fascinated him, he yet had a dream which clearly asked him, "What are you doing here in such a sense with a culture not your own, when your own Europe is sickening and in danger of collapse? Go home and do your own proper work with the common, everyday material given to you."

And this work, the dream said, was the resumption of his quest of the Grail. There on an island, in the dream, was a great castle as there was once on that island his fantasy had created and en-castled in the swift of the Rhine. But in this dream it was a castle awaiting the coming of the Grail. Jung and some friends went out to look for it since, though announced, it had failed to come. Appropriately with un- wavering dream precision they set out at sundown since we ourselves live in another sunset hour of our time. The scene became bleak and the nightfall bitter. For away from the castle they found the island divided by a broad channel of the sea, a split of collective unconscious proportions, and the Grail was beyond. One by one Jung's companions fell asleep, succumbed to that lack of awareness of which sleep is the fatal image, as it was in a garden in Gethsemane nearly two thousand years before. It was a cryptic dream, summing up what his own life had been and recording how often he had been abandoned by others as he was in the sleep of his companions. Undismayed, he stayed awake, took off his clothes and prepared to swim the channel to find the Grail. This stripping off is one of the most significant aspects of the dream. It symbolises how over the long years he unmasked himself of pre- tensions, discarded all worldly presumptions and preconceived atti- tudes, and could stand the man he was, naked as he was born, and vulnerable as a child again made innocent, simple and ready as Parsifal, through self-confession of his own inadequacies and acceptance of his shadow. Only then was he fit to swim this great rift in himself, this abyss between the two great opposites, this gap in-between his Number One and Number Two personalities. And so at last the dream showed him prepared to cross over his own divide to a self that was more than the sum of himself, a Grail overflowing with light of the ultimate mystery of creation.

I said goodbye to Jung with so much of this and more in turmoil within myself. As always with that innate sense of good manners the French call *politesse de cœur*, he came down the path leading to the gate with me. He stood there for a moment, leaning perhaps more heavily than usual on his stick, and waved goodbye saying, in his schoolboy English, "I'll be seeing you."

But some weeks later Jung was dead. I do not know the medical diagnosis of the immediate cause and in a sense I really do not need to know, because it is irrelevant. I know that he was dead because he had done his work and his life had come to its natural end. I have always thought that there is a profound link between longevity and the greatest forms of genius. It may be true that many of those whom the gods love die young. Even then I believe they do not die before they have done what the gods meant them to do, or that if they die young, it is because only through dying they can achieve the impact they were intended to make. But it is also just as true that those whom the gods loved most, live longest. In some mysterious way the length of their life is commensurate to the scale of the work they have to accomplish. They too tend not to die before that work is done. In that regard the length of Jung's life and the timing of his death is as compulsive as it is awesome.

He worked up to some three days before his death to finish some writing which was, I believe, on symbolism. He finished and said he was rather tired, and went to rest. The evening before he died, Ruth Bailey, who had been a companion on his journey to Africa and to whom all who loved Jung owe such an immense debt for the way she went to look after him and his household after his wife's death, left him for a moment with his son.

Jung said something to this effect: "Quick, help me out of bed before she comes back or she'll stop me. I want to look at the sunset."

And he looked out of his window and saw the sun setting behind the Alps, and in this completed the full circle of his vision of life on earth. He was back in a moment that had never left him when as a child he had had his first view of the form and spume of snow smoking over the blue swell of the storm-tossed Alps going red on the far horizon in the sunset. He was restored to that moment when he was in all that is symbolised by the garden at our beginning. He was back in the garden at Laufen where, lying in his pram looking at the sun dripping like crystal water from the green leaves, he was filled with a sense of wonder and utter belonging. The banishment and journey from that garden, more than fourscore years long in that last view of the Alps, I believe was over, for otherwise he could not have gone so content back to his bed. And I say that because I know in myself and in many others beside whom I am insignificant, as well as from what he himself had so often told me, that in this pattern of departure and return I have mentioned, all our separation and traffic and travail in-between our several beginnings serve only to enable us to see with a clarity we could never have achieved any other way how departure and return are one and our home is where we started from.

The afternoon on which Jung died, a great thunderstorm raged over his house at Küsnacht, as if nature itself were mobilised to acknowledge the event. Just about the time of his death lightning struck his favourite tree in the garden.

One of the earliest rituals to reconcile men to the death of those dearest to them was to burn not only their bodies but all their most precious belongings with them. They did this so that, through the fire which brought light, what was imperishable in matter could be re-leased from the perishable to accompany on the journey beyond the spirit freed from bondage, however loving in flesh and blood. The wood that makes the fire, the body that nourishes the flame of the spirit burns out, but fire and spirit flame and flare on. It is almost as if nature itself sent the lightning to perform this task for Jung. But not only did this happen in nature. It was as if in the dreaming and vision-ary unconscious of numbers who had known him, an awareness like a kind of witnessing of a great ship going down appeared to draw all sort of portents and visions towards the vortex of his death like flotsam and jetsam on the sea marking the place of a titanic sinking.

I myself had an experience of this which I have long hesitated to make public. I had sailed from Africa profoundly distressed by the condition of my native country. I was obsessed with forebodings of Apocalyptic disaster. I did not recognise what my own people had become and they did not recognise me. As a result, the sea and ships, which have always given me one of my greatest feelings of belonging and rest, utterly failed me on this occasion. I could not sleep. Even the strongest of sleeping-draughts were of no use to me.

And then one afternoon alone in my cabin, worn out and hovering between waking and sleeping out of exhaustion, I suddenly had a vision of myself in a deep, dark valley in avalanche country, among steep, snow-covered mountains. I was filled with a foreknowledge of imminent disaster. I knew that even raising my voice in the world of this vision could bring down the bulging avalanches upon me. Sud-denly, at the far end of the valley on one Matterhorn peak of my vision, still caught in the light of the sun, Jung appeared. He stood there briefly, as I had seen him some weeks before at the gate, at the end of the garden of his house, then waved his hand at me and called out,

"I'll be seeing you." Then he vanished down the far side of the mountain.

Instantly I fell asleep and slept the whole evening and night through. I woke next morning just as the sun was rising, and pushed aside the curtains of the porthole of my cabin. I saw a great, white lone albatross gliding by it; the sun on fire on its wings. As it glided by it turned its head and looked straight at me. I had done that voyage countless times before and such a thing had never happened to me, and I had a feeling as if some tremendous ritual had been performed. Hardly had I got back into bed when my steward appeared with a tray of tea and fruit and, as he always did, the ship's radio news. I opened it casually. The first item I saw was the announcement that Jung had died the previous afternoon at his home in Zürich. Taking into consideration the time, the latitude and longitude of the ship's position, it was clear that my dream, or vision, had come to me at the moment of his death.

But far more important than my own or other people's premonitions and visions were the last dreams experienced by Jung himself. Just before he died, he dreamt that he saw "high up on a high place" a boulder of stone in the full sun. Carved into it were the words, "Take this as a sign of the wholeness you have achieved and the singleness you have become."

The symmetry of meaning conveyed in this dream is as complete as it is final. All Jung's life was a dialogue, first with a stone, through stone with himself, then with all life, history and time, continued and fulfilled through moulding, shaping and carving its quintessentials in stone at Bollingen, and finally a dialogue with God himself as if from the heap of ashes of himself and his time. Nothing could have been more fitting in this great process of question and answer that is life in flesh and blood, than the fact that the conclusion of the last dialogue of Jung accessible to us, his dialogue with death, was also in terms of sunlit stone—that stone which is so great an image of what is lasting and indestructible.

Hard on this he had another dream in which he saw a square and trees growing in it. The roots of the trees were intertwined with green and gold.

The square in itself is a symbol of wholeness and needs no voice to proclaim it. It is the wholeness that is consciously achieved and asserted in the flux and welter of appearances and things. The trees of course carry the image of life rooted in the authentic earth of the unconscious and the promise of its increase; the green and gold around the roots which nourish the trees are the image of the alchemical property of the ultimate in sublimation and transfiguration, as he had once seen them in that vision of Christ standing at the foot of his bed. It was as if the master-pattern itself was saying to Jung at the very moment of transition and translation: "You have earned the freedom to move on! You have done your work. You have done it well and it will grow."

That this is not just a fanciful and highly subjective reading of mine of the event of death in the life of somebody I loved and to whom I owe much, was finally confirmed for me by another intrusion of the symmetry of meaning through a different sort of coincidence. I was making a film of the story of the life of Jung some years ago. The time schedule for the film had been determined nearly a year before we started filming. The final sequence on the last day of all was to be filmed in Jung's old house. We had worked all morning in his home and all day long the cameraman, producer and myself, without mentioning it to one another, had an indescribable feeling that Jung was near to us. I heard the cameraman saying to an assistant, half jokingly at the time, "You know, I had a feeling as if Jung was looking over my shoulder all day."

It was a dry, hot, blazing afternoon as we left the house to do some background filming in the old city of Zürich, intending to return for the filming of the final scene, by his home at sunset. On our way from Zürich to Küsnacht to do so, suddenly out of the hot blue sky, thunderclouds tumbled without forewarning, as if in a great hurry. By the time we reached Küsnacht, the lightning was flashing, the thunder rumbling and the rain pouring down.

When the moment came for me to speak to the camera about Jung's death, and I came to the description of how the lightning demolished Jung's favourite tree, the lightning struck in the garden again. The thunder crashed out so near and loud that I winced, and to this day the thunder is there in the film for all to hear just as the wince and slight impediment of speech it caused can be seen, while the lightning flashes over the storm-tossed lake and the wind-whipped trees.

As far as I am concerned, confirmation of this kind is unnecessary enough to be irrelevant. But I am compelled to mention it because it would seem as if it is in some sort testimony of how that great spirit lives on and will continue to show the way towards the transfiguration of life until the end of space and time.

EPILOGUE

The wind blows low on the mountains; the image of decay.

I-Ching on the symbol of *Ku* or the need
to work on what has been spoilt

Several years have gone by since the incident described at the end
of the previous chapter. In these years Jung and his work seem to have
loomed even larger and the man himself to have come nearer. That
remains for me one of the most significant consequences of this experience with which I continue to be concerned. Death does not seem
to have removed Jung further, nor to have diminished, strange as it
may seem, the physical presence of the man. By the year he draws
closer and by now stands so clear-cut beside one that it would seem
unreal to miss and mourn him.

Placed beside this new other clarity and nearness of Jung, one's own
slight remaining measure, however human, of wanting to hear him
and sit with him in his garden of Küsnacht or in the sunlit shelter of
the yellow stone of his own choosing at Bollingen to look out at the
wind-darkened water of the lake and hear him talk in a way that
invested the most insignificant of things with significance, shrinks into
a weightless triviality. And I can only take it all as signs of how man
and work were hewn into such an imperishable oneness as few lives
have been in recorded history; how the greatest necessity of our time
called and continues to call for just such a person with such a being
and a vision, and how swiftly this need is ascending towards a fateful
climax.

Something of this I am certain compelled me, against the trend of
the necessities of my own work, to make the film mentioned, re-
inforcing an instinct that there was no time to lose in rendering both
the man and his work more accessible to the ordinary non-specialist
and apparently normal, educated men and women; above all to the
young people of my day than they had hitherto been. The young in
particular, could not go on following the illusion that they had no
option but to turn to other cultures, Oriental religions, Whirling
Dervishes and alien esoteric practices and formulae to answer their
deepest needs, as they are in multiples of thousands. Neither they nor
we can afford to lose their exertion in any other area of action in life

than the field of battle into which they were born. Not only are there no answers for them or us at the end of the road from Kew to Katmandu, Minneapolis to Ajunta or other highways and byways to Middle and Far East, but only a great and dangerous evasion of their first obligation to fulfil themselves in their own context and place in time. Through Jung they have one key at hand for all the answers they need, not for magical transformation and abolition of the problems imposed on them by life but for a way of living them out without sacrifice of the values they have inherited.

In Jung these values are converted into a contemporary currency and interpreted in such a way that their history is forged into a living instrument of reality, capable of renewing both themselves, their decaying societies and the sick spirit of their day. What negatively observed appears as decay and danger, interpreted this way can become seed of modern growth and opportunity for far greater increase than life has yet known.

That the hunger for this new meaning in an idiom of our own is there was proved for me by the reception of even this inadequate film of Jung. It is still in constant demand and, in America in particular, continues to be shown to crowded university halls, lecture rooms and churches. The increased demand that follows the film for Jung's books, particularly *Memories, Dreams, Reflections*, and also the *I-Ching* wherever it continues to be shown, added more substance to the proof of how he expresses and fulfils the necessities of our day. And yet as time went by and this sense of his nearness increased, I felt I had not done all I had to do.

In the first place the film showed only a narrow section consisting of an hour and a half of material which took thirteen hours to film and which we thought was the minimum necessary for conveying the essence of Jung. The Foundation which acquired the rest of the film on the understanding that it would make a longer film of the story of Jung from it, inexplicably reneged on its undertaking. So what was to me even as a full film still an inadequate representation of Jung, was reduced for public consumption to this fragment so much in demand.

Somehow this fact, added to the other that even in the full film I had not attempted to describe the whole of Jung as I had experienced the man and his work, would not leave me at peace. I could not and of course never attempted to describe the whole of Jung. Even Jung could not do that, great as his achievement was. Until the end he too was more than he could express in words and work. But I could at least try to define the whole of my experience of him and his work. In addition, there is this growing acceleration of deterioration and proliferation of decay as I see it all round me to add to my sense of this inner duty only partially done.

Men by the day have become more bigoted, sloganised, abstracted from their natural selves, and caught-up in shallow collective power groups, at a rate I would not have thought possible even three years ago. The individual man made specific in a self capable of holding out against collective and totalitarian pressures, which is such a unique creation of the West, is in greater danger than he has been for centuries. As his danger increases, so does the peril to the cultures and free societies which once contained him and provided him with his communal foundation for growth.

As the mental asylums become increasingly overcrowded; as the churches empty; as one dictatorship of man and tyranny of state after the other take over new and larger segments of the international scene, it would seem as if the world itself had gone insane. All the signs of an international schizophrenic seizure are multiplying. The feeling values, considerations of love and emotion not only are fast vanishing but people appear increasingly incapable not just of experiencing them but even recognising and honouring their reality in others; all symptoms of schizophrenic man.

Moreover there is a strange incapacity abroad for experiencing real grief or allowing ourselves the tragic awareness commensurate with our general and particular plight—an I-could-not-care-less attitude to the suffering of others. The great cathartic role of tragedy in life and art, and the reclamation of human suffering in the discovery of its position in the progression of universal meaning, seems for the moment to have been abolished.

In so far as it is acknowledged in art anyway, it is more and more as a kind of sick joke played by life on man, if not a meaningless farce. It is as if the human spirit is increasingly in the grip of an age of ice and cold, impersonal indifference in command of its values. The free exercise of fantasy which is the imagination unsevered from its instinctive roots at play, has gone from literature and art. Characters no longer bubble up fountain-wise in the art of fiction but have been replaced by men and women who have been "researched" as novelists proudly assert, and so are not individual conceptions any more but statistical abstracts of humanity that live only as a form of dead accountancy. The visual arts more and more have withdrawn from the objective without, severed its links with its counterpart within and see and portray in this dark averted dimension the symptoms of anger, rebellion and dissociation caused by stubborn neglect of our natural spirit. D'Annunzio's resounding objection to the science of his day, because it presupposed a corpse, could be applied to the immense, laborious exercise of dissection which occupies so much of the spirit of our time and prevents it from a renewal and re-integration of its wounded, fragmented self.

Moreover, the world watches, as a matter of course, displays of violence and the taking of human life on television screens or reads about them in newspapers with a comparative absence of feeling that would have been unthinkable at the end of the last war. Less and less do we seem to be aware, as we review the daily casualty list of this new disordered spirit, that each one on that roll-call of the dead was a miracle of life extinguished without sound reason or meaning. The natural reverence for life which the first man took for granted in himself is vanishing from all but a few. All the symptoms, of which these are the more obvious examples, are of an invasion of consciousness that we call disturbance, delinquency or madness.

"Insanity", Jung said already in the 'thirties, "is a state of mind possessed by an unconscious content which, as such, is not assimilated to consciousness, nor can it be assimilated, since consciousness itself has denied the existence of these contents. Religiously expressed, the attitude is equivalent to saying that we no longer have any fear of God and believe that everything is to be measured in terms of human standards. This hubris, that is the narrowness of consciousness, is always the shortest way to the insane asylum."

All the evidence of such a narrowing of consciousness in modern man is here for those who can still be aware. Already in a country like Britain which I love, and which one might have thought more immune to this disorder of spirit and depletion of values, politics are increasingly politics of power and less and less a free institution designed to serve the greatest values and highest aspirations of an uniquely intuitive people. If there were one nation, one unique complex of races and cultures alive to the truth that politics worked for the human good, if only in service of a truth greater than itself, which by definition therefore could neither be a political one nor one directed merely to a political end, it was the British. Yet on the British scene, not only in Parliament but in churches and universities, splintered into increasingly specialised and compartmentalised faculties, incapable of relation of communication with one another, there is a growing tendency to make their highest value political as well. And all this is happening despite mounting social evidence of how discredited and bankrupt a development it is.

I deliberately use Britain as an example because it is one that I know well but it would be dangerously misleading to think it is exceptional. I travel the world more than most and can testify that I have found no race, culture or nation in the modern world which is not suffering in its own way from a similar profound affliction, and in one significant dimension shares the same common symptoms. In all countries there is the same wide gulf between young and old and, as a result, two archaic polarisations of two opposites in the forces of the collective unconscious in man. In the young there is a tendency towards a total submission to the Dionysian elements of the spirit and a rejection of the validity of the "ego" without which no individual awareness let alone existence is possible, hence the outbreak of tribalism and upsurge to hunt in packs which one sees among young people from the Isle of Man to the Californian coast, and Leningrad to Tokyo; among the older there is a compulsion to stand fast in an over-egotistical law and order stance, ignoring the profound shift of focus in the collective unconscious and the clamour for change from underneath. The greater the clamour the wider and closer the grouping to compensate for the sense of insecurity caused by the struggle for a change of ground below.

Even the world economic scene bears striking evidence of the failure of such an approach to administer to the real necessities of our day. One would have thought by now that the grave labour unrest everywhere could have testified irrefutably to the fact that its causes are not to be found in what are called inadequate living standards and social insecurity because this unrest and a new, subtler and more lethal kind of feeling of insecurity has grown with geometric progression as living standards have risen and social security increased. I would have thought it obvious by now that what makes not only labour, but societies, churches, doctors, historians and even the least specialised or ordinary human hearts alone with themselves in the silence of night full of a fearful unease, is the fact that there is no discernible meaning for man in what he is asked to do, and no overall and honourable value in the evolution of the society or culture to which he belongs to compensate him for the meaninglessness which affects him in his personal work and condition of being.

The crisis, I believe, is plainly one caused by an almost total loss of meaning, both individually and collectively. The human heart, as history proves, I believe, can endure anything except a state of meaninglessness. Without meaning it dies like a fish without water on the sands of a wasteland beach.

Maynard Keynes in my youth in London once said to me that ultimately economics made no sense except in a supreme human context and failed if its own material instrumentally was not related to ultimate and classical humanistic preconsiderations. He had not long before written a book that made his reputation, *The Economic Consequence of the Treaty of Versailles*. I wish he were here today to write on the economic consequences of, say, the inferiority complex, or another, for that matter, on the totality of complexes which represents the loss of meaning men find in themselves, their institutions and societies. The loss of output on the factory floor, the loss of attendances in church, all I am certain are directly proportionate to the decline in the input of meaning from the life of our time.

For the highest price men have always paid and still pay for all they acquire, whether of matter or spirit, is a psychological one. Human cultures at their most creative best have tried to ensure that whatever was bought or earned or sought after was also psychologically or spiritually or, at the very least, aesthetically worth it, and of some abiding value unconnected with any functional significance of the moment. But all these considerations have tended to vanish from contemporary values, and man is increasingly regarded as output or export fodder, and the reward he earns in the process more and more exclusively calculated in materialistic terms. Behind all this, there seems to me to be a betrayal of the most reprehensible kind, subversion of a kind not spun by some subtle Russian with snow on his boots in some unheated basement of the Kremlin, but by the institutions and the vocations which Western man has evolved precisely in order to protect him against this sort of treason. It is, of course, in a more obvious social dimension the treason so aptly described by the French, who are experts in the matter, as *trahison des clercs*, but this treason in itself is more mongrel offspring of a master betrayal, as it were, in the fourth-dimension betrayal of man by the guardians of his spirit, the churches, priests, doctors and teachers of his day.

I lump them together because they are uniquely charged by life with the task of keeping man and his societies whole. Perhaps at the beginning of this century still they could have pleaded justification for their failure because of ignorance of its causes. But they can do so no longer because, since Jung, his rediscovery of the collective unconscious and his empiric demonstration of its imperative role in the life of man, they cannot excuse themselves by a claim of ignorance of the causes of failure, they continue to promote instead of arresting and correcting it.

The priest, the doctor, the psychiatrist living seventy years after Jung first cured a schizophrenic—taking only one extreme of his endeavour—from his split and sick soul and demonstrated how the pattern of God in man was a scientific fact and a mighty activity, bear a crushing moral responsibility for the sickness of men and their societies because they have today the means for healing at their disposal, but refuse to apply it. It is a scandal of a moral kind so great and general that no-one will proclaim it as it ought to be from the housetops. Yet wherever men are and work they have only to listen and look and see it as some dry-rot in the basements of their surroundings or hear it at work as some death-watch beetle in the hollow wainscots of their spirit. Unless the keepers of the spirit of man at this hour, so much later than they think, will reassess their vocation in its ancient as well as its most contemporary of terms, life as always in these arrested moments will be compelled to call in the most terrible of all healers to do their work for them—the disaster cataclysmically proportionate to the centuries of neglect of their calling and failure to follow on the Pentecostal light into the darkness of unknowing ahead of which they have been guilty.

This cataclysm could be so great that they and their societies may well vanish forever. And yet one does not believe this because there is an answer to all this by following the way Jung pioneered in his own life and work. Sooner or later he will be seen by all for what he is, one of the great turning points in history, as he is already being recognised by growing numbers in Old and New Worlds, West and East and even in my own native Africa.

One day soon now man will come to reappraise the whole of recorded history in order to uncover, as archaeologists uncover the ruined cities of the crumbled civilisations buried in the dust behind us, the decisive role the collective unconscious has played in it. They will see the decline and fall of civilisations at last in their true light as partial expressions of the human spirit which, valid as they were for brief moments of time, perished because, in their own specialised establishment, they became increasingly separated from the natural forces of the collective unconscious that initially raised them so high until the support of this primordial world of infinite energies was totally alienated and withdrawn and they had to fall. History, no matter how remote, re-examined in terms of this great hypothesis, will show precisely how not the uncertainties of physical environment and external disaster but the inadequacy of men's conscious relationships with their collective unconscious and their failure constantly to renew, deepen and widen them were the real causes of decline and fall.

Once this point is reached, the road to a more meaningful future will be clear again because history for the first time will not only be as precise and honest as the best of historians have always tried to make it but it will also be whole. Without a history that is as whole as it is precise and honest, aware of all the forces that have gone into its making, our future cannot possess the sanity which is wholeness. Since Jung, no true historian any longer has either excuse or lack of means for doing the whole of his vital task for the first time on record, and our future be brighter than ever before. But the hour is late.

And indeed it is because there is no time to be lost for Jung in this as in so many other fields to be the beginning of our unique contemporary way, I found it imperative to express the meaning he has for me and the extent to which his example confirmed my own natural endeavour in life and added meaning to what I have tried to do.

Indeed, so much did I want this to be a record of my own experience of both the man and our own day that I have done practically no academic research in writing this account. I have consulted none of the numbers of my friends who knew and worked with Jung. I have read no books about him in this period and only turned to his own work as I remembered what was significant to me in it and wished to confirm it.

This record therefore is as fallible as I am myself, but none the less it is the greatest truth of which I am capable. Anything else from me would have been pretence and would have failed because the time has come when men can only truly communicate with one another out of what they themselves have experienced and suffered. For they can no longer speak to one another out of pure knowledge alone. The knowledge which is peddled in so great abundance in so ready a market today, seeing that it is bartered without human commitment, historical evaluation or moral obligation, is no longer a vehicle of legitimate exchange because it only communicates the facts and statistics of itself and nothing of the person who passes it on, nor anything of the one who receives it, let alone trails along with it a curl of the cloud of the aboriginal meaning which somewhere below the horizon of our time once inspired it and which alone can feed the great hunger we feel.

In any case, I could not do more. Even in the process of doing the little I have done, the immensity of my subject has shown up my own inadequacies, so that at times I could hardly continue. Yet strangely enough, out of this archetypal pattern of meaning which is the proper dimension of my subject, it is striking how often the relevant coincidences have come to encourage me. Only last night for instance, above the reddening snow on the highest peaks, its marble head bland and broad over the valley among the mountains of Switzerland which Jung loved and among which I am writing, I saw the planets Venus and Jupiter close to each other as they have not been since 1859, so that some starry images of the greatest masculine god of all, Zeus, as I prefer to call him in his aboriginal Greek, and the goddess of the feminine, Aphrodite, who has the principles of love, the Eros, in her keeping, and once rose out of the mist and spray of a wine-dark sea of morning at our European beginning, shone there close and reconciled, bright and trembling with their nearness, as if set deliberately there to remind me how they are forever united in the self Jung rediscovered for his time.

Then, on a day of particular despondence, when I had just finished the account of the meaning of *The Odyssey* for me and come to the pattern of the wise old man in Jung, the owner of this hotel who is an old friend, appeared with a large magnified copy, faithful even in colour to the original, of a detail from a Greek vase some 3,500 years old. It was an illustration of an old Greek shepherd leaning on his staff by a Classical fluted marble column, as the old shepherd in Ithaca might have done when patient, resolved, and uncomplaining he stared out to sea, for signs of his master's safe return. He was looking out of infinitely experienced eyes as if from the other side of the world there were stirring into movement towards him something of overwhelming import. I had only to look up from my writing table to see that wise old face and feel that between him and me some thread of meaning was intact and, though unrecorded, and names and faces in-between unknown, I had appropriate and great company in what I was trying to do. Indeed, no personification of a great archetype could have been more accurate or vivid, nor so timely.

But most of all, though perhaps least in itself, something happened high up on the side of a great white mountain when I was on my way to meet a guide to take me to the top one afternoon. I found two little Swiss boys full of life and mischief, waiting by the track across a steep slope for their own teacher. Tired of teasing one another and some rather pompous, over-fleshed adults going inexpertly by on their skis, one turned to the other and asked in his Graubunden dialect, "What is the difference between theology and psychology?"

"You're showing off!" the other exclaimed, taken aback. "I bet you don't know yourself."

"I do," his friend replied, suddenly solemn and rather shy. "Theology is the knowledge and study of God; psychology is the knowledge and study of the soul."

My immediate reaction was that this could only have happened in Switzerland, but coming down the mountain on skis at sunset to a darkening valley, with a vortex of crows tormented in the calm of evening over its deep centre, tossed like crumpled sheets of black, burnt-out paper in a current of heat rising from the ashes of a dying fire, the incident struck me another way. If these questions and the differences implied could be of concern to so young a boy, late as the hour was, there was both time and material to work on the decay of our day and restore it. I felt instantly that we all owed life itself all we could do to prevent the child of the future from being educated out of the natural spirit that had prompted question and answer, as indeed so many children are being educated out of it today.

For it seems to me that it is precisely out of these questions with their deep roots in our remote origins in the search for their truthful answer that the human spirit has always derived its clearest inspiration and found its greatest meaning, and will continue to do so until the end of time, despite all impediments of confusion and partialities of unawareness thrown in its way by no matter how disorientated, determined and powerful men and societies. And I could not say this with such certainty were it not for Carl Gustav Jung, through whom the universe dreamt a dream, giving him the capacity and the courage to live it, and our desperate time the vision that could save it from itself.

Post Hotel,
Valbella,
Switzerland
February 1975